Indigenous Peoples Rise Up

Global Media and Race

Series Editor: Frederick Luis Aldama, The Ohio State University

Global Media and Race is a series focused on scholarly books that examine race and global media culture. Titles focus on constructions of race in media, including digital platforms, webisodes, multilingual media, mobile media, vlogs, and other social media, film, radio, and television. The series considers how race—and intersectional identities generally—is constructed in front of the camera and behind, attending to issues of representation and consumption as well as the making of racialized and antiracist media phenomena from script to production and policy.

Bronwyn Carlson and Jeff Berglund, eds., *Indigenous Peoples Rise Up: The Global Ascendency of Social Media Activism*

Matthew David Goodwin, *The Latinx Files: Race, Migration, and Space Aliens*

Hyesu Park, ed., *Media Culture in Transnational Asia: Convergences and Divergences*

Melissa Castillo Planas, *A Mexican State of Mind: New York City and the New Borderlands of Culture*

Monica Hanna and Rebecca A. Sheehan, eds., *Border Cinema: Reimagining Identity through Aesthetics*

Indigenous Peoples Rise Up

The Global Ascendency of Social Media Activism

EDITED BY BRONWYN CARLSON AND
JEFF BERGLUND

Rutgers University Press

New Brunswick, Camden, and Newark, New Jersey, and London

Library of Congress Cataloging-in-Publication Data
Names: Carlson, Bronwyn, editor. | Berglund, Jeff, editor.
Title: Indigenous peoples rise up: the global ascendency of social media
    activism / edited by Bronwyn Carlson and Jeff Berglund.
Description: New Brunswick: Rutgers University Press, 2021. | Series: Global media
    and race | Includes bibliographical references and index.
Identifiers: LCCN 2020045031 | ISBN 9781978808775 (paperback) | ISBN 9781978808782
    (cloth) | ISBN 9781978808799 (epub) | ISBN 9781978808805 (mobi) |
    ISBN 9781978808812 (pdf)
Subjects: LCSH: Indigenous peoples—Communication. | Internet and indigenous peoples. |
    Social media. | Social media—Political aspects. | Indigenous peoples—Politics and government.
Classification: LCC GN380 .I5343 2021 | DDC 302.23/1089—dc23
LC record available at https://lccn.loc.gov/2020045031

A British Cataloging-in-Publication record for this book is available from the British Library.

♾ The paper used in this publication meets the requirements of the American National
Standard for Information Sciences—Permanence of Paper for Printed Library Materials,
ANSI Z39.48-1992.

www.rutgersuniversitypress.org

Manufactured in the United States of America

Contents

Indigenous Peoples Rise Up

Introduction

■■■■■■■■■■■■■■■■■■■■■

BRONWYN CARLSON AND
JEFF BERGLUND

The impetus for this project dates back to 2015, when the Forum for Indigenous Research Excellence (FIRE) hosted the "Reterritorialising Social Media: Indigenous People Rise Up" symposium.[1] FIRE is an international network of scholars interested in Indigenous research. Both editors and several contributors to this volume are members of this network. The symposium focused on Indigenous social media spaces and social and cultural connectedness, and Indigenous social movements and global solidarity. The presenters included a wide range of people active in Indigenous activism, both online and off. As it became more and more evident that Indigenous peoples were utilizing the technology offered by social media platforms, three Indigenous scholars (also FIRE members) collaborated on a special edition of the *Australasian Journal of Information Systems* on Indigenous activism on social media (see Carlson et al., 2017).

Not too long after this special issue was published, the idea for this book was born. Jeff Berglund was concluding his visit to Macquarie University to meet with honors and graduate students from the Department of Indigenous Studies helmed by Bronwyn Carlson. In a café near the Sydney International Airport, we (Jeff and Bronwyn) sketched out the idea for expanding our scope of social media activism that included the expressive arts, that foregrounded the function of Indigenous feminism and queer Indigenous perspectives, and that considered the affective impact of online environments, in short, its possibilities and constraints. We knew, importantly, that we wanted to include the insights of active, engaged social media activists, and we were pleased to retain

2 • Bronwyn Carlson and Jeff Berglund

Alex Wilson's involvement in our efforts—as someone at the center of the Idle No More movement—and to eventually secure interviews with Carly Wallace, known online as comic CJay's Vines, and Debbie Reese, the originator of the influential blog *American Indians in Children's Literature*. We knew, too, that we wanted to be able to represent perspectives from Indigenous scholars and scholars working in Indigenous Studies in Australia, Canada, Aotearoa (New Zealand), the United States, and beyond. While this book was in production, many of the contributors to this volume previewed their work in progress at a symposium at Northern Arizona University in Flagstaff. There, Indigenous scholars from Australia, Canada, Morocco, Aotearoa, and the United States shared their thinking and engaged in discussions with symposium participants in a packed gathering room in the Native American Cultural Center.

While Indigenous peoples continue to make use of social media, there remains a paucity of scholarly literature on the topic. Recent research indicates that Indigenous populations are avid social media users, but there has been little focus from researchers on the topic. In recent times, there have been publications on the general subject of social media and activism, such as Manuel Castells's 2015 *Networks of Outrage and Hope* and, in 2012, *Tweets on the Streets* by Paolo Gerbaudo. Neither have any Indigenous content. In 2017, Marisa Elena Duarte, one of our contributors, published *Network Sovereignty: Building the Internet across Indian Country*, which establishes an important foundation for thinking about the potential and limits of access to social media and the online world, more broadly. The focus of these three books is primarily the United States. To date, there have been no books that focus specifically on Indigenous social media use and activism in a globalized context. Yet as we were finishing this project, an important book on Indigenous peoples' use of technology and social media was published: Jennifer Gómez Menjívar and Gloria Elizabeth Chacón's impressive *Indigenous Interfaces: Space, Technology, and Social Networks in Mexico and Central America*; this book makes a vital contribution to understanding how Indigenous peoples in this region are using social media as part of their sovereign and autonomous ways of being Indigenous in the twenty-first century. *Indigenous Peoples Rise Up: The Global Ascendency of Social Media Activism*, extends the focus on Indigenous peoples and activism in an international context that includes North America, Australia, Aotearoa, and North Africa.

Over the past decade, social media technologies, particularly handheld devices and social media apps, have gradually become part of our everyday lives. Researchers have shown that Indigenous peoples have always been early adopters of technology, and the present moment demonstrates that this is indeed the case with social media (Carlson and Frazer, 2018). Platforms such as Facebook, Twitter, YouTube, Vine, Snapchat, Instagram, and TikTok, blogs with social media interfaces, and mobile technology generally, have expanded the nature of Indigenous empowerment, communities, and social movements. For example, social media has allowed Indigenous artists to expand audiences for their work and afforded opportunities outside of traditional curatorial structures like galleries and museums. The brilliant Indigenous artist who created this book's cover image, Charlotte Allingham, is a twenty-six-year-old Wiradjuri, Ngiympa queer Blak woman from New South Wales, Australia. They have over fifty-three thousand followers as @coffinbirth on Instagram, with a considerable following on Twitter @drawnbysoymilk. With great frequency, Allingham's vibrant, thought-provoking, and memorable art circulates globally, sending messages of empowerment, body positivity, strength, power, and Indigenous self-love. Their work emphasizes the brutality of colonization but the resilience and possibilities of resistance and a commitment to Indigenous futures.

Diné writer Natanya Ann Pulley, in an essay titled "Indigetechs: The Original Time-Space Traveling Native Americans," notes, "A Native American presence online is always a political act. It is a testament to our staying power and to the people's ability to surge onward. . . . I no longer need to open a book or work through my mother's memory of Navajoland to reach my people (though I deeply miss its sand and growing winds). I simply have to open an app. And I am not faced with static images, but with emergent and pulsing paths of inclusion and action" (2014, p. 100). David Treuer's critically acclaimed *Heartbeat of Wounded Knee: Native America from 1890 to the Present* (2019), a book written for a mainstream audience about the resilience of and resistance by American Indians in the twentieth century and beyond, includes a chapter titled "Digital Indians," in which he profiles individuals whose work is often supported by social media, including activist efforts that coalesced at Standing Rock and the #NoDAPL movement, a subject taken up by Nicholet Deschine Parkhurst's contribution to this volume.

Social media technologies bridge distance, time, and nation-states to mobilize Indigenous peoples to build coalitions across the globe to stand in solidarity with one another (including, for example, other social movements such as Black Lives Matter). From #IdleNoMore in Canada to protests defending sacred sites to publicizing the plight of missing and murdered Indigenous women, opposition to building projects at Mauna Kea and at Standing Rock by Water Protectors, #SOSBlakAustralia, which protested the closure of Indigenous communities, the Australian #ChangeTheNation campaign to protest the annual celebration of Australia Day on January 26, commemorating the arrival of the British and subsequent colonization of Aboriginal peoples, and social media campaigns driven by Māori to protect Ihumātao in Aotearoa, activist movements have succeeded and gained momentum and traction precisely because of the strategic use of social media. As we wrapped up the first draft of our manuscript in February 2020, social media was one vital force being used to galvanize the world's attention and support around the Wet'suwet'en First

Nation's resistance to the construction of TC Energy's Coastal GasLink pipeline set to cut through their unceded territory in northern British Columbia. Protests across Canada proliferated, shutting down trains and bringing traffic to a halt in major cities, all after social media—including the Twitter hashtags #Wetsuwetn and #WetsuwetenSolidarity—showed violent police raids targeting land defenders. And we saw how social media campaigns and activist causes continue to converge as defenders and protestors highlighted how the extraction industries are linked to #MMIWG and the epidemic of missing and murdered Indigenous Women and Girls in Canada and beyond.

Social media—Twitter and Facebook in particular—has also served as a platform for fostering health, well-being, and resilience, recognizing Indigenous strength and talent, and sustaining and transforming cultural practices when great distances divide members of the same community. And it has been used as a platform to provide and promote knowledge for Indigenous peoples about the law, Indigenous languages, and economic opportunities. It has also been fertile ground for consciousness-raising debates within publishing and the literary arts about the representation of Indigenous histories and lives by non-Indigenous artists and authors (some with very public specious claims), not to mention long-running debates about sports mascots and national founding myths and public memorials and holidays that support those myths of conquest, "discovery," and nation-state building. Individuals and groups use social media to shape new understandings about Indigenous peoples. May through July 2020, the period when the final draft of this book was completed, saw reinvigorated and lively social media coverage of global actions in the #BlackLivesMatter movement that questioned these very issues, including the name change of the Washington, D.C., NFL franchise, ongoing systemic racism, and the removals of statues commemorating colonizers, genocidal actors, and members of the Confederacy in the United States.

One vital way that social media resists and refashions stereotypes of Indigenous peoples is through the seemingly simple tactic of making and sharing memes. By using familiar images and/or memes but changing them up, Indigenous peoples are controlling the conversation, inspiring each other, and reaching Indigenous social media users with a positive message, using both humor and contemporary, current language. The framework of "woman yells at cat" meme, popular in 2019, is a case in point: Indigenous social media users employed this in myriad ways. This meme, for example, was transformed on a calico ribbon skirt, with an Indigenous woman on one side of the skirt yelling at a cat stitched on the other side of the skirt. Aqqalu Berthelsen, an Inupiaq musician from Greenland, "Inukified" or "Indigified" the meme as a woman yelling at a seal and offered it up through Instagram without text to interested users (figure I.1). Numerous examples proliferated. A recent meme, using the iconic image of Victor and Thomas from Chris Eyre's 1998 film *Smoke Signals*,

Aqqalu
@uyarakq

It's a template. My gift to all of you if you wanna make a meme.

11:29 PM · Nov 19, 2019

♡ 3.8K   ♡ 863 people are talking about this

FIG. I.1 Meme template created by Aqqalu Berthelsen. (Credit: Screenshot by authors of Instagram post @uyarakq.)

considers memes as "good medicine." Their powers to make people laugh, to reach deeper understandings of themselves and the world around them, and to revise negative cultural scripts are a testament to their impact (figure I.2).

While memes in and of themselves are not social media, they exist only if they proliferate and circulate; their lifeblood is social media, and it's through their dissemination on social media that they participate in activist capacities through engaged dialogue. Social media also serves as a vehicle for artists, comedians, filmmakers, and musicians to share their work and expand the ways that Indigenous peoples find entertainment and artistic reflections that are relevant and responsive and accurate. Aboriginal comedian Carly Wallace, for example, circulates her work through CJay's Vines on Facebook and YouTube to fans who eagerly await her next installment of hilarious and revealing commentary about herself and others in the Indigenous community. Similarly, the 1491s, an American Indian comedy troupe, disseminates its work via YouTube

"INDIGENOUS PEOPLE ARE POWERFUL PEOPLE VICTOR. THEY CAN EVEN TURN MEMES INTO MEDICINE"

FIG. I.2 *Smoke Signals* viral meme. (Credit: Screenshot by authors, origin unknown.)

and lampoons simultaneously the Native community and settler colonialism and the entertainment industry; from this comedic platform, with an established fanbase in the hundreds of thousands, the 1491s have launched other celebrations of resilience and resurgence that honor the vibrancy and creativity of Indigenous peoples. In short, social media has afforded the possibility of claiming the means of production to restore to the center Indigenous viewpoints and paradigms too often relegated to the margins by mainstream media formats.

One barometer of the sphere of influence exerted by social media technologies in Indigenous communities is its representation in literature. If new fiction is any indication, it's a vital component of everyday reality. Readers of Aboriginal novelist Anita Heiss have seen the contemporary reality of Indigenous life reflected in the pages of her books. Her 2014 novel *Tiddas*, for example, features a cast of five women, four of whom are Aboriginal, who provide love, support, and understanding to one another and maintain their connection with each other in Brisbane, Queensland, through texting and following goings-on on blogs and Twitter. This is an unremarkable and realistic reflection of life as we know it today, but in the history of literature featuring or about Indigenous peoples, it's remarkable to see the deep integration of technology as a force for connection in everyday life. Tommy Orange's (Cheyenne) critically acclaimed novel *There There* (2018), set in contemporary Oakland, California, similarly features a large cast of mainly Indigenous characters who text, chat online, reconnect to family via Facebook and Facebook Messenger, tweet, Facetime, and use phone apps to control camera drones as well as a character, the teenager Orvil Red Feather, who learns about tribal cultural traditions and pow-wow dancing via YouTube. One character, Edwin Black, after finishing a graduate degree in Native American studies and literature, dives deep into an online world (its own "there" that some may consider "unreal"), and it threatens to swallow him up. He is agoraphobic and inactive and separates himself from the offline world, until one day when he grabs a lifeline that connects him with a tribal community organization and a job that capitalizes on his knowledge and his interests that the online world has further fostered. He rejoins the face-to-face "there" that is located, placed, and part of the now that is continuous with the past, another "there." Like *Tiddas*, Orange's fictional meditation on the urban experiences of Indigenous peoples from many tribal nations living in one West Coast American city looks at the multiple ways that identity is understood and that community is fostered, both online and offline, in the "real" world.

This edited volume on Indigenous social media activism begins with Alex Wilson and Corals Zheng's "Shifting Social Media and the Idle No More Movement." In the early winter of 2012, the landscape of activism for Indigenous peoples in North America dramatically changed, and Wilson was there as a leader and participant. At the end of November of that year, four women began to organize Idle No More (INM), an Indigenous and environmental protection movement. INM grew with remarkable speed, powered by the founders' use of social media to reach out to Indigenous peoples throughout Canada and across the globe. For the first time, Indigenous peoples—particularly Indigenous women and two-spirit people—had a significant and impactful presence on social media. Indigenous peoples in the Americas have engaged in activism and resistance since their lands were first colonized, but Idle No More helped change the nature of that activism and resistance by encouraging Indigenous people to take leadership and organize locally to address issues that affect us and our communities, directly challenging and working outside of the systems and institutions that oppress us. Wilson and Zheng discuss the importance of social media to INM and analyze how social media has changed over the past six years since the group's inception. The monetization of social media platforms has created a new extraction industry, one that mines and markets data about Indigenous (and non-Indigenous) users and renders the platforms far less useful or safe for Indigenous (or any other) organizing and activism. Idle No More has now shifted its focus to providing support for on-the-ground actions such as Tiny House Warriors, Standing Rock, Mauna Kea, Missing and Murdered Indigenous Women, and One House Many Nations.

In our second chapter, Nicholet A. Deschine Parkhurst shares how the movement to protect the Standing Rock Sioux Tribe's primary source of clean water, sacred cultural heritage sites, and burial sites from the Dakota Access Pipeline emerged in 2016 and how it was supported by social media through the #NoDAPL and #StandwithStandingRock hashtags. "Mni wiconi, water is life" was chanted at the frontlines, and "Mni wiconi" adorned banners in Instagram photos, was chanted in the background of Facebook Live stories, and even became a hashtag on social media platforms. The #NoDAPL movement demonstrates how Indigenous peoples' use of social media for activism extends beyond recognition and consciousness raising to building virtual and physical communities around the value of #MniWiconi and is a call to action for people to #StandwithStandingRock in their demand for their treaty rights to be honored. "From #Mniwiconi to #StandwithStandingRock: How the #NoDAPL Movement Disrupted Physical and Virtual Spaces and Brought Indigenous Liberation to the Forefront of People's Minds" focuses attention on the ways the #NoDAPL movement garnered solidarity across the United States and the world, drawing thousands of people to converge in the rural area home to the Standing Rock Sioux Tribe in North Dakota. By examining the #NoDAPL movement from a decolonizing perspective, Deschine Parkhurst highlights the ways that social media can be harnessed to disrupt public spheres, center Indigenous voices, challenge political processes, and create communities of change.

In our next chapter, "Anger, Hope, and Love: The Affective Economies of Indigenous Social Media Activism," Bronwyn Carlson and Ryan Frazer draw on Sara Ahmed's notion of "affective economies" to explore the political affordances of emotions in Indigenous activism. For Ahmed, emotions are never private but always political—they "work to shape the 'surfaces' of individual and collective bodies" (Ahmed, 2004, p. 10). Building on Ahmed's conceptual work, they follow two social-media-driven cases of Indigenous activism in Australia (#SOSBlakAustralia and #IndigenousDads), interrogating what the emotions of anger, hope, and joy do in agitating for change. While emotions are absolutely central in forging political solidarities and mobilizing action, they are also highly volatile and even dangerous things, moving in unexpected ways and often leading to unforeseen and undesirable outcomes. Carlson and Frazer argue that different emotions have different political affordances for Indigenous activists and that there exists a difficult balance between political expediency and care. Emotions are often effectively mobilized to galvanize and animate people into progressive action, but they can equally be leveraged against activists, with anger and hatred often being pathologized by reactionary groups.

Steve Elers, Phoebe Elers, and Mohan Dutta continue this examination of affective economies in "Responding to White Supremacy: An Analysis of Twitter Messages by Māori after the Christchurch Terrorist Attack." On March 15, 2019, an Australian white supremacist, Brenton Tarrant, shot dozens of Muslim worshippers at two mosques in Christchurch, New Zealand, resulting in the deaths of fifty-one people and the serious injury of many others. The first seventeen minutes of this act of terrorism was livestreamed using Facebook. Elers, Elers, and Dutta draw attention to the ways that social media, namely Twitter, was used as a communication tool by Māori for antiracist activism, to express their whakaaro (thoughts/opinions) of racism and white supremacy in Aotearoa (New Zealand) after the Christchurch terrorist attack. In the hours, days, and weeks that followed this tragedy, many New Zealanders took to Twitter to vent and share their frustrations about hate speech, racism, and white supremacy—tangata whenua (people of the land) have experienced all of these since colonization. Indigenous voices on social media during this time reworked the meaning of Aotearoa, grounding it in the Māori concepts of invitation, openness, and dialogue and, in doing so, worked to disrupt strategies of whiteness that erase conversations on white supremacy under the pretense of dialogue.

Vital conversations about maintaining and reinvigorating Indigenous culture, language, and identity are the focus of Mounia Mnouer's "The Imazighen of Morocco and the Diaspora on Facebook: Indigenous Cultural and Language Revitalization." Mnouer examines how three Moroccan Amazigh associations have turned to Facebook as a social media space to connect with other Amazigh people (once referred to as Berbers by colonizers) in Morocco and in the diaspora. Specifically, she examines three Facebook sites: the National Federation of Amazigh Associations (FNAA), which encompasses a large number of activists who work on issues related to Imazighen; La Voix de la Femme Amazighe (VFA), which means the Voice of the Amazigh Woman in English and focuses on the matters of Amazigh women and their role in the preservation and revitalization of the cultural heritage of the Amazigh; and Tamazgha Voice Media (TVM), created by activists living outside of Tamazgha to support activism through language and cultural revitalization in North Africa and in the diaspora. Mnouer shares how these associations use their pages as a way to connect with Amazigh communities and to revitalize the language and the cultural aspects of the Amazigh people. These Facebook pages, Mnouer contends, also serve as a reminder for everyone in the lands of Imazighen and in the diaspora to be held accountable for the status of Tamazight.

The next set of chapters in our collection foregrounds how gender and sexuality impact social media activist spaces and how related issues are represented. First, Marisa Elena Duarte and Morgan Vigil-Hayes offer readers a theorization of Indigenous feminist approaches to digital studies by offering a meditation on the ways that researchers should take up methodological concerns regarding inclusion, voice, and representation. By adopting feminist Indigenous approaches within social media studies, a reconfiguring of advanced digital methods will occur because it takes into account a feminist ethics of care in understanding the political and social exigencies of Indigenous women and girls engaging in activities, from sustaining family and friend groups at a distance to social protest, community well-being, and individual self-expression. This work helps us all discern how we create intellectual, spiritual, political, and social connections—and the limitations of those connections—through our approaches to science and technology as well as through our mediated interactions.

In "Indigenous Social Activism Using Twitter: Amplifying Voices Using #MMIWG," Taima Moeke-Pickering, Julia Rowat, Sheila Cote-Meek, and Ann Pegoraro explore how social media can be a positive source to amplify voices and create a sense of mobilization and collective conscientization among users around the national crisis of murdered and missing Indigenous women and girls in Canada. They set this epidemic against the backdrop of subversive texts about Indigenous women on social media that perpetuate racialized and violent discourse. This information circulates and is consumed by Indigenous social media users and non-Indigenous social media users alike and further subjugates Indigenous women and girls and vilifies and dehumanizes them, leading to victim blaming and a refusal to address systemic, colonial, and institutional causes.

Cutcha Risling Baldy's "Radical Relationality in the Native Twitterverse: Indigenous Women, Indigenous Feminisms, and (Re)writing/(Re)righting Resistance on #NativeTwitter" traces how Indigenous women's activism has led the way in (re)claiming land, life, history, and futures, from early memoirs and autobiographies written by Indigenous women to the contemporary activism of Indigenous women on social media. In particular, Baldy analyzes Indigenous women's voices on Twitter and centers how Indigenous women use social media to dismantle and shift dominant narratives and settler-colonial claims to legitimacy through a type of storytelling that (re)claims and (re)stories land, life, and history to not only "make space" but create new spaces of connection and "radial relationality."

In our ninth chapter, "The Rise of Black Rainbow: Queering and Indigenizing Digital Media Strategies, Resistance, and Change," Andrew Farrell explores the development of Black Rainbow, a grassroots collective of lesbian, gay, bisexual, transgender, intersex, and queer (LGBTIQ) Aboriginal and Torres Strait Islander peoples. Through the affordances of social media, Black Rainbow has developed meaningful and impactful strategies to address the communities' needs and desires—from individual and community support through an online presence to structural change that lobbies for competent, inclusive, and safer services. The health and well-being of Aboriginal and Torres Strait Islander LGBTIQ peoples is considerably underrecognized and underresourced and lacks a policy framework that identifies and ensures that the gender and sexual diversity of Indigenous peoples are considered. Black Rainbow, Farrell argues, addresses the many needs of a community who seeks justice and healing from violence, isolation, and a range of ill effects from queerphobia and racism.

The last section of *Indigenous Peoples Rise Up* concentrates attention on the activist potential and reach of social media to support Indigenous art, literature, music, and expressive arts generally, including comedy. In many respects, such forums provide ways for Indigenous epistemologies and ideologies to entertain and move people, to trade in the affective economies of empathy and understanding that will lead to action and change. For example, in chapter 10, Miranda Belarde-Lewis highlights the ways several activist movements—specifically #MMIW (Walking with Our Sisters and the Urban Indian Health Institute's report on MMIW) and #WaterIsLife (various art inspired by the #NoDAPL movement)—have employed the arts and leveraged their impacts through the use of specific social media strategies. Tristan Kennedy's "United Front: Indigenous Peoples' Resistance in the Online Metal Scene," our twelfth chapter, explores how Indigenous metal fans and bands are using social media platforms to disseminate messages of resistance and truth telling that bypass traditional mainstream record industry channels and that resist Western hegemonies. Specifically, attention garnered by the Sydney-based band Homesick in the online metal scene illustrates the efficacy of social media platforms such as Facebook and YouTube in solidifying a political presence for Indigenous peoples. Kennedy concludes that digital communication technologies afford heightened degrees of permanence and visibility to interactions between metalheads in these disintermediated, digital social spaces.

Two key components of this section are in-depth interviews with social media practitioners Debbie Reese and Carly Wallace. Reese, who is Nambé Owingeh, is an expert in children's literature and educational curriculum as well as a former professor; in 2006 she launched the now greatly influential blog *American Indians in Children's Literature.* In her interview Reese discusses her move to start a blog after listservs flamed out and the eventual migration to Twitter as an adjunct platform. In addition to reflecting on some important books and key debates, Reese shares the ups and downs of activist engagement online and through social media. Similarly, Wallace, a Dulguburra Yidinji woman, reflects on the positive and negative components of being on social media as an Indigenous comic. When she started posting her videos—always using a filter to create a screen between herself and the persona she was projecting—Wallace had no idea that her personal stories and silliness would resonate among viewers and lead to CJay's Vines, with nearly forty thousand followers and over two million views. She reckons that people have connected with her because "Blackfella humour is just that little bit different and it's a real part of our kinship."

In our last chapter, "'We're Alive and Thriving . . . We're Modern, We're Human, We're Here!' The 1491s' Social Media Activism," Jeff Berglund offers a parallel inquiry about the activist role of comedy in his examination of work on YouTube and other social media spaces by the comedy troupe named the 1491s. Since 2009 the 1491s have used the positive energy of comedy to galvanize others, with a particular emphasis on shaping the ways Indigenous peoples are seen, how Indigenous peoples see themselves, and how changes might lead Indigenous people to think critically about the conditions under which they are living. In addition to examining their comedic output, Berglund discusses their videos, which honor Indigenous resilience and advocate for political causes; these efforts are also supported by their production infrastructure and disseminated via their YouTube channel. Strategically disseminating their videos to a global audience through YouTube, Berglund contends, the 1491s should be seen as a major force in social change, inspiring Indigenous and non-Indigenous audiences alike, many of whom interact and form a core fanbase despite being separated by time and space.

Social media is ever-changing. The platforms are constantly being updated and functions are added and removed; and the way that Indigenous people use them is under continual transformation and innovation. While we present fourteen informative chapters in this collection, we know that the experiences of Indigenous social media users are too diverse to ever contain within a single book.

It would be remiss of us not to signpost how social media was leveraged in late May and early June 2020 to rally a movement that continues to build across the globe. As this collection reached the final stage prior to production, we find the world has been changed. In the midst of the fifth month of the global COVID-19 pandemic, around the globe we all watched footage documenting the death of George Floyd at the hands of the Minneapolis, Minnesota, police on May 25, 2020. The video, filmed on a bystander's phone, showed Floyd lying face-down, struggling to breathe. One officer held his feet, and he was handcuffed. Derek Chauvin, a white police officer, knelt with his knee firmly lodged in Mr. Floyd's neck. Bystanders heard Mr. Floyd saying, "You're going to kill me, man." Four police officers had arrested Floyd. He did not resist being taken into custody yet was forced to the ground. As a Black man he no doubt understood the ramifications of resisting arrest. Chauvin held the position for eight minutes and forty-six seconds until Mr. Floyd was unconscious and unresponsive. He continued to apply pressure for a full minute after the paramedics arrived (Hill et al., 2020). About an hour later at a medical center, Floyd was pronounced dead.

The video of George Floyd's killing in this midwestern city went viral across social media and was quickly shared worldwide. It sparked unprecedented global anger about this injustice and others, resulting in protests around the world. The hashtag #BlackLivesMatter, which emerged first in 2013, was used to express anger not only about the unlawful death of Mr. Floyd but also about the structural racism that results in the killing of Black and Indigenous peoples globally. In the United States, Native Americans have the highest proportion of fatal encounters with law enforcement of any minority group, yet their deaths result in little media attention (Hansen, 2017; Schroedel and Chin, 2020). Similarly, in Australia, the unlawful deaths of Aboriginal and Torres Strait Islander people rarely result in media focus. The rise of the #BlackLivesMatter movement, which continues to reverberate—has by no means come to an end. It profoundly demonstrates, though, how social media platforms have provided a means for our stories to be told, where we can rally support for injustices we face and come together to support each other in our trauma, our anger, our joy, our hope.

Note

1   To view videos of the symposium, see https://www.mq.edu.au/research/research -centres-groups-and-facilities/resilient-societies/centres/forum-for-indigenous -research-excellence/journal-of-global-indigeneity.

References

Ahmed, S. (2014). *Cultural politics of emotion*. Edinburgh: Edinburgh University Press.

Carlson, B., and Frazer, R. (2018). *Social media mob: Being Indigenous online*. Macquarie University. https://research-management.mq.edu.au/ws/portalfiles/portal /85013179/MQU_SocialMediaMob_report_Carlson_Frazer.pdf.

Carlson, B., Sciascia, A., and Wilson, A. (2017). Indigenous activism on social media. *Australasian Journal of Information Systems*, 21. https://pdfs.semanticscholar.org /f9ad/4c43935fcb7020ad936998c472547b72da60.pdf.

Hansen, E. (2017). The forgotten minority in police shootings. *CNN*. https://edition .cnn.com/2017/11/10/us/native-lives-matter/index.html.

Heiss, A. (2014). *Tiddas*. Cammeray, NSW: Simon & Schuster.

Hill, E., Tiefenthäler, A., Triebert, C., Jordan, D., Willis, H., and Stein, R. (2020, May 31). 8 minutes and 46 seconds: How George Floyd was killed in custody. *New York Times*. https://www.nytimes.com/2020/05/31/us/george-floyd -investigation.html.

Orange, T. (2018). *There There*. New York: Knopf.

Pulley, N. A. (2014). Indigetechs: The original time-space traveling Native Americans and our modern world hyper-pow-wow. *Western Humanities Review*, *68*(2), 95–101.

Schroedel, J. R., and Chin, R. J. (2020). Whose lives matter: The media's failure to cover police use of lethal force against Native Americans. *Race and Justice*, *10*(2), 150–175.

Treuer, D. (2019). *The heartbeat of Wounded Knee: Native America from 1890 to the present*. New York: Riverhead Books.

1

Shifting Social Media and the Idle No More Movement

■■■■■■■■■■■■■■■■■■■■■■

ALEX WILSON AND CORALS ZHENG

Indigenous peoples in the Americas have engaged in activism and resistance since our lands were first invaded. In the late fall and early winter of 2012, however, the landscape of that activism changed dramatically. In mid-October that year, the Canadian government put forward a series of bills that together, if passed, would amend or repeal existing legislation to remove legally required environmental protections for nearly all of Canada's fresh water bodies, reduce requirements for environmental assessments associated with the permit process for activities such as pipeline development, and erode Indigenous and treaty-based rights. In response, four women based in Saskatchewan began to organize community teach-ins and rallies to quickly share information about the impacts of the proposed legislation. This was the start of Idle No More (INM), a movement to affirm Indigenous sovereignty and to protect lands and waters.

INM has maintained an online and social media presence since its start, but the ways that it uses these platforms have changed significantly. This chapter discusses INM's use of social media and explores the nature and reasons for these changes. These include ethical concerns about the corporate practices of Facebook and other social media companies and, in particular, the extent to which social media platforms mine and market data about their users, rendering the platforms far less useful or safe for Indigenous peoples' (or any other group's) organizing and activism. Changes to INM's online presence are also linked to a shift in the group's focus, which is now directed primarily to supporting community-led on-the-ground actions, such as the Tiny House Warriors, Mauna Kea, One House Many Nations, and Missing and Murdered Indigenous Women and Girls (MMIWG) and Two-Spirit People (in their chapter in this volume, Moeke-Pickering et al. discuss the role of Twitter and other social media in movements to raise awareness of MMIWG).

INM's vision statement "calls on all people to join in a peaceful revolution, to honour Indigenous sovereignty, and to protect the land and water" (2013b). Throughout its history, INM has worked closely with Defenders of the Land (a network of Indigenous communities and people engaged in land struggles across Canada) and allied with and actively supported other campaigns, network and movements. In 2013, INM and Defenders of the Land jointly called upon federal, provincial, and territorial governments in Canada to make changes in six specific areas. The calls for change demand that systems and institutions abandon practices that oppress Indigenous people and nations and instead take action that is "in accordance with the principles of coexistence and mutual respect between Indigenous and non-Indigenous Peoples" (Idle No More and Defenders of the Land, 2013):

1 Repeal provisions of Bill C-45 (including changes to the Indian Act and Navigable Waters Act, which infringe on environmental protections, Aboriginal and Treaty rights) and abandon all pending legislation which does the same.

2 Deepen democracy in Canada through practices such as proportional representation and consultation on all legislation concerning collective rights and environmental protections, and include legislation which restricts corporate interests.

3 In accordance with the United Nations Declaration on the Rights of Indigenous Peoples' principle of free, prior, and informed consent, respect the right of Indigenous peoples to say no to development on their territory.

4 Cease its policy of extinguishment of Aboriginal Title and recognize and affirm Aboriginal Title and Rights, as set out in section 35 of Canada's constitution, and recommended by the Royal Commission on Aboriginal Peoples.

5 Honour the spirit and intent of the historic Treaties. Officially repudiate the racist Doctrine of Discovery and the Doctrine of Terra Nullius, and abandon their use to justify the seizure of Indigenous Nations lands and wealth.

6 Actively resist violence against women and two-spirit people and hold a national inquiry into missing and murdered Indigenous women, girls

and two-spirit people, and involve Indigenous women and two-spirit people in the design, decision-making, process and implementation of this inquiry, as a step toward initiating a comprehensive and coordinated national action plan. (Idle No More and Defenders of the Land, 2013)

INM is a non-hierarchical movement in which leadership and power are dispersed. Indigenous people are encouraged to take leadership in their own communities; to organize, participate in, and take ownership of locally based actions; to respond to and support national and international mobilizations that address shared concerns and issues; and to directly challenge and work outside of the systems and institutions that oppress them. INM's conveners and early organizers committed to communication strategies that reflect the movement's dispersed leadership and power model. These include supporting multiple people to assume the role of a spokesperson and represent INM in the media and reaching out to connect with and support (rather than compete with) similar emerging or established campaigns and solidarity movements. As a result of these choices, the majority of leaders and organizers who have emerged in the movement have been Indigenous women, two-spirit people, and youth.

While INM is Indigenous-led at both national and local levels, it also opens space for settler Canadians and other non-Indigenous people to ally with Indigenous people and actively participate in and contribute to the teach-ins, rallies, drum dances, flash mobs, online discussions, webinars, and other actions organized through the movement. This approach, as one person explained, invites everyone and anyone to join "an actual dialogue about how to be a good neighbour and family member, and what it means to be a country where indigenous peoples have always led, always taught and always gifted newcomers a future" (Sinclair, 2014).

Irlbacher-Fox (2012) observes that settler Canadians might ally with INM for reasons that include a sense of "moral responsibility, or self interest." If the movement is to achieve its goals, however, settler Canadians (and she includes herself in this group) must be willing to transform the nature of their relationships with Indigenous people:

Co-existence through co-resistance is the responsibility of settlers, and we achieve it in part by making change in our own systems and among other settlers, taking our cue from Indigenous action and direction. For settler allies, having a place to land relationally creates a stronger rationale for unsettling established systems: knowing and being with Indigenous peoples, even if it is just to be welcomed to stand alongside at marches and rallies, or to join the drum dance circle, creates a tangible bond. Relationship creates accountability and responsibility for sustained supportive action. This does not mean requiring Indigenous energies for creating relationship with settlers; it means settlers taking initiative to live on a personal level what they claim on a political one. (Irlbacher-Fox, 2012)

Social Media as a Tool for Resistance

INM's use of "democratized digital tools" (Blevis, 2013, p. 2) such as Twitter and Facebook has been widely studied and reported (Blevis, 2013; Callison and Hermida, 2015; Donkin, 2013; Raynauld, Richez, and Boudreau Morris, 2018; Tupper, 2014; Wood, 2015). When the internet and, in particular, social media first appeared, enabling people to connect across distances, share, discover, and discuss, these technologies held the promise of becoming "an empowering and emancipatory force" (Zuboff, 2019b, p. 11). The INM conveners recognized and quickly made the most of this potential. Social media activities enabled the movement to reach Indigenous peoples and non-Indigenous allies throughout Canada, the Americas, and elsewhere, connecting diverse and widely dispersed people in a common cause.

The movement's starting place was a teach-in on the omnibus Bill C-45, held in Saskatchewan in October 2012 and organized by Jessica Gordon (Saulteaux/Cree), Sylvia McAdam Saysewahum (Cree), Sheelah McLean (settler Canadian), and Nina Wilson (Nakota and Plains Cree). The four women mobilized their own personal and professional networks and social media for information campaigns about the pending legislation, teach-ins, rallies, and land-defense activities. They reached out to Indigenous people and allies throughout Canada, the Americas, and beyond, inspiring them to join, commit to, and organize "ongoing resistance against neo-colonialism" (Idle No More, 2013a). The first tweet with the hashtag #IdleNoMore was sent in early November 2012; the Idle No More Facebook group (@IdleNoMoreCommunity) was launched on November 29; and the movement's Twitter account (@IdleNoMore4) and web page (idlenomore.ca) were set up in the first week of December. Using social media and word of mouth, INM put out a call for a National Day of Action on December 10, and in response, Indigenous people, allies, and solidarity groups throughout Canada promoted and organized actions in their own communities. Images and descriptions of actions that took place that day (including the public announcement by Chief Theresa Spence of the Attawapiskat First Nation that she would begin a hunger strike to draw attention to the concerns about conditions in her home community, Bill C-45, and other issues affecting First Nations people and in support of the INM movement) were posted and shared on social media. The movement also received significant coverage in mainstream media. After footage of a flash mob round dance in a mall organized by activists in Regina was posted and circulated on social media, similar actions were organized at public sites in other cities, including round dances (some of which blocked roads or rail lines) in nine different Canadian cities on December 21.

The movement grew with astonishing speed. On December 1, 2012, the hashtag #IdleNoMore appeared on Twitter only ten times. On December 10, the National Day of Action, when thirteen protest actions took place across Canada, INM was mentioned in as many as 14,600 tweets, including 11,416 uses of the hashtag (Blevis, 2013; Donkin, 2013; Wood, 2015). On December 21, 79 round dances and other actions were held across the country. Over the week beginning December 23, the movement was mentioned more than 12,260 times on Facebook and more than 144,215 times on Twitter, with as many as 24,815 tweets in a single day. At the end of 2012, INM had existed as a movement for less than two months. Over that relatively brief period, INM organizers documented 191 actions in Canada, the United States, Central America, Europe, Australia, New Zealand, the Middle East, Africa, and Southeast Asia. By January 2013, roughly 45,000 people had joined the INM Facebook group, adding to the page their photos from rallies, protests, and actions throughout the globe (CBC News, 2013; Donkin, 2013). On January 11, INM's first Global Day of Action, 265 INM events were scheduled at locations around the globe, and references to INM appeared in 56,954 tweets, the greatest number in any given single day (Blevis, 2013). Over the movement's first six months, the total number of tweets referencing INM exceeded 1,215,000.

INM has been described as "the most focused use of social media in aboriginal activism" (Donkin, 2013). INM has been able to connect with diverse and dispersed Indigenous peoples and non-Indigenous allies from throughout the world and bring them into a grassroots movement that honors Indigenous sovereignty and protects the land and water. For some, involvement in INM has been their first directly political engagement. The Sisseton-Wahpeton Oyate scholar Kim TallBear observed that "there are people who have never left their home communities but have been on top of the movement through Facebook and Twitter" (cited in Wood, 2015, p. 616). INM's use of social media enabled Indigenous people to organize around the issues affecting them, drawing on their own local networks, connecting with activists in other communities, and gaining inspiration about the ways in which they might organize and take action at both local and national levels.

The Cree activist Erica Lee (an early INM organizer) has pointed out that prior to INM's founding, when mainstream media wanted to present the "voice" of Indigenous people in Canada, it was First Nation Chiefs or other Indigenous people in positions of power who were invited to speak. In the INM movement, social media became a space where all Indigenous people were invited to speak and to be heard (Donkin, 2013). Lee's comments and those of others were presented in an article in a nationally read newspaper in Canada, and as the movement grew, mainstream media in Canada increasingly turned to INM organizers to get their story straight. To guide their contacts with mainstream and other media and their social media and online activities, INM's national organizers drew on lessons learned in a successful campaign to remove the racist name and mascot of a high school sports team in Saskatoon. Their communication strategy emphasizes the importance of focusing on short, clear, and consistent messages; the use of hashtags such as #IdleNoMore, which makes it easier for people to find information about the movement and to trace circulation of this information in social media platforms; avoiding contests between individuals or groups of people who are experiencing oppression over whose experiences are the most oppressive; having multiple spokespersons to represent the movement; and connecting to other similar campaigns (McLean, Wilson, and Lee, 2017). As the chief executive of the national Indigenous television network APTN stated, "This is new and it's pushing change in the community. . . . And it's coming from the bottom" (Wood, 2015, p. 616).

To better understand the extent to which INM's social media presence facilitated the movement's rapid growth, Wood (2015) looked closely at INM's use of social media in its first two months. Indigenous people constitute around 5 percent of Canada's total population. The Indigenous population is dispersed, growing rapidly, and, in comparison to the country as a whole, relatively young. Slightly more than half of First Nation, Inuit, and Métis people live in urban centers. Of the nearly half who live in rural areas, a significant proportion are located in First Nation reserves or other small communities in remote and/or northern territories. Dense networks of social ties exist within individual reserves or other Indigenous communities, and at an individual level, many people maintain strong ties to relatives, close friends, and associates living outside the community. Indigenous communities also have ties to political networks, including those associated with the formal, top-down governance systems imposed by the settler government. These include, for example, Chief and Council in individual First Nations, the Assembly of First Nations (a national body representing First Nation Chiefs and Councils throughout Canada), and federal, provincial, territorial, and municipal governments. At an individual level, Indigenous people may also be connected to grassroots networks, campaigns, and movements that focus on asserting and protecting Indigenous sovereignty, rights, and lands, such as Defenders of the Land (the Indigenous-led network with which INM allies) and INM. Wood (2015) observes, "This combination of a young population who are enthusiastic users of social media, a shared threat, perceptions that existing governance structures were not successful advocates, and bottom-up political networks produced a fertile context for spreading the movement nationally, despite a diversity of interests, marginalization and a sparse population" (p. 617). Donkin (2013) has also taken note of the high rate of youth participation in INM, commenting that "while youth may not have started Idle No More, they're the people that have 'captured' the movement."

In addition to its website and its presence in mainstream media, a significant portion of INM's communication and organizing have taken place on Facebook and Twitter. There are some notable differences between the two platforms. Facebook "puts offline relationships online" (Wood, 2015, p. 618). Because people interact with "friends" on the platform, they may be more confident that what they see or read there is truthful, valid, and relevant than they are with what they see or read on other platforms or in mainstream media. Facebook is designed for interaction, so any user can comment on or repost a post, initiate or jump into a discussion about a post, signal with a click or an emoji their approval of or emotional response to a post, or share their own experiences or opinions in a post. In the context of INM, Facebook was a particularly effective way for people to learn about the national issues that drove the movement's formation, and to make the link between those issues and their own experiences at a local level. Online discussions and the circulation of event announcements, photos, and videos from specific actions and other INM-related posts engaged and mobilized people to initiate actions in their own communities, supporting the rapid spread of specific tactics: "The mechanisms happen almost simultaneously. An image or clip of a round dance would be shared, along with some sort of commentary or introduction like, 'Wow! Imagine doing this in our city!' or 'Check this out!' Sometimes such introductions would also adapt or recode the information for a new audience—linking it to local campaigns or contexts" (Wood, 2015, p. 618). Wood describes this cycle as a "diffusion mechanism" (p. 619). It moves an expanding group of Facebook users from identification (the post came from a Facebook "friend" or group) to certification (if a "friend" or group shared it, it must be important and trustworthy info), deliberation (what does this mean to me?), and adaptation (how can we use this here?). Organizers' ability to adapt and mobilize information and tactics gathered from social media has been a critical component of INM's growth. It helped the movement to quickly broaden, diversify, and deepen, opening the door for more people (both Indigenous people and non-Indigenous allies) to see themselves as part of the movement. It also facilitated people to organize and take part in actions that joined their local struggles with what was happening at national and international levels, to contribute to the developing collective understanding of what Indigenous sovereignty and protection of the land and waters might entail, and, as Wood reminds us, to lay down "infrastructure [for Indigenous activism] that can continue to be used" (p. 620).

Blevis (2013) and Callison and Hermida (2015) have studied INM's Twitter presence. Blevis (2013) compiled data analytics on Twitter users who incorporated the #IdleNoMore hashtag in their tweets during the movement's first six months. As noted earlier in this chapter, his analysis shows (perhaps unsurprisingly) that INM's Twitter mentions are linked closely to specific events. For example, in December 2012, Twitter mentions grew rapidly in association with INM's National Day of Action, tapered off, and then climbed dramatically again, peaking on INM's Global Day of Action on January 11, 2013. INM's Twitter mentions declined significantly (by as much as 50 percent) on January 12 and continued to decline over the next few months, with the exception of a few bumps around individual events organized by or associated with INM. By the beginning of April, the average number of INM-referencing tweets issued on a daily basis had stabilized, sitting somewhere around a few thousand throughout those months. Similarly, the rate at which new participants joined the Twitter "chatter" about INM increased throughout December 2012 and then peaked and plateaued in January 2013.

Blevis (2013) analyzed the level of engagement of the 143,000 Twitter users who included the #IdleNoMore hashtag in their tweets over the movement's first six months. He established three categories of engagement: low engagement users (those referencing INM in one to 15 tweets over the six-month period), medium engagement users (referencing INM in 16–500 tweets), and high engagement users (referencing INM in more than 500 tweets). Nearly 94 percent of all users fell into the low engagement category, each sending, on average, only two INM-referencing tweets and accounting for only 23 percent of all INM-referencing tweets. Blevis describes this group as consisting of "members of the public . . . who appear to have limited interest in the movement, whether they are supporters, critics or indifferent" (2013, p. 3). "Medium engagement" users constituted 6 percent of the total group, each sending an average of 67 INM-referencing tweets and accounting for 51 percent of the total tweets. He considers this group "to be actively interested in the movement, or at least interested enough to openly express their views" (p. 3). It includes some of the movement's more public figures, media organizations (which he characterizes as generally neutral in their views of the movement, a characterization that, as discussed later in this chapter, other researchers have contested), labor groups, and researchers or analysts. While "high engagement" users constituted only 0.2 percent of the total group, each sent an average of 1,128 tweets and together contributed more than a quarter of the total tweets. This group includes "some of the most passionate supporters of the movement" (p. 3) as well as some media employees or organizations. It also includes spambots that use the #IdleNoMore hashtag to draw attention to their own online content, which typically did not relate to the movement.

Blevis's (2013) analysis of INM-referencing Twitter data also considered whether participants were individuals or organizations and, for individuals, their gender identity. In instances where these aspects of identity could not be determined from the information included in a user's Twitter identity, he established the category of "unspecified." Together, users identified as "unspecified" or as organizations (including "national, regional, local and alternative media outlets as well as community, labour, political and activist organizations" [p. 16]) accounted for roughly one-quarter of the participant group. Blevis notes that the "unspecified" category likely also includes spambots.

INM was initiated by women and as a movement has, to a great extent, been driven by women and two-spirit people (an identity not included in any of Blevis's analytic categories). Blevis (2013) points out that while males typically generate about 70 percent of online political chatter, in INM's Twitter feed women contributed more tweets than men did, a pattern also found in the Twitter activity associated with other Indigenous resistance movements (Baldy, this volume). Blevis also analyzed the sentiment reflected in individual tweets, categorizing them as positive, neutral, or negative. Throughout the six-month period, the vast majority of the tweets were positive, particularly in the last two months of the study period. While both men and women contributed positive tweets, women were somewhat more likely to do so. Men were more likely than women to contribute negative tweets.

Blevis (2013) observes that as the movement grew, the nature and sources of what was discussed in INM-related tweets shifted. Between December 2012 and January 2013, nearly all of the INM-related tweets came from Canada and typically discussed either the nature of the movement itself or promoted or documented (often in the form of photos and videos) specific INM-related actions or events. A few critical tweets that, for example, questioned Chief Spence's fast or expressed frustration with actions that impeded or blocked traffic appeared in the feed. Toward the end of January, public participation in both on-the-ground actions and INM-referring tweets began to decline, and a growing percentage of tweets featured news headlines. At the same time, the percentage of tweets originating from and/or referring to events outside of Canada (e.g., United States, Brazil, Ecuador, New Zealand) grew. With this geographic expansion, the range of topics included in INM-related Twitter also expanded to include, for example, threads related to issues or concerns that affect Indigenous peoples (such as the Alberta tar sands, Keystone XL pipeline, and environmental protection) and that challenge and demand changes to the policies and actions of both government and the corporate sector.

While Blevis was interested primarily in the metrics of INM's Twitter presence, Callison and Hermida (2015), in a study of tweets that included the #IdleNoMore hashtag and that were sent from December 2012 to January 2013, explored how use of the hashtag involved citizens in the "flow, framing and interpretation of news" (p. 695).

Callison and Hermida (2015) recognize the potential of Twitter and other social media platforms to function as "a tool to articulate a counter narrative and to contest selective or dismissive framing by mainstream media" (p. 696). It is a much needed tool. A recent study of nine Canadian print media publications' reporting on INM in its first month found that any positive or supportive coverage was "overwhelmed by anti-INM rhetoric advanced by Postmedia Network and its affiliate titles" (Chen, 2017, p. 144). Postmedia publishes one of Canada's two daily national newspapers as well as dailies in thirty-three Canadian cities. It is an influential and consistently conservative news provider with close ties to the oil and gas sector, an industry whose operations frequently directly conflict with Indigenous sovereignty, Indigenous land rights, and the protection of the land and waters. These issues, of course, are at the center of the INM movement.

For INM, Twitter's usefulness as a tool relies, to a considerable extent, on the use of the #IdleNoMore hashtag. As Callison and Hermida (2015) explain, "The mechanism allows users to find and follow a particular stream of messages from a high volume of information. The inclusion of a hashtag indicates a desire to participate in a specific communicative exchange and make such content more visible on the network, beyond a user's immediate circle of followers. . . . Hashtags create a macro layer of communication on twitter that facilitates the rapid forming of ad hoc issue publics" (p. 698). Like other movements that have made effective use of social media, such as Occupy and the Arab Spring, INM does not focus on a single issue or demand (Callison and Hermida, 2015). Rather, it focuses on broad and deep concerns related to Indigenous sovereignty, the protection of the land and waters, and the reframing and transformation of relationships between Indigenous and non-Indigenous nations, people, and private interests. In its vision statement, INM commits to ongoing alliance building and the inclusion of grassroots perspectives, issues, and concerns (Idle No More, 2013b). Twitter is one way the movement expresses this commitment, harnessing "a form of network power that allows individuals to make connections across networks and leverage resources to contest hierarchical power . . . a mechanism for loosely knit groups to debate, formulate and articulate meaning" (Callison & Hermida, 2015, p. 699).

Callison and Hermida's (2015) study asks and answers an important question: whose voice has helped shape the meaning of INM? They analyzed the most influential users (where level of influence is calculated using an algorithm that incorporates number of followers as a central factor) and the most retweeted users (those whose commentary is most widely circulated) in the virtual community gathered around the #IdleNoMore hashtag. The twenty-five most influential voices consist primarily of mainstream media organizations and employees and institutional elites, a group that includes Indigenous and non-Indigenous musicians, authors, and other celebrities. Alternative voices, a category that includes bloggers, individual activists, and activist organizations, can also be found on the list. Only one Indigenous person was identified on the top twenty-five list. While the list of the twenty-five most influential voices does not include any members of the general public, they are the largest single group within the list of the top five hundred most influential voices, occupying more than one-quarter of the spots, followed by the alternative voices group, which occupies only slightly less than one-quarter of the spots. Only 2 percent of the users on the list of top five hundred influencers were identified as Indigenous.

Findings from Callison and Hermida's (2015) analysis of the most retweeted accounts tell a very different story. The two most retweeted are INM and the hacktivist movement Anonymous, part of a larger group of alternative voices that includes Indigenous and non-Indigenous activists, bloggers, and alternative media and occupies nearly half of the top twenty-five most retweeted list. Indigenous and non-Indigenous performers, artists, and other celebrities hold nearly one-third of the spots, and the remaining spots are split between mainstream media and members of the general public. Indigenous people or organizations occupy more than half the spots on the list. Only three representatives of mainstream media are included in the top twenty-five retweeted accounts, and two of these users are part of the conservative Postmedia Network, discussed earlier in this chapter. Within the much longer list of top five hundred retweeted voices, alternative voices occupy nearly one-third of the spots, the general public nearly one-quarter, and institutional elites (now including researchers/experts along with performers, artists, and other celebrities) slightly more than one-fifth. More than two-fifths of the users on the top five hundred list were identified as Indigenous.

Social media, Callison and Hermida (2015) remind us, "is a chance to be seen, heard, and listened to outside the established channels for news and information" (p. 710). The #IdleNoMore hashtag provided the mechanism for this, bringing members of the public and alternative voices together with institutional elites in an online conversation in which they shared, gathered, and cocreated knowledge and awareness about the meaning of the movement, about local and national concerns and issues the movement might address, and about actions and tactics that might be an effective way to address them. Because a user's number of followers is typically the weightiest factor in calculations of Twitter influence, mainstream media, celebrities, and other institutional elites appear to be the most influential users in the #IdleNoMore community. As Callison and Hermida point out, mainstream media, celebrities, and other institutional elites "inherit structural power [and] do not necessarily retain their influence on the hashtag" (p. 713). Twitter users typically retweet what is most relevant and resonant for them. In this way, users whose tweets are most frequently and widely retweeted become a "crowdsourced elite" or influencer (p. 713), amassing significant clout within the online #IdleNoMore community. Arguably, they become the most influential voices in the ongoing collaborative development of the movement's identity, concerns, and actions. It is reassuring, then, that Indigenous people and organizations occupy more than half the spots on the list of top twenty-five retweeted accounts and that members of the public and alternative voices constitute more than half of the top five hundred retweeted accounts.

Rethinking Social Media

As the research discussed above makes clear, social media in the INM movement provided essential tools that enabled the movement to connect and engage with diverse and widely dispersed populations, including, importantly, those most directly impacted by the issues and concerns the movement addresses. Online exchanges and conversations in the community that formed around the #IdleNoMore hashtag nurtured the development of a collective identity and shared consciousness that animated the movement and "helped to diffuse the tactics and to push the wave of protest" (Wood, 2015, p. 616). Without a doubt, social media played a critical role in INM's development. However, over the eight years since the movement began, social media platforms have become increasingly monetized, making them far less useful or safe for Indigenous (or any other) organizing and activism.

The monetization of social media platforms was possible because every time we (knowingly or unknowingly) have a presence on the web, we leave some kind of data residue or debris behind. These data have become a valuable resource that is scraped up in the new extraction industry, one that mines and markets data about Indigenous (and non-Indigenous) users. "Privacy," Birchall observes, "is like the light we see from an already dead star. We cling to it even though we live in what our digital conjuncture has essentially rendered a post-privacy paradigm" (2017, p. 25). In most circumstances, we have no meaningful control over what information is collected or how or by whom that information is accessed or used (Cinnamon, 2017). We now live under a new economic regime, one in which "the earlier dream of digital technology as an empowering and emancipatory force" (Zuboff, 2019b, p. 11) has become the nightmarish state of "surveillance capitalism," in which social media and smart devices have become "supply chain interfaces for the flow of raw material to be translated into data, to be fashioned into prediction products, to be sold in behavioral futures markets so that we end up funding our own domination" (Zuboff, in Biddle, 2019).

Social media raises many ethical concerns (Pilar, 2017). It lacks transparency and accountability about the ways in which data are gathered and (mis)used by those who have access to them (Doward, Cadwalladr, and Gibbs, 2017); about its refusal to monitor and remove fake news, fake posts, and fake identities (Hachman, 2017); and about its use of algorithms to predict and manipulate users' behaviors, a practice that validates and entrenches users in their own positions and perceptions of the world (Jones, 2018). Social media also has had significant environmental impacts. The five largest companies in the world today are all in the information and communications technology (ICT) sector—Apple, Amazon, the Google conglomerate Alphabet, Microsoft, and, of course, Facebook (Jones, 2018). Both internet traffic and the electricity demands of this sector have grown rapidly, and its carbon footprint now equals that of the entire aviation industry's emissions from fuel (Clifford, 2019). It is estimated that by 2030 the ICT sector will be responsible for as much as 20 percent of the world's electricity demand. While each company has publicly committed to reduce energy consumption through strategies such as developing more efficient data centers purchasing renewable energy (Jones, 2018), the five largest companies have each joined and/or financially contributed to groups that actively engage in climate change denial (Merchant, 2019).

Law enforcement and governments are invaluable markets for surveillance capitalists. Currently, dissent and protest are increasingly criminalized. Indigenous land protectors have been identified by governments as "radicalized environmentalists" (Bronskill, 2014), "environmental rights extremists," and a "domestic terrorist threat" (Kusnetz, 2018). Law enforcement's access to an individual activist's online personal data and photos (invaluable data when coupled with facial recognition technology) places land defenders at risk. In 2018 in northern British Columbia, Indigenous land defenders in Wet-suwet-en First Nation set up an encampment and blockade in the path of a proposed pipeline in their traditional territory. The following year, Royal Canadian Mounted Police (RCMP) officers, using social media to monitor the land defenders, were authorized to use lethal force in their raid of the camp (Dhillon and Parrish, 2019a, 2019b). In 2017, after a court refused his request for a search warrant to gain access to a Facebook page on the NoDAPL movement (Parkhurst's chapter in this volume discusses this movement protesting construction of the Dakota Access Pipeline), a prosecutor in Washington State worked around that prohibition by requesting and receiving access to the page from federal officials (Bitar, 2018).

In their review of government documents released in response to Access to Information and Freedom of Information requests, Crosby and Monaghan (2016) determined that INM has been identified "as both a criminal and a national security threat" (p. 37) and has been consistently monitored by multiple government departments and agencies in Canada. The RCMP, Canadian Security Intelligence Service (CSIS), Department of National Defense, Public Safety Canada, Transport Canada, Canada Border Services Agency, Aboriginal Affairs, Northern Development Canada, and provincial and municipal police services contributed resources to what CSIS called "a fusion centre for Native problems" (Crosby and Monaghan, 2018), an expanded security apparatus and coordinated effort (through, for example, the creation of fake social media accounts to monitor and interfere with INM's online activities) to monitor, surveille, catalogue, and silence the movement. Ultimately, the center surveilled and reported on more than one thousand INM events. As Crosby and Monaghan explain, this response to INM cannot be separated from Canada's status as a settler colonial state: "Government and policing agencies have attempted to neutralize and criminalize Idle No More precisely because it is an Indigenous movement that threatens the material and immaterial values of settler colonialism by asserting self-determination and land and treaty rights" (p. 42). As the creation of the "fusion centre for Native problems" illustrates, the settler-colonial state is willing to use any means possible (including communications technologies that most in the general public have adopted as a way to strengthen their social connections) to intensify the violence it directs toward Indigenous bodies.

A Renewed Focus

In Canada and other nations, settler colonialism persists and INM continues its work to honor Indigenous sovereignty and to protect the land and water. In published interviews and commentaries, individual organizers involved with INM in its early days have reflected on what the movement has accomplished. They point to the increased organization, motivation, and readiness to respond at a grassroots level with collective action led by Indigenous people; increased carefulness and attention to Indigenous and treaty rights, Indigenous sovereignty, and nation-to-nation status on the part of governments; more responsible media coverage; and a deepened understanding of the need for non-Indigenous people to transform their relationships with Indigenous people (Monkman and Morin, 2017; Sinclair, 2014).

INM has strategically shifted its use of social media to more directly activate and support people to engage in action in their own local settings, while avoiding online engagements that reveal activists' networks or relationships and put individuals at further risk. On its website, INM provides access to webinars, policy papers, solidarity statements, calls to action, and other resources it has developed to support activist responses to specific issues as they arise, such as a 2018 bill introduced by the federal government that threatened Indigenous sovereignty and collective rights (Defenders of the Land, Truth Campaign, and Idle No More Networks, 2018). INM remains on Facebook and Twitter and uses its extensive networks (approximately 400,000 people) on social media and email to alert people to these resources.

INM continues to actively support allied movements that affirm Indigenous sovereignty in their traditional territories and that protect the land and waters. These include the Tiny House Warriors, who are building small houses in Secwepemc Territory, strategically placed along the route of the Trans Mountain Pipeline "to assert Secwepemc Law and jurisdiction, and block access to this pipeline" (Tiny House Warriors, n.d.); the Mauna Kea land defenders, who have also set up an encampment and road blockade to halt the construction of a telescope on a sacred site (Chávez, 2019; Idle No More, 2015); and many other localized actions.

INM also established the One House Many Nations (OHMN) campaign to address the inadequate quality and availability of housing in First Nations across Canada and the resultant significant overrepresentation of Indigenous people in the population experiencing or at risk of homelessness, both on and off reserve (Standing Senate Committee on Aboriginal Peoples, 2015). The first OHMN project was to build a home for an unhoused Elder in the Big River First Nation in northern Saskatchewan. Tapping into its networks and drawing on the infrastructure for actions developed over the course of the movement, INM launched a crowdfunding call that raised donations of money, materials, and labor and was able to build the house within three weeks. The next OHMN project, a collaboration with the American Decentralized Design Lab and with Opaskwayak Cree Nation (OCN), was to develop a model for a sustainable community village within the larger community of OCN. OCN Elders, knowledge keepers, leaders, and community members worked with designers, architects, and builders to design and build housing that responds to local needs and to the current climate crisis. The design for each housing unit incorporates modular building techniques, locally sourced materials, and sustainable water and waste management. The first home has been built by a team of volunteers that included the person who now inhabits the house, and modular components have been assembled for a second home. The Muskrat Hut, designed and built in 2019, is another component of the OCN sustainable village. It is a mobile, off-grid, sustainable washroom and kitchen unit that will function as part of the core infrastructure of the village. Because it is mobile, it will also be available to support the development of additional housing and land-based activities.

The OHMN campaign also raises awareness about the appalling housing conditions in First Nations and pressures the federal government to honor its treaty, legal, and ethical responsibilities to provide adequate housing on reserve. The on-reserve housing crisis is rooted in settler colonialism. Its starting place was "the forced resettlement of Indigenous people into villages, the reorganization of their communities, and the reformation of their housing practices, . . . instruments wielded by both missionaries and governments to impose, maintain, and extend their supervision and social control of Indigenous peoples" (Wilson and Mans, 2019, p. 171). Housing constructed on reserve by the federal government may have met the needs of an assimilationist regime, but it has not met the needs of First Nations people. On-reserve housing has routinely been built from inadequate materials, unfit for the frequently challenging environmental conditions of the Canadian north, and often began to deteriorate immediately after construction.

The OHMN campaign and the development of OCN's sustainable village are offline "hacks" of the colonial system that makes and keeps Indigenous people houseless. It brings together Indigenous people and their non-Indigenous allies to create Indigenous-led solutions to address problems and issues generated by settler colonialism, shifting the too often pathologizing discourse around Indigenous homelessness to the action of sharing and building knowledge and resources. In this and other ways, the INM movement continues its fight to affirm and extend the sovereignty of Indigenous people.

Acknowledgments

The authors would like to acknowledge and thank the Jackman Humanities Institute, University of Toronto for supporting this work. We would also like to thank Janet Sarson for reviewing and providing feedback on drafts of this chapter.

References

Biddle, S. (2019, February 2). "A fundamentally illegitimate choice": Shoshana Zuboff on the age of surveillance capitalism. *The Intercept*. https://theintercept.com/2019/02/02/shoshana-zuboff-age-of-surveillance-capitalism/.

Birchall, C. (2017). *Shareveillance: The dangers of openly sharing and covertly collecting data*. Minneapolis: University of Minnesota Press. https://manifold.umn.edu/projects/shareveillance.

Bitar, J. (2018, February 6). 6 ways government is going after environmental activists. *ACLU Speak Freely*. https://www.aclu.org/blog/free-speech/rights-protesters/6-ways-government-going-after-environmental-activists.

Blevis, M. (2013, June). Idle No More at six months: Analysis of the first six months of the Idle No More movement. *Full Duplex*. http://digitalpublicaffairs.com/wp-content/uploads/2013/06/IdleNoMoreAtSixMonths.pdf.

Bronskill, J. (2014, September 28). Spy watchdog's past oil ties spark concerns in civil liberties complaint case. *Canadian Press*.

Callison, C., and Hermida, A. (2015). Dissent and resonance: #IdleNoMore as an emergent middle ground. *Canadian Journal of Communication, 40*(4), 695–716.

CBC News. (2013, January 5). 9 questions about Idle No More. https://www.cbc.ca/news/canada/9-questions-about-idle-no-more-1.1301843.

Chávez, A. (2019, July 24). Activists camped at Hawaii's Mauna Kea face government opposition as they attempt to block telescope construction on sacred land. *The Intercept*. https://theintercept.com/2019/07/24/hawaii-mauna-kea-telescope-protest/.

Chen, S. (2017). How to discredit a social movement: Negative framing of "Idle No More" in Canadian print media. *Journal of Environmental Communication, 13*(2), 144–151.

Cinnamon, J. (2017). Social injustice in surveillance capitalism. *Surveillance & Society, 15*(5), 609–625.

Clifford, B. (2019, April 8). The alarming environmental impact of the internet and how you can help. *Medium*. https://medium.com/wedonthavetime/guest-blog-post

-the-alarming-environmental-impact-of-the-internet-and-how-you-can-help -6ff892b8730d.

Crosby, A., and Monaghan, J. (2016). Settler colonialism and the policing of Idle No More. *Social Justice, 43*(2), 37–57.

Crosby, A. C., and Monaghan, J. (2018). *Policing Indigenous movement: Dissent and the security state.* Winnipeg: Fernwood.

Defenders of the Land, Truth Campaign, and Idle No More Networks. (2018). Idle No More, Defenders of the Land & Truth before Reconciliation—Joint statement. http://www.idlenomore.ca/inm-dol-joint-statement.

Dhillon, J., and Parrish, W. (2019a, December 20). Exclusive: Canada police prepared to shoot Indigenous activists, documents show. *Guardian.*

Dhillon, J., and Parrish, W. (2019b, December 24). Indigenous people outraged at Canada police's possible use of lethal force. *Guardian.*

Donkin, K. (2013, January 11). Social media helps drive Idle No More movement. *Star.* https://www.thestar.com/news/canada/2013/01/11/social_media_helps_drive_idle _no_more_movement.html.

Doward, J., Cadwalladr, C., and Gibbs, A. (2017, March 7). Watchdog to launch inquiry into misuse of data in politics. *Guardian.* https://www.theguardian.com /technology/2017/mar/04/cambridge-analytica-data-brexit-trump.

Hachman, M. (2017, September 7). Just how partisan is Facebook's fake news? We tested it. *PC World.* https://www.pcworld.com/article/3142412/just-how-partisan -is-facebooks-fake-news-we-tested-it.html?page=2.

Idle No More. (2013a). The story. http://www.idlenomore.ca/story.

Idle No More. (2013b). The vision. http://www.idlenomore.ca/vision.

Idle No More. (2015, April 4). Indigenous land defenders protect sacred mountain Mauna Kea. http://www.idlenomore.ca/indigenous_land_defenders_protect _sacred_mountain_mauna_kea.

Idle No More and Defenders of the Land. (2013). Calls for change. http://www .idlenomore.ca/calls_for_change.

Indigenous Climate Action. (2017). Climate justice: Indigenous-led. https://www .indigenousclimateaction.com/.

Irlbacher-Fox, S. (2012, December 27). #IdleNoMore: Settler responsibility for relationship. *Decolonization: Indigeneity, Education & Society.* https:// decolonization.wordpress.com/2012/12/27/idlenomore-settler-responsibility-for -relationship/.

Jones, N. (2018, September 13). How to stop data centres from gobbling up the world's electricity. *Nature.* https://www.nature.com/articles/d41586-018-06610-y.

Kusnetz, N. (2018, August 22). How energy companies and allies are turning the law against protesters. *Inside Climate News.* https://insideclimatenews.org/news /22082018/pipeline-protest-laws-felony-free-speech-arrests-first-amendment -oklahoma-iowa-louisiana.

McLean, S., Wilson, A., and Lee, E. (2017). The whiteness of Redmen: Indigenous mascots, social media and an antiracist intervention. *Australasian Journal of Information Systems, 21.* https://doi.org/10.3127/ajis.v21io.1590.

Merchant, B. (2019, February 2). How Google, Microsoft, and big teach are automating the climate crisis. *Gizmodo.* https://gizmodo.com/how-google-microsoft-and -big-tech-are-automating-the-1832790799.

Monkman, L., and Morin, B. (2017, December 10). 5 years after Idle No More, founders still speaking out. *CBC News.* https://www.cbc.ca/news/indigenous/idle -no-more-five-years-1.4436474.

Pilar, P. (2017). Situating the web of the necro-techno complex: The Church of Nano Bio Info Cogno. *Performance, Religion, and Spirituality, 1*(1), 67–86.

Raynauld, V., Richez, E., and Boudreau Morris, K. (2018). Canada is #IdleNoMore: Exploring dynamics of Indigenous political and civic protest in the Twitterverse. *Information, Communication and Society, 21*(4), 626–642.

Sinclair, N. (2014, December 7). Idle No More: Where is the movement 2 years later? *CBC News.* https://www.cbc.ca/news/indigenous/idle-no-more-where-is-the -movement-2-years-later-1.2862675.

Standing Senate Committee on Aboriginal Peoples. (2015). *Housing on First Nation reserves: Challenges and successes.* Ottawa: Senate of Canada.

Tiny House Warriors. (n.d.). Our land is home. http://tinyhousewarriors.com.

Tupper, J. (2014, Winter). Social media and the Idle No More movement: Citizenship, activism and dissent in Canada. *Journal of Social Science Education, 13*(4), 87–94.

Wilson, A., and Mans, J. (2019). One House Many Nations: Indigenous project-based collaboration. In M. Henderson (Ed.), *Catch a fire: Fuelling inquiry and passion through project-based learning* (pp. 171–186). Winnipeg: Portage.

Wood, L. J. (2015). Idle No More, Facebook and diffusion. *Social Movement Studies, 14*(5), 615–621.

Zuboff, S. (2015). Big other: Surveillance capitalism and the prospects of an informa-tion civilization. *Journal of Information Technology, 30*, 75–89.

Zuboff, S. (2019a). *The age of surveillance capitalism.* New York: PublicAffairs.

Zuboff, S. (2019b). Surveillance capitalism and the challenge of collective action. *New Labor Forum, 28*(1), 10–29.

2

From #Mniwiconi to #StandwithStandingRock

•••••••••••••••••••••••

How the #NoDAPL Movement
Disrupted Physical and Virtual
Spaces and Brought Indigenous
Liberation to the Forefront of
People's Minds

NICHOLET A. DESCHINE

PARKHURST

It was the early fall of 2016 when I brought my husband and kids to visit my mother, Greta Conica (Standing Rock Sioux), who lived near the area of Cannonball of the Standing Rock Sioux Tribe in North Dakota. We had driven North Dakota state highway 1806, between the Standing Rock Sioux Reservation and the nearest city Mandan, many times before. While it is a scenic route of prairie and hills, there are generally very few vehicles to share the two-lane road with. However, the fall of 2016 was not like any other fall. We were driving south toward Cannonball when we came over a hill and suddenly could see a row of flags gently waving in the wind surrounded by an encampment. Vehicles lined each side of the small state highway. We pulled off the road, parked our car, unloaded, and walked toward an opening in the gate where we

FIG. 2.1 Flag Road in the Oceti Sakowin camp. Nicholet stands before a banner that states, "INTERNATIONAL intervention NEEDED to protect HUMAN RIGHTS of INDIGENOUS people of US and Canada," October 2016. (Credit: Wayne S. Parkhurst.)

could see flags lining a dirt road—Flag Road (figure 2.1). There was a slight chill in the wind, and my teenage kids were walking ahead of me. We walked to the top of what was then known as Facebook Hill, later renamed Media Hill. Standing atop Media Hill, I expressed what a sight the Oceti Sakowin camp was. It was breathtaking. Tipis, tents, cars, and RVs were clustered together, and to the east was the Missouri River and to the south the Cannonball River. The size of the camp had grown considerably from when photos I had seen posted on Facebook and Instagram had been taken.

My kids have heard our Lakota family's history before, but I wanted to remind them. During the summers of my childhood, my mother would bring my siblings and me to live with our grandmother, Marie Conica, in Cannonball. My mom would take us on walks down the hill alongside the Missouri River. She would talk about how her paternal grandparents, Henry and Annie Conica, lived in north Cannonball on the lower land close to the confluence of the Missouri and Cannonball rivers. My mother's maternal grandparents, Joseph and Dora Two Bears, lived in the same area. Both sets of my great-grandparents were relocated due to the Oahe flood caused by the Oahe Dam of the Pick-Sloan Plan.[1] My mom would take us to the bushes along the river to pick chokeberries. She pointed out the location of the eagle's nest, and we would stare at the sky, squinting our eyes, to catch a glimpse of a flying eagle. There was hardly anyone else out there aside from another family or two whom we would share the location of chokeberries with. Some summers we would wade in the river and my cousins would fish.

So seeing such a gathering of people, the Water Protectors of the #NoDAPL movement, living in the Oceti Sakowin (Seven Council Fires or Great Sioux Nation) camp invoked a lot of feelings and thoughts. I felt awe and astonishment that people, those living in the camps, even knew where the Standing Rock Sioux Tribe was located and were there because they wanted to #StandwithStandingRock in the tribe's demand for their treaty rights to be honored as they challenged the legality and construction of the Dakota Access Pipeline. Not to mention, I was amazed that mni wiconi, water is life, had become a unifying message not only for people on the ground of the #NoDAPL movement but also in the various circles I was part of both online and off. Having my family visit the Oceti Sakowin camp meant a lot to me, so they could understand my connection and my people's connection to that land and water, but also to provide context to everything they were observing through social media (figure 2.2).

My experiences in the Oceti Sakowin camp and participation in the #NoDAPL movement are my own. I am not a leader of the movement in the way that the movement's leaders and spokespersons have been described. I did not live in the camps because I lived with my family in the nearby community. I contributed to the movement in ways that are not often talked about in scholarly articles or shared on social media. I attended tribal hearings and district meetings. I gave educational presentations to college students and delivered talks in communities. I used social media to connect people in my various networks to support the Oceti Sakowin camp with physical, financial, and professional resources. I participated in community building in the Oceti Sakowin camp and made sure my friends had food. And I provided support to my family who were on the receiving end of racial microaggressions in the towns and cities surrounding the #NoDAPL camps. These acts inform my experience and understanding of how social media activism of the #NoDAPL movement extended beyond recognition and consciousness raising to garnering solidarity in virtual and physical spaces across the United States and the world, drawing thousands of people to converge in the very rural area near the Standing Rock Sioux Tribe.

During the fall and winter of 2016, I was a graduate student studying public policy and access to the internet for Native Americans. I was inquisitive about how the #NoDAPL movement was using social media as a tool to facilitate such a historic movement and moment, and how social media was being used to disseminate information. There is growing scholarship on the #NoDAPL movement that situates the movement within a historical context

FIG. 2.2 Water Protectors from all nations came to live in the Oceti Sakowin camp to support the #NoDAPL movement, December 2016. (Credit: Nicholet A. Deschine Parkhurst.)

about the federal-tribal relationship (Estes, 2019), discusses the flawed environmental regulatory processes (Gilio-Whitaker, 2019; Johnson, 2019), and examines news coverage of the movement (Hunt and Gruszczynski, 2019; Moore, 2018). There is little research discussing the ways in which social media is used as a mechanism to disrupt public spheres (both online and off), to center Indigenous voices, and to challenge political processes and create communities of change.

While I strongly believe that Native scholars will be writing about Standing Rock and the #NoDAPL movement as long as we have been writing about the Native activist movements of the 1960s and 1970s, there is a need to identify how the "connective actions" and collective actions (Bennett and Segerberg, 2012) through social media facilitated social change. There are debates and criticism among social media theorists about the real effects online behavior can have in creating and actualizing mass political action and change such as the exposure of messages outside ideological clusters (Himelboim, McCreery, and Smith, 2013) and whether stakeholders, such as policy decision makers, are listening (Dreher, McCallum, and Waller, 2016). To this end, this chapter is an Indigenizing project that aims to ground the online actions in an "alternative conceptions of world view and value systems" (Smith, 2012, p. 147) and suggests that rather than measure the success of the movement on whether or not the DAPL (DAPL) construction was stopped, we instead should ask in what ways the movement caused disruptions of existing colonial systems.

The #NoDAPL Movement

The #NoDAPL movement was an Indigenous-led movement in opposition to Energy Transfer Partners (ETP) and the construction of the $3.8 billion DAPL that was almost twelve hundred miles in length, crossing through four states (North Dakota, South Dakota, Iowa, and Illinois). More specifically, the movement coalesced around the portion of the pipeline that crosses the Missouri River, within half a mile of the Standing Rock Sioux Tribe's (SRST) reservation located in North Dakota. The SRST was concerned because the DAPL threatened the "Tribe's environmental and economic well-being, and would damage and destroy sites of great historic, religious, and cultural significance to the Tribe" (*Standing Rock Sioux Tribe v. U.S. Army Corps of Engineers*, 2016). Further, the tribe asserted concerns about infringement of tribal sovereignty and the failed consultation between the federal government and the tribe, required as part of the government-to-government relationship and federal government's trust responsibility (Archambault, 2016).

The #NoDAPL movement is most recognized for events during the fall and winter of 2016, when thousands of Water Protectors converged and lived in camps near Cannonball, North Dakota, and engaged in nonviolent direct action to stop the construction of the DAPL through the SRST's historical treaty lands. But the opposition to the pipeline was made known on September 30, 2014, at the Standing Rock Sioux Tribal Council meeting where the tribe informed DAPL and ETP representatives that it has a "standing resolution that was passed in 2012 that opposes any pipeline within that treaty [Fort Laramie Treaties of 1851 and 1868] boundary" (Estes, 2019; Standing Rock Sioux Tribe, 2016); a video file of audio from the Tribal Council meeting was uploaded by the tribe to YouTube. While the #NoDAPL movement has often been portrayed as an environmental movement, it is in fact a larger movement about tribal sovereignty.

The mobilization of the #NoDAPL movement has been attributed to the reaching of a critical mass, a culmination of Indigenous resistance movements to U.S. colonial policies (Estes, 2019), violations of tribal sovereignty (Archambault, 2016; Curley, 2019; Ellis, 2019; Whyte, 2017), environmental injustice (Archambault, 2016; Gilio-Whitaker, 2019; Whyte, 2017), opportune moments of inter-tribal and cross-movement solidarity (Gilio-Whitaker, 2019; Steinman, 2019), and old and new media such as traditional/mainstream news media and social media (Brígido-Corachán, 2017; Hunt and Gruszczynski, 2019; Moore, 2018). Conferences in Indian Country and scholarship have focused on tribal sovereignty to consent to projects that impact customary homelands (Boxer, 2017; Purdon, 2017), tribal intergovernmental relations (Purdon, 2017), the intersection of tribal religion and environmental claims (Smith, 2017), the role of Indigenous women (TallBear, 2019), the human rights violations of individuals by ETP and the North Dakota Morton County Law Enforcement (Toelupe, 2017), and the centering of Indigenous environmental justice (Gilio-Whitaker, 2019; Whyte, 2017). A smaller body of media studies examined how journalism shaped and influenced coverage and representations of American Indians and the DAPL conflict (Bacon, 2019; Moore, 2018).

Nick Estes (Lower Brule Sioux Tribe), in his book *Our History Is the Future* (2019), provides perhaps the most in-depth account situating the #NoDAPL movement within a historical context of Indigenous resistance to settler-colonial expansionism and U.S. colonial policies of land grabs, removal, and relocation. Vine Deloria Jr. (SRST) and Clifford M. Lytle state, "History . . . cannot be divorced from an analysis of American Indian life" (1983, p. 1). Estes's book examines the complexities of the contemporary political reality for Natives that contributed to the origins of the #NoDAPL movement. Further, Estes and Jaskiran Dhillon, in the introduction to their edited book *Standing with Standing Rock* (2019), state, "#NoDAPL, however, was not a departure from so much as it was a continuation—a moment within a longer movement, but also a movement within a moment—of long traditions of Indigenous resistance deeply grounded in place and history" (2019, p. 2). The edited book centers Indigenous resistance through documentation of the voices of #NoDAPL leaders, sets the movement within a U.S. historical and contemporary context of state violence and resource extraction, and discusses movement building with other resistance efforts such as #BlackLivesMatter.

The #NoDAPL movement drew widespread intertribal, national, and international support and solidarity from organizations and various municipalities. In the early fall of 2016, the SRST received eighty-seven resolutions and letters expressing solidarity with the tribe (*Indian Country Today*, 2016). During my time living in the area from October to December 2016, I stood with Water Protectors and often recorded and shared video via social media that welcomed groups who came to stand in solidarity with Standing Rock Sioux. On October 11, 2016, we welcomed horseback riders who had just returned from a spiritual ride to the source of the oil in Tioga, North Dakota. On November 3, 2016, over five hundred clergy members and people of faith arrived in solidarity with the tribe and Water Protectors. On November 5, 2016, we welcomed Native youth of Perseverance for Preservation who completed an honor run from Flagstaff, Arizona, to the Oceti Sakowin Camp. And on December 3, 2016, we welcomed thousands of veterans who came to serve as a shield and barrier to protect peaceful Water Protectors from militarized police force. Other groups included the Dakota 38 memorial riders and spiritual runners. Aside from the groups I personally witnessed, a group of Indigenous Sami people met with then-SRST chairman Dave Archambault II on September 30, 2016 (Hardy, 2016), and Māori people across New Zealand were uploading videos of themselves performing haka as a message of solidarity (Wanshel, 2016), demonstrating the international attention the #NoDAPL movement was generating.

The #NoDAPL Movement, Social Media, and Connectivity

Advocates of Native American political issues are increasingly using social media as a tool to extend contemporary grassroots activism. This was apparent during the #NoDAPL movement as evidenced through live video streaming, social media campaigns, Facebook check-ins, crowdsource funding, and posts to social media or blogs to share personal experiences and disseminate information (Johnson, 2017). There were many key moments in the #NoDAPL movement (Hersher, 2017), but the most contentious, such as the September 3, 2016, bulldozing of culturally significant sites and attack of the DAPL private security's dogs, were livestreamed by citizen journalists, independent media, and Indigenous organizations and went viral. In particular, the bulldozer incident was recorded by *Democracy Now!*'s Amy Goodman (*Democracy Now!*, 2016). Until this point in time, the #NoDAPL movement had largely been ignored by national mainstream news media outlets, such as NPR, CNN, CBS, and NBC, and ensuing coverage was inaccurate, was misleading, or misrepresented Indigenous-centered claims (Moore, 2018; Moore and Lanthorn, 2017).

One moment that garnered attention of international news media was the confrontation between militarized police and Water Protectors that happened in the middle of the night on November 20, 2016. This incident has been known as the Battle of Backwater Bridge (a.k.a. Backwater Sunday), as Water Protectors were met with an extreme display of militarized police violence. This incident was livestreamed through multiple Facebook accounts of individuals, citizen journalists, Indigenous organizations, and the independent media organization *Unicorn Riot* (Mari Birkett and Montoya, 2019; *Unicorn Riot*, 2016b). Live video streams of the incident showed militarized police using water cannons and firehoses and deploying rubber and plastic bullets on Water Protectors in subfreezing temperatures.

As mentioned earlier, in the years following the peak of the #NoDAPL movement there has been relatively extensive scholarship surrounding the movement as well as films and documentaries such as *Awake, a Dream from Standing Rock* (Fox, Spione, and Dewey, 2017) and *Akicita: The Battle of Standing Rock* (Lucich, 2018). But literature on the deployment of social media in specific online tactics and its role in facilitating social movement goals has been scant. Social media has become a valuable tool for raising awareness of injustices that our small, geographically disbursed, and often rural tribal communities often face. It has also become a place for us, Indigenous people, to find and advocate for common goals, whether advocating against cultural appropriation in film and entertainment (Risling Baldy, 2016), calling on the

Washington, D.C., NFL team to change its name (Blackhorse, 2013; Keeler, 2014), or calling for the protection of sacred sites such as the San Carlos Apache Tribe with Oak Flat in Arizona (Deschine Parkhurst, 2017) and Mauna Kea in Hawaii (Higa, 2019; Kuwada and Yamashiro, 2016). Ultimately these causes are decentering worldviews about who has the right to determine what is important to Indigenous peoples. Although individual tribes all have their own history of survival, there are similarities across Native Nations in the patterns of oppression and trauma that our people as a collective have faced. Social media has been a way to connect us across physical barriers and even time.

The affordances of social media platforms and the enablement of certain communication practices (Bucher and Helmond, 2018) are a materiality, a utility, a tool for individuals to interact with to connect with their networks for diffusing information, organizing, and mobilizing collective actions and connective actions to gain support of Native American causes. Social media by itself is not powerful, as Marisa Duarte (Pascua Yaqui/Chicana) says "it is the networks of devices and women [people] using them that are powerful" (2017, p. 25). In the case of #NoDAPL, it is the online networks of Native youth, tribal leaders, resistance leaders, organization leaders, and others who are powerful. Such leaders were able to successfully harness social media, prior to the onset of mainstream news media, to communicate the narrative and discourses of the movement and the representation of their cause and people (Johnson, 2017). This is particularly important as news media can marginalize the perspectives of Indigenous peoples by overreliance of stereotypical tropes and may simplify and thus inaccurately portray the complexities of federal-tribal relations and Indigenous environmental justice (Johnson, 2017; Moore, 2018; Moore and Lanthorn, 2017).

The #NoDAPL movement could be described as both a grassroots on-the-ground movement as well as an online social movement that aimed not just to engage in consciousness raising but also to gain recognition for the political issues the SRST faced. This hybrid movement, characterized by a need for organizational flexibility so the coordination of offline and online interactions could be facilitated, enabled a collective identity (Boler and Nitsou, 2014) for Indigenous supporters and allies to #StandwithStandingRock in place-based collective actions such as marches, flash mobs, and other nonviolent direct actions. Collective action is a mass mobilization of people usually facilitated by formal organizations where the collective group embodies a shared identity (Boler and Nitsou, 2014); the Native Nations Rise march in Washington, D.C., on March 10, 2017 (*Indian Country Today*, 2017) was a type of a collective action. In contrast, hybrid movements are characterized by features of cyberactivism such as horizontally structured and connective actions that enable individuals, through social media, to have a shared vision with a movement but that allow individuals to connect in ways that fit their lifestyle and to express opinions (Bennett and Segerberg, 2012; Boler and Nitsou, 2014; Valenzuela,

2013). Connective actions of the #NoDAPL movement include the sharing of movement-generated content (e.g., content created by Indigenous organizations) and the uploading of content such as videos, live video streams, photos, memes, and text through social media networks.

As a connective action of the #NoDAPL movement, over the weekend of October 31, 2016, over a million people remotely checked in to Facebook to express solidarity with Water Protectors (Hunt and Gruszczynski, 2019; Kennedy, 2016; *Unicorn Riot*, 2016a). Regardless of whether it was a tactic to circumvent social media monitoring and intelligence gathering by North Dakota law enforcement (Kennedy, 2016; Shoichet, 2016), it is an example of connective actions that raised national and international consciousness about the #NoDAPL movement and state violence to repress the movement (Hunt and Gruszczynski, 2019). This "disembodied presence" of supporters increased the visibility of bodies on the ground in Standing Rock (Deem, 2019).

Disruptions

Native Americans' use of information communication technology to facilitate information flows has been happening since the late 1880s, when Lakota people sent messages, by way of train, to boarding school students about the Ghost Dance, an anticolonial resistance movement. Estes states, "Without this means of dissemination, the Ghost Dance would not have been so widespread" (2019, p. 127). During the rise of American Indian activism, the American Indian Movement (AIM) and Red Power of the 1960s and 1970s, other modes such as radio and television broadcasts were used to mobilize Native peoples (Duarte, 2017). Duarte suggests that the strategic use of such technologies had long-term consequences of benefit to Indian Country: "The generation of Native leaders who are now running major political organizations, such as the National Congress of American Indians, and directing the operations of tribal colleges and other national-level forums were in their teens when the AIM occupation of Alcatraz and the federal government blockade at Pine Ridge were shown on television. Both of these broadcasts irrevocably shaped the nature and ethos of intertribal organizing and activism in Indian Country" (2017, p. 78). In the case of Standing Rock, social media was used by formal organizations, citizen journalists, and individuals to disseminate news about the nonviolent direct actions of the day and to provide information for individuals coming to join the encampments, coordinate caravans, and organize solidarity events. There were calls to action to divest from banks that provided funds to the DAPL and to create communities of change, such as Stand with Standing Rock solidarity groups, some of which have evolved into lasting activist communities of their own being.

Not only have the affordances of digital technology facilitated information flows, but in the case of Standing Rock, digital traces of online activity such as the sharing of live video streams, tweets, and posts represent online connective actions. However, describing these acts simply as connective actions makes them almost devoid of political significance. Drawing from Leanne Betasamosake Simpson (Anishinaabe), these online actions are inherently political because the issues Indigenous movements are responding to, "these 'social issues' are not social" (2017, p. 227), are political consequences of settler colonialism. Furthermore, Duarte reminds us, "First-world technologies become, not a weapon, but a means of working toward decolonization" (2017, p. 25). Thus, it becomes imperative to reconsider the role of online connective actions within Indigenous resistance—these actions do more than simply connect people to raise awareness of a cause and can disrupt and transform individuals and systems because Indigenous resistance is a tradition of disrupting the colonial system.

These online actions, or rather disruptions, then have a role in the larger context of the #NoDAPL movement by collectively disrupting the digital and physical landscapes that the movement is embedded in. They have consequences on individual thoughts and systems, and although some may have negatively impacted Water Protectors, they need to be considered in relation to the purpose of Indigenous resistance movements to refuse settler colonialism and work toward Indigenous liberation. We can then think about the ways in which disruptions took place within state systems and at the nation-state and international levels.

The #NoDAPL movement disrupted individual people's preconceived notions about contemporary Native people, tribal governments, and historic realities of the Great Sioux Nation. These disruptions introduced a complexity about U.S. colonial history with Native peoples that is rarely discussed in U.S. school textbooks—the building of a nation based on the slow genocide (Huseman and Short, 2012) of its Indigenous peoples (Estes, 2019). There were disruptions of systems at the state level. For example, North Dakota invoked the Emergency Management Assistance Compact (EMAC) to request law enforcement assistance from neighboring states—nine states responded, with North Dakota covering their expenses (Dresslar, 2016; Sammon, 2016)—and to deploy the North Dakota National Guard (Hersher, 2017; Rickert, 2016). At one point the North Dakota court system was inundated with the arrests of Water Protectors, placing a strain on court workloads and costs and even on the federal court system (Associated Press, 2016; Sammon, 2016). Although the state's response resulted in further acts of injustice and human rights violations, there is no denying the state of North Dakota spent a considerable amount of resources (e.g., time, funds) in its response (Associated Press, 2017). It was reported, prior to the closing of the encampments, that North Dakota law enforcement expenses had reached $10.9 million and Morton County expenses were an additional $8 million (Sammon, 2016). Further, at the nation-state level, disruption happened within the system of the Army Corps of Engineers, apparent by their December 4, 2016, decision to deny the permit for construction of the DAPL that crossed under the Missouri River (Hersher, 2017; Rott and Peralta, 2016) and then later rescinding the Notice of Intent to Prepare an Environmental Impact Statement (Department of the Army, 2017; Hersher, 2017). At the international level, there were disruptions to the financial industry when calls for governments and organizations to divest from the banks that provided loans to the DAPL were enacted (Moore, 2018). Viewing the #NoDAPL movement in terms of the multitude of disruptions to individuals and to state, national, and international systems paints a different overall picture about how social media and grassroots social movements can effect change.

At the same time, these disruptions represent an alternate aspect of social change. Simpson (2017) reminds us that the measurement of success of an Indigenous movement should not be centered on the transformation of settlers and whiteness. In this regard, we should rethink whether the transformation of the federal government and ETP, in terms of stopping the construction of the pipeline and rerouting it, should be how the success of the #NoDAPL movement is measured. The success or failure of the #NoDAPL movement is an ongoing, and sometimes tiring, conversation in activist circles I am part of. But when we look outside of transforming ETP's behavior, we can see alternate ways in which the #NoDAPL movement was transformative by raising consciousness of people and solidarity around the world, building virtual and physical communities, centering Indigenous voices and representations, disrupting public spheres, and creating communities of change.

Moving Forward

At the time of this writing, it has been three years since the peak of the #NoDAPL movement, when militarized state police officers enacted violence, such as the use of water cannons in below-freezing temperatures and rubber bullets against Water Protectors at the Battle of Backwater Bridge. Every year about this time, I receive notifications from Facebook and Instagram reminding me of the digital traces, "memories," I made in 2016. There are photos and videos that show the solidarity and support of people as they arrive at the Oceti Sakowin. There are videos of my family and me attempting to pass barricades manned by the North Dakota National Guard just to reach our home. And there are even more media artifacts that show Morton County police enacting violence and state repression on Water Protectors praying and engaging in nonviolent direct action. These digital traces made years ago remind me not to become complacent because the fight for my tribe's water and recognition of their tribal sovereignty is still ongoing. In fact, a Public Service Commission hearing was held November 13, 2019, to gather public testimony regarding the DAPL's request for a permit to build a pump station that would double the capacity of oil that flows through the pipeline (North Dakota Public Service Commission, 2019; Nickel, 2019). On that day, Greta Conica, my mother and current sitting Cannonball District Chairperson, gave testimony. I share with you a bit of her testimony where she says, "I strongly oppose any expansion of the Dakota Access Pipeline." She further states,

> I am Greta Conica. My parents are Tidell Conica, a Korean War veteran, and my mother is Marie Two Bears, daughter of a Code Talker. I am currently the District Chairperson of Cannonball District. . . . I grew up in an era where I did see those trees. I sat on a hilltop and watched them play baseball below what is now a riverbed. I was born on the hill directly across from where the Dakota Access Pipeline is. I was born on November 30th in the wintertime. So, my mom was walking back from where her parents lived down in the riverbed back up to the house and she had me outside, along that hill. I can no longer access that area where I grew up on, where I played. And that is from flood waters. When you put that pipeline in, now you have more chances of that land that we still live on, our grandchildren, our great grandchildren, may not even have that opportunity to play on that land because if our water is destroyed, we will have to move again.

She ends her testimony describing a recent water pipe break in Cannonball and how people in their community had to boil their water for a couple days until the pipe was fixed. She states, "Our community is very poor. And not many people have the means to go out and buy this water for when there is no water for us to drink." Watching a live video stream of Greta's testimony during the Public Service Commission hearing made me ever so proud to be her daughter. She centered her experience as a Standing Rock Sioux woman and as a leader of her community. She asserted and used her voice to disrupt this process by grounding her testimony in her experience and truth.

While it is upsetting and concerning that oil is flowing through the DAPL, there have been positive long-term outcomes from the #NoDAPL movement, one of which includes my mother running for public office and serving as Chairperson for the Cannonball District. This is one of the ways I personally see how transformative the #NoDAPL movement was.

Note

1 The U.S. Flood Control Act of 1944 authorized the Pick-Sloan Missouri Basin Program, which resulted in the construction of the Oahe Dam that flooded the Missouri River. The Pick-Sloan Plan consequently relocated 190 families of the Standing Rock Sioux Tribe, destroyed 55,994 acres of Standing Rock lands, and affected wildlife, plant life, and the Standing Rock people's way of life (Lawson, 1976; Estes, 2019).

References

Archambault, D., II. (2016, August 24). Taking a stand at Standing Rock. *New York Times*. https://mobile.nytimes.com/2016/08/25/opinion/taking-a-stand-at -standing-rock.html.

Associated Press. (2016, November 30). North Dakota courts strained by pipeline protest arrests. *CBS News*. https://www.cbsnews.com/news/dakota-access-pipeline -standing-rock-protest-arrests-north-dakota-courts/.

Associated Press. (2017, December 16). More than $600,000 spent in North Dakota on police gear for pipeline protest. *Des Moines Register*. https://www .desmoinesregister.com/story/news/2017/12/16/more-than-600-000-spent-north -dakota-police-gear-pipeline-protest/958422001/.

Bacon, J. M. (2019). Dangerous pipelines, dangerous people: Colonial ecological violence and media framing of threat in the Dakota Access Pipeline conflict. *Environmental Sociology*. https://doi.org/10.1080/23251042.2019.1706262.

Bennett, W. L., and Segerberg, A. (2012). The logic of connective action: Digital media and the personalization of contentious politics. *Information, Communication and Society, 15*(5), 739–768.

Blackhorse, A. (2013, March 8). Why the R*dsk*ns need to change their name. *Huffington Post*. https://www.huffpost.com/entry/washington-nfl-name-change _b_2838630.

Boler, M., and Nitsou, C. (2014). Consciousness-raising and connective action in hybrid social movements. In M. McCaughey (Ed.), *Cyberactivism on the participatory web* (pp. 232–256). New York: Routledge.

Boxer, E. (2017, February 2). AISA presidential address. Speech given at the 18th annual American Indian Studies Association Conference, Albuquerque, NM.

Brígido-Corachán, A. N. (2017). Material nature, visual sovereignty, and water rights: Unpacking the Standing Rock Movement. *Studies in the Literary Imagination, 50*(1), 69–90.

Bucher, T., and Helmond, A. (2018). The affordances of social media platforms. In J. Burgess, T. Poell, and A. Marwick (Eds.), *The SAGE handbook of social media* (pp. 233–253). London: SAGE.

Deem, A. (2019). Mediated intersections of environmental and decolonial politics in the No Dakota Access Pipeline Movement. *Theory, Culture and Society, 36*(5), 113–131.

Deloria, V., Jr., and Lytle, C. M. (1983). *American Indians, American justice*. Austin: University of Texas Press.

Curley, A. (2019). Beyond environmentalism: #NADAPL as assertion of tribal sovereignty. In N. Estes and J. Dhillon (Eds.), *Standing with Standing Rock: Voices from the #NODAPL movement* (pp. 158–168). Minneapolis: University of Minnesota Press.

Democracy Now! (2016, September 3). Dakota Access Pipeline company attacks Native American protestors with dogs and pepper spray. https://www.youtube.com/watch ?v=kuZcx2zE04k.

Department of the Army. (2017, January 18). Notice of intent to prepare an environmental impact statement in connection with Dakota Access, LLC's request for an easement to cross Lake Oahe, North Dakota. *Federal Register*. https://www .federalregister.gov/documents/2017/01/18/2017-00937/notice-of-intent-to-prepare -an-environmental-impact-statement-in-connection-with-dakota-access-llcs.

Deschine Parkhurst, N. (2017). Protecting Oak Flat: Narratives of survivance as observed through digital activism. *Australasian Journal of Information Systems, 21*. http://dx.doi.org/10.3127/ajis.v21i0.1567.

Dreher, T., McCallum, K., and Waller, L. (2016) Indigenous voices and mediatized policy-making in the digital age. *Information, Communication and Society, 19*(1), 23–39.

Dresslar, T. (2016, November 30). How many law enforcement agencies does it take to subdue a peaceful protest? *ACLU*. https://www.aclu.org/blog/free-speech/rights-protesters/how-many-law-enforcement-agencies-does-it-take-subdue-peaceful?redirect=blog/speak-freely/how-many-law-enforcement-agencies-does-it-take-subdue-peaceful-protest.

Duarte, M. E. (2017). *Network sovereignty: Building the internet across Indian country*. Seattle: University of Washington Press.

Ellis, E. (2019). Centering sovereignty: how standing rock changed the conversation. In N. Estes and J. Dhillon (Eds.), *Standing with Standing Rock: Voices from the #NODAPL movement* (pp. 172–197). Minneapolis: University of Minnesota Press.

Estes, N. (2019). *Our history is the future: Standing Rock versus the Dakota Access Pipeline, and the long tradition of Indigenous resistance*. New York: Verso.

Estes, N., and Dhillon, J. (2019). The Black Snake, #NoDAPL, and the rise of a people's movement. In N. Estes and J. Dhillon (Eds.), *Standing with Standing Rock: Voices from the #NODAPL movement* (pp. 1–10). Minneapolis: University of Minnesota Press.

Fox, J. (Director), Spione, J. (Director), and Dewey, M. (Director). (2017). *Awake, a dream from Standing Rock*. Bullfrog Films.

Gilio-Whitaker, D. (2019). *As long as grass grows: The Indigenous fight for environmental justice, from colonization to Standing Rock*. Boston: Beacon.

Hardy, K. (2016, October 8). A pipeline protest meets a spiritual movement. *Des Moines Register*. https://www.desmoinesregister.com/story/news/2016/10/08/near-standing-rock-dakota-access-pipeline-protest-meets-spiritual-movement/91567854/.

Hersher, R. (2017, February 22). Key moments in the Dakota Access Pipeline fight. *NPR*. https://www.npr.org/sections/thetwo-way/2017/02/22/514988040/key-moments-in-the-dakota-access-pipeline-fight.

Higa, S. (2019, August 8). Sterling Higa: The social media movement behind the Mauna Kea protests. *Honolulu Civil Beat*. https://www.civilbeat.org/2019/08/sterling-higa-the-social-media-movement-behind-the-mauna-kea-protests/.

Himelboim, I., McCreery, S., and Smith, M. (2013). Birds of a feather tweet together: Integrating network and content analyses to examine cross-ideology exposure on Twitter. *Journal of Computer-Mediated Communication, 18*, 154–174.

Hunt, K., and Gruszczynski, M. (2019). The influence of new and traditional media coverage on public attention to social movements: The case of the Dakota Access Pipeline protests. *Information, Communication and Society*. https://doi.org/10.1080/1369118X.2019.1670228.

Huseman, J., and Short, D. (2012). "A slow industrial genocide": Tar sands and the Indigenous peoples of northern Alberta. *International Journal of Human Rights, 16*(1), 216–237.

Indian Country Today. (2016, August 23). Native nations rally in support of the Standing Rock Sioux. https://newsmaven.io/indiancountrytoday/archive/native-nations-rally-in-support-of-standing-rock-sioux-mlt8Ck6mgUajgGp9x1OqyA/.

Indian Country Today. (2017, March 23). Native nations march to Trump's White House draws huge crowds. https://newsmaven.io/indiancountrytoday/archive /native-nations-march-to-trump-s-white-house-draws-huge-crowds-video -sQLTEJ7sqkKUeIei84Ux-Q/.

Johnson, H. (2017). #NoDAPL: Social media, empowerment, and civic participation at Standing Rock. *Library Trends, 66*(2), 155–175.

Johnson, T. N. (2019). The Dakota Access Pipeline and the breakdown of the participatory processes in environmental decision-making. *Environmental Communication, 13*(3), 335–352.

Keeler, J. (2014, February 8). Inside the #NotYourMascot Super Bowl Twitter Storm. *Indian Country Today.* https://newsmaven.io/indiancountrytoday/archive/inside -the-notyourmascot-super-bowl-twitter-storm-jegA1JWdCkqJUibl_pN82w.

Kennedy, M. (2016, November 1). More than 1 million "check in" on Facebook to support the Standing Rock Sioux. *NPR.* https://www.npr.org/sections/thetwo-way /2016/11/01/500268879/more-than-a-million-check-in-on-facebook-to-support-the -standing-rocksioux.

Kuwada, B. K., and Yamashiro, A. (2016). Rooted in wonder: Tales of Indigenous activism and community organizing. *Marvels and Tales 30*(1), 17–21.

Lawson, M. (1976). The Oahe Dam and the Standing Rock Sioux. South Dakota State Historical Society. https://www.sdhspress.com/journal/south-dakota-history-6-2 /the-oahe-dam-and-the-standing-rock-sioux/vol-06-no-2-the-oahe-dam-and-the -standing-rock-sioux.pdf.

Lucich, C. (Dir.). (2018). *Akicita: The Battle of Standing Rock.* Firestarter Films.

Mari Birkett, T., and Montoya, T. (2019). For Standing Rock: A moving dialogue. In N. Estes and J. Dhillon (Eds.), *Standing with Standing Rock: Voices from the #NODAPL movement* (pp. 261–280). Minneapolis: University of Minnesota Press.

Moore, E. (2018). *Journalism, politics, and the Dakota Access Pipeline: Standing Rock and the framing of injustice.* New York: Routledge.

Moore, E. E., and Lanthorn, K. R. (2017). Framing disaster: News media coverage of two Native American environmental justice cases. *Journal of Communication Inquiry, 41*(3), 227–249.

Nickel, R. (2019, November 13). Dakota Access oil pipeline eyes expansion over Tribe's objections. Reuters. https://www.reuters.com/article/us-energy-transfer-oil -pipeline/dakota-access-oil-pipeline-eyes-expansion-over-tribes-objections -idUSKBN1XN2IB.

North Dakota Public Service Commission. (2019, August 21). Notice of Hearing for Dakota Access, LLC (Case No. PU-19-204). https://psc.nd.gov/public/meetings /agenda/2019/171-010.pdf.

Purdon, T. Q. (2017, April 6). Sharing power: Tribal, local, state, and federal coopera-tion. Presentation at the 42nd annual Indian Law Conference, Scottsdale, AZ.

Rickert, L. (2016, November 20). North Dakota calls up more National Guard to assist law enforcement at DAPL site. *Native News Online.* https://nativenewsonline .net/currents/north-dakota-calls-national-guard-assist-law-enforcement-dapl-site/.

Risling Baldy, C. (2016). The new Native intellectualism. #ElizabethCook-Lynn, social media movements, and the millennial Native American studies scholar. *Wicazo Sa Review, 31*(1), 90–110.

Rott, N., and Peralta, E. (2016, December 4). In victory for protestors, Army halts construction of Dakota Pipeline. *NPR.* https://www.npr.org/sections/thetwo-way /2016/12/04/504354503/army-corps-denies-easement-for-dakota-access-pipeline -says-tribal-organization.

Sammon, A. (2016, December 4). How did police from all over the country end up at Standing Rock? *Mother Jones*. https://www.motherjones.com/environment/2016/12/standing-rock-police-militarized-emergency-management-assistance-compact-north-dakota/.

Shoichet, C. E. (2016, October 31). Why your Facebook friends are checking in at Standing Rock. *CNN*. https://www.cnn.com/2016/10/31/us/standing-rock-facebook-check-ins/index.html.

Simpson, L. B. (2017). *As we have always done: Indigenous freedom through radical resistance*. Minneapolis: University of Minnesota Press.

Smith, G. A. (2017, April 6). Pillars of sovereignty in the era of the #DAPL: The intersection of tribal religion and environmental claims. Presentation at the 42nd annual Indian Law Conference, Scottsdale, AZ.

Smith, L. T. (2012). *Decolonizing methodologies* (2nd ed.). London: Zed Books.

Standing Rock Sioux Tribe. (2016, December 3). Sept 30th DAPL meeting with SRST. https://www.youtube.com/watch?v=ZlwdtnZXmtY.

Standing Rock Sioux Tribe v. U.S. Army Corps of Engineers, No. 1:16-cv-01534 (U.S. Dist. July 27, 2016). http://earthjustice.org/sites/default/files/files/3154%20 1%20Complaint.pdf.

Steinman, E. (2019). Why was Standing Rock and the #NoDAPL campaign so historic? Factors affecting American Indian participation in social movement collaborations and coalitions. *Ethnic and Racial Studies, 42*(7), 1070–1090.

Taliman, V. (2016, August 16). Dakota Access Pipeline standoff: Mni wiconi, water is life. *Indian Country Media Network*. https://indiancountrymedianetwork.com/news/native-news/dakota-access-pipeline-standoff-mni-wiconi-water-is-life/.

TallBear, K. (2019). Badass Indigenous women caretake relations: #StandingRock, #IdleNoMore, #BlackLivesMatter. In N. Estes and J. Dhillon (Eds.), *Standing with Standing Rock: Voices from the #NODAPL movement* (pp. 13–18). Minneapolis: University of Minnesota Press.

Toelupe, B. (2017, April 7). Energy development, DAPL, and tribes: What's next. Presentation at the 42nd annual Indian Law Conference, Scottsdale, AZ.

Unicorn Riot. (2016a, November 1). DAPL resistance continues despite advancing construction. https://unicornriot.ninja/2016/dapl-resistance-continues-despite-advancing-construction/.

Unicorn Riot. (2016b, November 21). Video on #NoDAPL Highway 1806 standoff. https://livestream.com/unicornriot/events/6668525/videos/142426670.

Valenzuela, S. (2013). Unpacking the use of social media for protest behavior: The roles of information, opinion expression, and activism. *American Behavioral Scientist, 57*(7), 920–942.

Wanshel, E. (2016, October 31). New Zealand's Native people are showing their support for Standing Rock in a powerful way. *Huffington Post*. https://www.huffpost.com/entry/maori-facebook-haka-standing-rock-sioux-dakota-access-pipeline_n_58177018e4b0990edc325e0f.

Whyte, K. (2017). The Dakota Access Pipeline, environmental injustice, and U.S. colonialism. *Red Ink, 19*(1), 154–169.

3

Anger, Hope, and Love

■ ■ ■ ■ ■ ■ ■ ■ ■ ■ ■ ■ ■ ■ ■ ■ ■ ■ ■ ■

The Affective Economies
of Indigenous Social
Media Activism

BRONWYN CARLSON AND

RYAN FRAZER

There have been growing concerns that social media is facilitating the break-down of the principles underpinning liberal democracy, with many online spaces seeing the rise of fascist, racist, misogynistic, and otherwise illegal and violent collectives (Chertoff, 2017; Jardine, 2015). But for Indigenous peoples living under settler-colonial regimes, the "norms" of a liberal democracy have never quite been a material reality. Instead, the disruptive force of social media has provided powerful pathways through which Indigenous collectives can express and enact political agency, in a context where this agency has been violently suppressed (Castells, 2013; Duarte and Vigil-Hayes, 2017). Social media has enabled new voices to rise, new emotional relations to emerge, and new political collectives to form in opposition to settler-colonial power (Petray, 2011; Saramo, 2016).

In this chapter, we attend to the place of emotions in animating, consolidating, and reinventing Indigenous Australian activism in two social media movements: #SOSBlakAustralia and #IndigenousDads. Following the work of Sara Ahmed (2008, 2015), we ask the following: What do emotions *do* in the context of Indigenous social media activism? What are the emotional and affective forces pushing along and pulling apart these "movement moments" (Barker, 2015)? Through the analysis that follows, we argue that the online elicitation and circulation of emotion works to conjure particular political publics into being. We show also that emotions are *differentially* political, depending both on which social group they "stick" to and which kind of emotional expression is made.

Indigenous Social Media Activism

Indigenous political groups have often been the vanguard of online activism (Landzelius, 2006; Wolfson, 2012). Blending strategies in "conventional" activism with the affordances of new digital media, Indigenous peoples globally have used social media as "one tool in the greater array of Indigenous repertoires of contention" (Duarte, 2017, p. 2). Particular scholarly attention has been paid to how social media figures into the so-called small "p" politics of Indigenous representation. Postcolonial scholars have long explored the ways in which pejorative racial stereotypes, perpetuated by state power, mainstream media, and everyday settler discourse, work to position Indigenous people as the "dangerous" or "lesser" *other* in need of containment, control, and elimination (Wolfe, 2006).

In this context, the more decentralized forms of social media provide opportunities for Indigenous peoples to subvert these racist stereotypes, undoing and challenging settler notions of what it means to be Indigenous. Salazar (2003) argues online media has been embraced by Indigenous Mapuche activists as "a field of symbolic and political struggle" (p. 19)—what they describe as a "counter public sphere." They found online media was used by activists in countering "mainstream media's distorted construction of a Mapuche conflict" (Salazar, 2003, p. 19) in Chile. More recently, Chen (2019) explores how the #IdleNoMore movement against new colonial policy measures in Canada was discredited by legacy media campaigns through positioning the debate not as between a violent colonial state and First Nation sovereignty, but between "progress" and unsatisfied "natives."

This same "symbolic struggle" over Indigeneity is taking place in Australian social media (Petray, 2011). Looking at the Twitter account of expressly political Aboriginal hip-hop group A.B. Original, Hutchings and Rodger (2018, p. 86) argue that "social media platforms like Twitter are important tools that can be utilised by Indigenous peoples to make explicit and powerful challenges to Settler ideas of what defines contemporary Aboriginality." Likewise,

Dreher, McCallum, and Waller (2016) document how rotating Twitter account IndigenousX provides opportunities to diversify mainstream understandings of Indigeneity, by giving control of the account to a different Indigenous Australian each week. Through participating in (relatively) free self-expression and finding space to articulate their own lived realities, Indigenous social media users are working to challenge, undo, and reconfigure what it means to be "Indigenous," and in the process are refuting the logic that sustains settler power.

Alongside this symbolic politics of Indigenous identity, discourse, and representation, social media has also affected the more "traditional" systems processes of politics—the so-called big "P" politics. A growing body of work has followed how social media has been used by Indigenous groups to increase voter turnout (Waitoa, Scheyvens, and Warren, 2015), inform people of current Indigenous issues (Duarte and Vigil-Hayes, 2017), and get bodies on the ground in acts of physical protest (Carlson and Frazer, 2016).

Many recent analyses have focused on hashtag-driven campaigns that have corralled national and international support toward their movements, including the #NoDAPL protest against an oil development on Sioux land in the United States (Deschine Parkhurst, this volume; Steinman, 2019), the #IdleNoMore movement against Canadian policy disenfranchising First Nations people (Raynauld, Richez, and Boudreau Morris, 2018; Wilson and Zheng, this volume), and the #MMIW movement shedding light on the crisis of "missing and murdered Indigenous women" across Canada (Felt, 2016; Moeke-Pickering et al., this volume). Cappelli (2018, p. 1), for instance, explores how activists "deployed digital media platforms to mobilize individuals from diverse geographical locations and diverse social, racial, political, and economic backgrounds to share their artistic expression and to stand in solidarity with The Standing Rock Sioux Tribe"—connected through the hashtags #NoDAPL and #IStandWithStandingRock (see also Steinman, 2019). Likewise, in Canada, Dahlberg-Grundberg and Lindgren (2014) argue the #IdleNoMore campaign not only was a significant and powerful Canadian First Nations movement but eventually became a global "pan-Indigenous" movement against colonial policy. They demonstrate how "locally situated social movements can use social media to deploy *translocally networked* forms of protests" (p. 49, emphasis added). The hashtag acted as a node, they argue, through which the heterogeneous and decentralized movement was able to establish and sustain bonds across geographically dispersed political networks. It produced what Barker (2015, p. 43) describes as "a renewed assertion of Indigenous sovereignty in opposition to settler colonisation." In this way, more than simply "gathering" together otherwise disparate peoples, social media can work to intensify entirely new publics, producing what Callison and Hermida call a new "middle ground" (2015, p. 695).

Emotion in Political Activism

Social media, then, is not just some new "conduit" or "container" for already existing forms of political activism; rather, it has produced entirely new forms of political movements (Castells, 2013). Seeking to make sense of this profoundly altered political landscape, recent scholarship has turned to theories of affect and emotion. While historically relegated to the "irrational" realm of domestic life, the importance of feeling in politics can hardly be overstated. "Emotions are present in every phase and every aspect of protest," writes Jasper (2011, p. 286). Emotion is what *moves* people; it is through emotion that we touch and are touched by others. Advancing beyond earlier structuralist political theories, a focus on affect and emotion affords a range of lenses through which to conceptualize politics as always processual, provisional, and embodied; it highlights the myriad ideas, bodies, and performances that compose contemporary political movements.

Significantly, emotion and affect are generated and circulated through webs of ties forged through social media technology, producing what Döveling, Harju, and Sommer (2018, p. 1) describe as "a globally mediatized emotional exchange." Social media can circulate and transform emotive discourse, elicit complex, powerful emotional expressions from users, and bring forth new kinds of political collectives. Outpourings of grief after a terrorist attack, the fractionalized organization of online hate groups, and the spread of messages of pride for marginalized groups all constitute what Papacharissi (2016) calls an "affective public," which are "soft, networked structures of feeling that help us tell stories about who we are, who we imagine we might be, and how we might get there" (p. 311). These emotional and affective publics are complex, contingent networks that often lack any recognizable hierarchy or organizational structure. This is particularly significant for political movements. Shared emotions are the "glue" of identity (Persson, 2017): they can call forth different collectives into being, can reinforce, challenge, and rework stereotypes, and can glue people together in a different way.

Only a small body of work has attended to the affective and emotional registers of Indigenous activism. Felt (2016), for instance, exploring the affective politics of the hashtag movement #MMIW (murdered and missing Indigenous women), reveals that hope, anger, and disgust were the most common affective expressions through the #MMIW campaign and were central in developing and sustaining affective solidarity among activists. In an analysis of the protest materials of Standing Rock activists, Cappelli argues that artistic expression works to "politically align indigenous and non-indigenous protestors together in affective solidarity and artful resistance" (2018, p. 1). And in their analysis of the dynamics of pain and pride in Indigenous social media use, Carlson et al. (2017) show that just as traumatic content can circulate and intensify online, so too Indigenous social media users can generate, circulate, and intensify more joyful affects—converting shame into pride, for instance.

The Affective Economies of Indigenous Activism

This chapter charts the dynamics of emotion in the two Indigenous political arrangements: #SOSBlakAustralia and #IndigenousDads. Both of these movements were significant national events. The former constituted what has been described as the first truly global Indigenous Australian movement (Cook, 2015); it garnered the support of hundreds of thousands of people and on more than one occasion drew major Australian cities to a standstill. In contrast, #IndigenousDads was remarkable for its cultural impact. It offered an entirely different path through the racist logic underpinning Australian politics, banding together people through expressions of Indigenous love, pride, and joy.

To unpack the "soft, networked structures of feeling" (Papacharissi, 2016) that compose these two movements, we draw on Sara Ahmed's (2015) notion of "affective economies." Ahmed encourages us to see emotions neither as entirely private nor entirely social, but as collective feelings that move *between* people, "sticking" to some bodies and gliding off others. Importantly, for Ahmed, this motion of emotion is what makes the "skin" of the individual and collective self felt, known, and sensible. "The objects of emotion take shape as *effects* of circulation," Ahmed writes. "It is through emotions . . . that surfaces or boundaries [of bodies] are made" (2015, p. 10, emphasis added). This economic model of emotion draws attention to how, on the one hand, the circulation of different emotions both *moves* and *moves between* bodies and how, on the other hand, it works to *consolidate* and bind together different publics.

Taking this model as a starting point, we are guided by two main questions. First, we ask, what are the emotional forces pushing along and pulling apart these movements? In other words, how do the various emotions of Indigenous activism work to animate and consolidate antisettler publics? And second, what strategies are deployed by others to contain and eliminate these affective economies?

#SOSBlakAustralia: Indigenous Dispossession and the Affective Economies of Anger

The Announcement

On November 12, 2014, Colin Barnett, the premier of Western Australia, announced that up to 150 of the state's 274 remote Aboriginal communities would be closed. Responsibility for funding basic services was being transferred from the national to the state government. Despite being the nation's richest state—a state whose wealth derives almost entirely from the extraction of minerals from the ground—these homelands were, in the words of Barnett, "not viable" (Wahlquist, 2015c).

While the announcement sent waves of fear and anger throughout the state, it was a comment on March 10, 2015, by the then prime minister Tony Abbott—self-instated minister for Indigenous affairs—that became what was later described as "the trigger needed to polarize a nation" (#SOSBlakAustralia, 2015). On radio, Abbott supported Barnett's decision, explaining, "What we can't do is endlessly subsidise lifestyle choices if those lifestyle choices are not conducive to the kind of full participation in Australian society that everyone should have" (ABC, 2015).

The Emergence of a Movement

It was this characterizing of Aboriginal connection to Country as an economically unsustainable "lifestyle choice" that became the "tinder needed" (#SOSBlakAustralia, 2015) to inflame political action. On the evening of March 12, a small group of mainly remote Kimberley women were convening in person and online. And by two o'clock the following morning, a clear action was initiated. Both a public Facebook page, "Stop the Forced Closure of Aboriginal Communities," and a private member page for activist organizers were established (Cook, 2015). Gathering under the hashtag #SOSBlakAustralia, the campaign was an urgent call of distress: Save Our Souls. It aimed "to support the Aboriginal communities in Australia to remain in their homelands and on country and enable them to self-determine their own futures" (#SOSBlakAustralia, 2015). In response to the claim that living on Country is a lifestyle choice, the organizers instead explained that they "hold significant cultural obligations to our Ancestors to maintain Sovereign ties to our lands" (#SOSBlakAustralia, 2015). There would be two arms to the movement: a garnering of support and a challenging of the logic of the settler state spread online, and a physical show of solidarity against the policy circulated offline.

Activists were mobilized across every state and territory; there was a shared Google Drive document for coordinating protests actions, and all actions were informed by a "Cultural Code of Conduct," which emphasized the shared responsibility protesters had for maintaining cultural integrity. Emotion, particularly anger, is volatile. Thus the code called for unity, focus, and clarity of movement. "Let us hold our combined power and move together as one," it explained (#SOSBlakAustralia, 2015).

In seven hours, the Facebook page had two thousand followers, up to fifty thousand a fortnight later. A drove of celebrities and civil rights activists jumped on board. Indigenous groups, unions, and political parties across the world lent their support. The UN permanent forum on Indigenous issues supported a submission from the Kimberley Land Council, describing the policy as "a discriminatory and race-based erosion of their rights and the attempted assimilation of Indigenous people into white Australia" (Wahlquist, 2015a).

The first national day of action took place just seven days later, mobilizing over thirty communities across the nation. At least eight hundred people in Sydney and four thousand in Melbourne marched, shutting down both CBDs during peak hour traffic. Melbourne lord mayor Robert Doyle dismissed the protesters as "self-indulgent," and the major newspaper of Victoria, the *Sun Herald*, described them as "selfish rabble" across front-page headlines (Watson, 2015). The inconvenience to commuters was the core of the story in mainstream media. It made clear that protesters' anger was not an expression of injustice—it was not *righteous* anger—but was the petty complaints of a petulant child and could therefore be dismissed as self-indulgent and selfish.

With no change to policy yet announced, a second day of global action was called two weeks later. Some ninety-eight protests were held globally, involving over thirty thousand people, capturing every capital city in Australia, dozens of other cities and towns nationwide, and cities across Germany, the United States, New Zealand, Hong Kong, England, Hawaii, and Canada. The largest protest again took place in Melbourne's CBD, where an estimated ten thousand people marched toward the main transport station, shutting down the city during peak hour. Protesters shouted "No pride in genocide" and "Always was, always will be Aboriginal land." As day turned to night, parts of the crowd moved to Kings Domain and established a camp, which they occupied for two nights to hold smoking ceremonies, discussions, and information sessions. It was described as a "sovereign hub," "a place of smoking ceremony, information sessions, panel discussions, children's activities, music, and dance" (Davidson, 2015).

It was on this day that the movement emerged as truly global: by the afternoon, #SOSBlakAustralia was trending globally on Twitter. Across the major social media sites, supporters changed their profile pictures to the movement's characteristic poster featuring a "stop sign" in the colors of the Aboriginal flag: red, black, and yellow. The two arms to the protests were working together powerfully: resistance to the political discourse around the closures—rejecting the rationality, the justification—online, and resistance in the streets through disrupting the regular flow of city life in the colony offline. *New Matilda* described the emotional force of the movement: "The ability to mobilise so many across the country, not once, but twice, within two months of each other speaks to the outrage that will hopefully end up suffocating Barnett's plans to close these communities" (*New Matilda*, 2015).

Containing Indigenous Anger

But when asked again about the protestors, Premier Barnett sought to delegitimize them, asking, "Are they from Aboriginal communities? I doubt they are." He claimed those protesting "misunderstand what I'm saying and what we are doing as a government" (Wahlquist, 2015b). He took the opportunity to offer a new justification for their closure: child abuse and high rates of sexually transmitted infection in children in the communities, a claim that lacked credible evidence. Like so many times in the history of Australian colonization, the rights of Aboriginal children would be weaponized against the rights of Aboriginal people more broadly.

Considering its incredible scope, the second day of protest was barely covered by mainstream media, with the noted exception of the *Herald Sun*'s familiar story about petulant protestors punishing hardworking citizens. "For the second time in three weeks," they reported, "hundreds of thousands of people trying to get home on Friday were severely inconvenienced as an angry throng of more than 12,000 people jammed the streets" (Langmaid, Gillet, and Payne, 2015). They highlighted the tragedy of the "Friday night football fans" who "were among those caught up in the gridlock" (Langmaid et al., 2015). Mainstream media commentator Andrew Bolt described "feeling less reconciled and more threatened than ever, and wonder[ing] how much worse this divisiveness will get" (*New Matilda*, 2015). Indeed, he claimed that it was the protests that were in fact racist because they were delivering a "collective punishment of mainly white Australians in Melbourne in return for what white politicians on the other side of the country have allegedly done to black Australians" (*New Matilda*, 2015).

The Affective Force of Anger

Anger has a palpable affective force. As a response to the unjust suffering of others, it circulates rapidly between bodies, eliciting and consolidating a collective of people against that injustice whose actions and reactions stimulate affect. Anger is a force that demands attention and is therefore capable of generating far-reaching empathy and solidarity on social media. There is a symbiotic relationship between anger and social media whereby affect can be an immediate response. In other words there is an *immediacy* to both anger and social media that makes them work so well together. Anger calls for urgent action, justice, and restitution, and social media provides the instantaneous connections through which it might move.

#SOSBlakAustralia effectively circulated anger at the injustice of Aboriginal dispossession, putting out a direct call of distress: Save Our Souls. Through anger, a new collective was brought into being: the "selfish rabble" who could not tolerate the forced removal of Aboriginal people from Aboriginal Country. An angry public with no foreseeable pathway to justice, however, can be destructive and debilitating; it is incapable of being sustained. Importantly, then, #SOSBlakAustralia also gave vision and direction toward a potential recourse to justice. Through carefully coordinating organizers online, through setting up social media pages and groups and hashtags, and through developing a clear "code of conduct" for activists, #SOSBlakAustralia directed the anger of tens of thousands of bodies to the street, elicited loud demands for justice, and shut down city centers. #SOSBlakAustralia realized what Henderson (2008, p. 30) calls the "enabling function of anger."

It is important to recognize that there is a racial politics to anger that determines who is allowed to express anger and who is not. Once an affective economy of anger has stimulated a public into action, then, that public itself becomes an object of politics. And the anger of Black and Indigenous people has always elicited forceful responses from the white settler state. As Ahmed explains, the anger of Aboriginal publics destabilizes the illusion of the cohesive, happy, multicultural nation (2008, p. 6). Aboriginal scholar Chelsea Bond (2018) also notes that this anger is "a real threat to the colony."

In the above account, we can see how the power of categorizing this affective economy as "angry rabble" works. By labeling the collective in this way, their concerns can be pushed aside; they can be categorized as irrational, as needing to be "rational" and "sensible," as needing to "calm down." As Bond (2018) explains, "The angry black woman is a trope which insists that our emotional responses are irrational and unregulated, which then makes the oppression we experience seem like a rational outcome of our behaviour." This works as a strategy of containment, in which the original problem that led to the anger is obscured. The protestors are instead positioned as what Ahmed calls "killjoys," in which "certain bodies are seen as the origin of bad feeling, as getting in the way of public happiness" (2008, p. 1). The person who identifies a problem, who refuses to just "go along" with things—even their own oppression—*becomes* a problem, sabotaging the happiness of innocent others, blocking the flow of happiness throughout the social body of the settler state.

#IndigenousDads: The Affective Force of Indigenous Love

Australia's Shame

On July 25, 2016, an investigation by journalism program *Four Corners* aired on primetime TV. It was titled "Australia's Shame" and documented the horrific treatment of detainees in the Northern Territory's juvenile detention center, Don Dale. Footage smuggled out of the facility showed in vivid detail the cruel, violent practices of guards spraying tear gas into locked cells, stripping naked detainees, pouring water over their heads while prone and handcuffed, pushing and punching them, ordering them to fight one another. One image was so shocking it appeared the next day on the front page of every major newspaper in the country. It showed a teenager shackled to a chair, shirtless, with a "spit hood" secured over his head. The detainees were children and teenagers, ten to sixteen years old. Response from the public and politicians was immediate. The United Nations High Commissioner for Refugees announced the footage documented contraventions of both the Convention against Torture and the Convention on the Rights of the Child. In an unprecedented move, the prime minister announced a Royal Commission into the facility the very next day—one of the most powerful and far-reaching forms of public enquiry possible. Publicly, there were outpourings of grief, pain, trauma, and immense anger.

The fact that almost all the detainees were Indigenous—almost 97 percent in a territory with an Indigenous population of 25 percent—did not feature prominently in the public discussion that followed. Rather, it was framed as an issue of poor regulation, unprofessional practice by people in authority and poor oversight in detention institutions. It was, according to the primary narrative that emerged, an institutional and policy failing, as opposed to a direct manifestation of settler-colonial logic whereby, despite eliciting a discourse of "human rights," white supremacy continues to exert violence.

The Cartoon

A fortnight after the investigation went to air, Bill Leak, a resident cartoonist at Australia's national newspaper *The Australian*, published a single-panel cartoon depicting a white policeman, holding a young Aboriginal child by the collar of his shirt, telling the child's father that his son needed to be taught some responsibility (Carlson et al., 2017). In response, the father, barefoot and holding a beer can, asked the officer what the child's name was. The cartoon said nothing explicit about Don Dale, but the subtext was clear. According to Leak, the root cause of the situation at Don Dale was the neglectful Indigenous fathers, who don't take "proper" care of their children. Public reaction was immediate. The cartoon circulated rapidly across Facebook and Twitter throughout that day, carried by an incredible wave of anger directed toward the cartoon, its creator, and the newspaper that published it. It would have been difficult to be in Australia that day and not see the cartoon.

Leak responded a few days later, explaining that the cartoon was not offensive or racist. In fact, it was the opposite. Instead, he described his critics as "sanctimonious Tweety Birds having a tantrum" (Kerin, 2016); they were having an irrational, unreasonable reaction to a piece of important social commentary. "If a cartoonist's job is to provoke discussions of really important issues," he said, "then you'd have to say I did rather well." It was described by the paper's editor as a "contribution" to the "national conversation" around Indigenous issues—a debate that didn't and couldn't possibly include discussion of over two centuries of colonial violence, intergenerational trauma, the Stolen Generations, police racism, and the lack of state support for Indigenous families or the continued overrepresentation and incarceration of Indigenous fathers in the criminal "justice" system. By portraying Indigenous fathers as threats to their own children—a common trope perpetuated by the settler state (Hammond, 2010,

p. 23)—what becomes obscured is the disruption and destruction colonial interventions have wrought on Indigenous families, and the incredible loss of cultural knowledges, practices, and connections around fatherhood (Faulkner et al., 2018).

Indigenous people were put in an impossible position. How to respond effectively to such hurtful and racist depictions of Indigenous family life? How to respond to this mainstream media machine that thrives off attention, "controversy," and anger? How to respond to this violence disguised as concern, this hatred disguised as compassion, and this colonialism disguised as care?

The Love of Indigenous Dads

But while social media was implicated deeply in this affective economy of hatred and anger, it also afforded new forms of action: what Bennett and Segerberg (2012) describe as connective action, and what Papacharissi (2016) calls an "affective public." We don't ever know how a particular expression will be received; we don't know which will pass away unnoticed and which will catch fire. And in the noise anger of the cartoon's fallout, a single post catalyzed what became an island of pride, joy, and love. A single tweet was sent out by Indigenous man Joel Bayliss: "To counter the bill leak cartoon here is a pic of me & my kids. I am a proud Aboriginal father" (figure 3.1). Something evidently resonated, as this lone expression of love and pride emerged from the waves of anger, pain, and hatred. It was enthusiastically liked and retweeted and soon became a meme—with hundreds of users sharing tender moments of love, intimacy, and joy of their relationships with their fathers. "Aboriginal fathers and children shared personal family moments on social media, presenting an image of Aboriginal life mainstream society rarely sees," wrote chairman of the NSW Aboriginal Land Council Roy Ah See (2016). It was "a rare demonstration of positive father-child connections in Aboriginal families" (Faulkner et al., 2018, p. 3).

The love and joy spilled into print media too, with an opinion piece published in the *Coffs Coast Advocate*: "To all of our incredible #IndigenousDads in our community, including my dad, brother and partner. There are so many amazing #IndigenousDads in Coffs and I want you to know that you are appreciated and valued." Williams explained that the movement had struck the hearts of Indigenous people nationwide: "In highlighting the goodness that exists, we have been able to connect with the wider community, who have shared our joy and cried with us as we have shared our stories, celebrating and honouring our cherished #Indigenousdads" (Williams, 2016). "The campaign trended nationally," Elfie Shiosaki (2016) later explained, "creating a vivid digital archive."

This circulation of love stood in stark contrast to the politics that inspired it. As Goori writer and researcher Jack Latimore explained, the #IndigenousDads campaign "was imbued not only with compassion, but deeper, constructive

Joel B
@jb_bays

To counter the bill leak cartoon here is a pic of me & my kids.
I am a proud Aboriginal father. @IndigenousX #auspol

6:35 PM · Aug 5, 2016 · Twitter for iPhone

450 Retweets   **25** Quote Tweets   **910** Likes

FIG. 3.1 Joel Bayliss's original #IndigenousDads tweet. (Credit: Joel Bayliss.)

consideration" of the issues surrounding Don Dale (Latimore, 2016). Radically challenging the settler stereotype of the dangerous and neglectful Indigenous father, the campaign instead showed Indigenous families that are close, intimate, loving, caring. Anger was the obvious and most justified response to the cartoon and the racist discourse that produced it. But through the hashtag moment, anger against settler violence took another form, blooming into an affective economy of love, pride, and connectedness in Indigenous kin.

The Danger of Indigenous Love

However, much like the anger of #SOSBlakAustralia, it seems Indigenous people collectively expressing their love for and pride in their families was not acceptable to some people. In response to the campaign, conservative commentator Chris Kenny (2016) wrote in *The Australian* that while the #IndigenousDads campaign may have, in his words, "lifted the spirits of social media users," "the trouble is that [it] has been used to deny or distract from a serious social crisis." "This is disappointing and damaging," he continued, "because it diminishes a crucial debate." Kenny framed the response as irrational and distracting and argued that the issue instead required calm, "balanced" consideration: "Perhaps if more media organisations engaged in [an] intelligent national examination of indigenous issues, rather than emotive confrontation, they could tackle the underlying causes of indigenous disadvantage." According to Kenny, then, even the love of Indigenous dads is dangerous for Indigenous children, and the circulation of this love must then be contained and eliminated. Framing Indigenous political activism through the stereotypical force of the "angry" Native functions in this instance to blame Indigenous people for their own disadvantage; they become positioned as complicit in their own suppression. This tactic is very effective and is widely used to silence Indigenous politics.

Closing: Converting Anger to Action

To be Indigenous online is to be a political subject. It means being exposed to and entangled within the logics, actors, and processes of the settler state. In this context, social media both enables and contains the political agency of Indigenous users. The task, as Duarte and Vigil-Hayes (2017) argue, is to understand how social media technologies might be appropriated as effective tools of political expression, liberation, and cultural resurgence.

In this chapter, we have explored the work of emotion in Indigenous social media movements. We have argued that the affective economies of Indigenous protest involve both the *circulation* and *consolidation* of affect. Both protest moments were responses to the unjust treatment of Indigenous people, with anger circulating rapidly through social media platforms, through users sharing news, images, stories, and connecting through hashtags. Anger, however, needs somewhere to go; it's a "busy" emotion, and it demands hope for some kind of resolution. Anger is a powerful affective force, but from it something must grow.

Importantly, then, both movements offered different ways in which the righteous anger could be converted into a concrete political expression. In #SOSBlakAustralia, anger was converted into on-the-streets protest, in which city centers across Australia were shut down, while in #IndigenousDads, anger was converted into expressions of love and pride of family. These are the "points of conversion" (Ahmed, 2008) in affect—the transformation of affect and emotion from one form to another. While differentiating considerably in form, they were both expressions of a refusal to "go along" with things as they were. The conversion of anger into action in both movements challenged the material and discursive politics of the settler state: the physical removal of Aboriginal people from Aboriginal Country, and stereotypes of the dysfunctional Indigenous family and violent father.

Political affect does not arise in a vacuum; there are "feeling rules" that guide who is "allowed" to express which feelings, where and when. It seems that every time an Indigenous movement achieves a powerful affective economy—of anger, love, or pride—there are always others attempting to cut short these circulations of feeling that in some way threaten settler power. According to segments of mainstream media and mainstream Australia, Indigenous people are not allowed to express their righteous anger, or even their love or pride. It seems they are not meant to feel anything at all. The anger, love, and pride of Indigenous people will upset their position of power and privilege. The settler strategy of "just wanting to have a rational conversation," without all this feeling—is only an option as long as that conversation doesn't include any reference to the violent structures of settler colonialism. In conclusion, it is evident that social media sites have become powerful sites of political activism for Indigenous people. We have created viable platforms whereby users can express emotion in an affective manner that generates response, solidarity, and further political engagement. Despite consistent attempts to thwart Indigenous political forces and disrupt attempts to intervene in settler colonialism, social media platforms continue to be powerful mechanisms for resistance. It is our contention that the affect produced by the continued critique and anger of Indigenous activists will continue to generate disruptions to the force of settler colonial discourses.

Acknowledgments

The authors wish to acknowledge and thank the Aboriginal and Torres Strait Islander people who participated in this study. Your contributions, experiences, and anecdotes have enriched this area of research. Additionally, we would like to thank the research assistants in each community who generously provided us with information on local cultural protocols.

References

ABC. (2015, March 10). Prime Minister Tony Abbott's interview with the ABC Goldfields-Esperance. *ABC Goldfields Radio.* http://www.abc.net.au/local/videos /2015/03/10/4194973.html.

Ahmed, S. (2008). The politics of good feeling. *Australian Critical Race and Whiteness Studies Association Journal*, 4(1), 1–18.

Ahmed, S. (2015). *The cultural politics of emotion* (2nd ed). New York: Routledge.

Ah See, R. (2016, August 31). #IndigenousDads and Aboriginal health: Stereotyping a barrier to Aboriginal advancement. *NACCHO Communique.* https:// nacchocommunique.com/2016/08/31/naccho-indigenousdads-and-aboriginal -health-stereotyping-a-barrier-to-aboriginal-advancement/.

Barker, A. J. (2015). "A direct act of resurgence, a direct act of sovereignty": Reflections on idle no more, Indigenous activism, and Canadian settler colonialism. *Globalizations, 12*(1), 43–65.

Bennett, W. L., and Segerberg, A. (2012). The logic of connective action: Digital media and the personalization of contentious politics. *Information, Communication and Society, 15*(5), 739–768.

Bond, C. (2018, January 31). The audacity of anger. *Guardian.* https://www .theguardian.com/commentisfree/2018/jan/31/the-audacity-of-anger.

Callison, C., and Hermida, A. (2015). Dissent and resonance: # Idlenomore as an emergent middle ground. *Canadian Journal of Communication, 40*(4), 695.

Cappelli, M. L. (2018). Standing with Standing Rock: Affective alignment and artful resistance at the Native Nations Rise March. *SAGE Open, 8*(3), 2158244018785703.

Carlson, B. and Frazer, R. (2016). Indigenous activism & social media: A global response to #SOSBLAKAUSTRALIA. In A. McCosker, S. Vivienne, and A. Johns (Eds.), *Negotiating digital citizenship: Control, contest and culture.* Lanham, MD: Rowman & Littlefield.

Carlson, B., Jones, L., Harris, M., Quezada, N. and Frazer, R. (2017). Trauma, shared recognition and Indigenous resistance on social media. *Australasian Journal of Information Systems, 21,* 1–18.

Castells, M. (2013). *Networks of outrage and hope: Social movements in the internet age.* New York: John Wiley.

Chen, S. (2019). How to discredit a social movement: Negative framing of "Idle No More" in Canadian Print Media. *Environmental Communication, 13*(2), 144–151. https://doi.org/10.1080/17524032.2018.1546201.

Chertoff, M. (2017). A public policy perspective of the Dark Web. *Journal of Cyber Policy, 2*(1), 26–38. https://doi.org/10.1080/23738871.2017.1298643.

Cook, S. (2015, April 1). #SOSBlakAustralia: Stop the forced closure of Aboriginal communities—IndigenousX. *Guardian.* https://www.theguardian.com /commentisfree/2015/apr/01/sosblakaustralia-stop-the-forced-closure-of-aboriginal -communities-indigenousx.

Dahlberg-Grundberg, M., and Lindgren, S. (2014). Translocal frame extensions in a networked protest: Situating the #IdleNoMore hashtag. *IC Revista Científica de Informacióm y Communicación, 11.* https://icjournal-ojs.org/index.php/ic-journal /article/view/295.

Davidson, H. (2015, May 1). Melbourne city centre blocked by protests over closure of Indigenous communities—as it happened. *Guardian.* https://www.theguardian .com/australia-news/live/2015/may/01/protests-at-proposed-closure-of-remote -indigenous-communities-live.

Döveling, K., Harju, A. A., and Sommer, D. (2018). From mediatized emotion to digital affect cultures: New technologies and global flows of emotion. *Social Media and Society, 4*(1). https://doi.org/10.1177/2056305117743141.

Dreher, T., McCallum, K., and Waller, L. (2016). Indigenous voices and mediatized policy-making in the digital age. *Information, Communication and Society, 19*(1), 23–39. https://doi.org/10.1080/1369118X.2015.1093534.

Duarte, M. E. (2017). Connected activism: Indigenous use of social media for shaping political change. *Australasian Journal of Information Systems, 21,* 1–12.

Duarte, M. E., and Vigil-Hayes, M. (2017). #Indigenous: A technical and decolonial analysis of activist uses of hashtags across social movements. *MediaTropes, 7*(1), 166–184.

Faulkner, D., Hammond, C., Nisbet, L., and Fletcher, R. (2018). How do young aboriginal fathers in Australia "stay on track"?—Perspectives on the support networks of aboriginal fathers. *Journal of Family Studies.* https://doi.org/10.1080 /13229400.2018.1537193.

Felt, M. (2016, July). Mobilizing affective political networks: The role of affect in calls for a national inquiry to murdered and missing Indigenous women during the 2015 Canadian Federal election. In *Proceedings of the 7th 2016 International Conference on Social Media & Society* (p. 7). New York: ACM.

Hammond, C. (2010). Making positive resources to engage Aboriginal men/fathers. *Aboriginal and Islander Health Worker Journal, 34*(5), 23.

Henderson, V. L. (2008). Is there hope for anger? The politics of spatializing and (re) producing an emotion. *Emotion, Space and Society, 1*(1), 28–37.

Hutchings, S., and Rodger, D. (2018). Reclaiming Australia: Indigenous hip-hop group A.B. Original's use of Twitter. *Media International Australia, 169*(1), 84–93. https://doi.org/10.1177/1329878X18803382.

Jardine, E. (2015). The dark web dilemma: Tor, anonymity and online policing. *SSRN Electronic Journal, 21.* https://doi.org/10.2139/ssrn.2667711.

Jasper, J. M. (2011). Emotions and social movements: Twenty years of theory and research. *Annual Review of Sociology, 37,* 285–303.

Kenny, C. (2016). Outrage over Bill Leak cartoon misses the point. *The Australian.* https://www.theaustralian.com.au/commentary/opinion/outrage-over-bill-leak -cartoon-misses-the-point/news-story/db1a205b2d78ff61a309ced66df226ae.

Kerin, L. (2016, August 5). Bill Leak defends controversial cartoon against "sanctimo- nious Tweety Birds." *ABC.* Available: https://www.abc.net.au/news/2016-08-05 /bill-leak-defends-controversial-cartoon/7693244.

Landzelius, K. (2006). *Native on the net: Indigenous and diasporic peoples in the virtual age.* New York: Routledge.

Langmaid, A., Gillet, C., and Payne, N. (2015). Protesters shut down city centre and warn more chaos to come. *Herald Sun.* https://www.heraldsun.com.au/news /victoria/protesters-shut-down-city-centre-and-warn-more-chaos-to-come/news -story/4efa4a48b47053f31c2e3de12d3a5579.

Latimore, J. (2016, August 15). Gratuitous emphasis on race: Why Bill Leak's cartoon fails to be meaningful. *Guardian.* https://www.theguardian.com/commentisfree /2016/aug/15/gratuitous-emphasis-on-race-why-bill-leaks-cartoon-fails-to-be -meaningful.

New Matilda. (2015). In Andrew Bolt's world, Black is white and peaceful protest is war. https://newmatilda.com/2015/05/04/andrew-bolts-world-black-white-and -peaceful-protest-war/.

Papacharissi, Z. (2016). Affective publics and structures of storytelling: Sentiment, events and mediality. *Information Communication and Society, 19*(3), 307–324. https://doi.org/10.1080/1369118X.2015.1109697.

Persson, G. (2017). Love, affiliation, and emotional recognition in #kämpamalmö: The social role of emotional language in Twitter discourse. *Social Media and Society, 3*(1). https://doi.org/10.1177/2056305117696522.

Petray, T. L. (2011). Protest 2.0: Online interactions and Aboriginal activists. *Media, Culture & Society, 33*(6), 923–940. https://doi.org/10.1177/0163443711411009.

Raynauld, V., Richez, E., and Boudreau Morris, K. (2018). Canada is# IdleNoMore: Exploring dynamics of Indigenous political and civic protest in the Twitterverse. *Information, Communication and Society, 21*(4), 626–642.

Salazar, J. F. (2003). Articulating an activist imaginary: Internet as counter public sphere in the Mapuche movement, 1997/2002. *Media International Australia Incorporating Culture and Policy, 107*(1), 19–30.

Saramo, S. (2016). Unsettling spaces: Grassroots responses to Canada's missing and murdered Indigenous women during the Harper government years. *Comparative American Studies, 14*(3–4), 204–220. https://doi.org/10.1080/14775700.2016 .1267311.

Shiosaki, E. (2016). Hand on heart. *Overland.* https://overland.org.au/previous-issues /issue-233/feature-hand-on-heart/.

#SOSBlakAustralia. (2015). http://www.sosblakaustralia.com/.

Steinman, E. (2019). Why was Standing Rock and the# NoDAPL campaign so historic? Factors affecting American Indian participation in social movement collaborations and coalitions. *Ethnic and Racial Studies, 42*(7), 1070–1090.

Wahlquist, C. (2015a, April 23). UN forum backs fight against closure of remote Aboriginal communities in WA. *Guardian.* https://www.theguardian.com /australia-news/2015/apr/23/un-forum-backs-fight-against-closure-of-remote -aboriginal-communities-in-wa.

Wahlquist, C. (2015b, May 1). Colin Barnett shrugs off protests against WA's remote community policy. *Guardian.* https://www.theguardian.com/australia-news/2015 /may/01/colin-barnett-shrugs-off-protests-against-was-remote-community-policy.

Wahlquist, C. (2015c, June 28). Sydney streets blocked by protest against WA remote community closures. *Guardian.* https://www.theguardian.com/australia-news /2015/jun/28/sydney-streets-blocked-by-protest-against-wa-remote-community -closures.

Waitoa, J., Scheyvens, R., and Warren, T. R. (2015). E-Whanaungatanga: The role of social media in Māori political empowerment. *AlterNative: An International Journal of Indigenous Peoples, 11*(1), 45–58.

Watson, M. (2015). The *Herald Sun* has dismissed 4,000 Indigenous rights protesters as a "selfish rabble." *Junkee.* http://junkee.com/the-herald-sun-has-dismissed-4000 -indigenous-rights-protestors-as-a-selfish-rabble/54833.

Williams, G. (2016). My #indigenousdad would never forget my name, he was the epitome of love and honour. *Sydney Morning Herald.* https://www.smh.com.au /opinion/my-indigenousdad-would-never-forget-my-name-he-was-the-epitome-of -love-and-honour-20160809-gqo9uv.html.

Wolfe, P. (2006). Settler colonialism and the elimination of the Native. *Journal of Genocide Research, 8*(4), 387–409.

Wolfson, T. (2012). From the Zapatistas to Indymedia: Dialectics and orthodoxy in contemporary social movements. *Communication, Culture & Critique, 5*(2), 149–170. https://doi.org/10.1111/j.1753-9137.2012.01131.x.

4

Responding to White Supremacy

■ ■

An Analysis of Twitter
Messages by Māori after the
Christchurch Terrorist Attack

STEVE ELERS, PHOEBE ELERS,
AND MOHAN DUTTA

Christchurch in Aotearoa New Zealand was the site of a racist terrorist attack by an Australian white supremacist, Brenton Tarrant. On Friday, March 15, 2019, Tarrant shot Muslim worshippers at two mosques in Christchurch, killing fifty-one innocent people and seriously injuring others. The first seventeen minutes of this act of terrorism were livestreamed using the social media platform Facebook. Tarrant was apprehended by police and is, at the time of writing, awaiting trial on fifty-one charges of murder, forty charges of attempted murder, and one charge under the Terrorism Suppression Act. The video footage from the livestream and the terrorist's seventy-four-page manifesto were banned by the chief censor, David Shanks (Office of Film and Literature Classification, 2019).

This was the first terrorist attack in Aotearoa New Zealand in recent times, but it was not the first terrorist attack, nor was it the first white supremacist terrorist attack in Aotearoa New Zealand. We should not forget the colonial violence inflicted upon Māori (Indigenous peoples of Aotearoa New Zealand) despite many Pākehā (white people in Aotearoa New Zealand) refusing to frame colonial violence within the discourse of terrorism. For many Pākehā, terrorism is an "Other" event, not something enacted by their forebears on Māori. An overseas visitor at an Aotearoa New Zealand conference challenged a national counter terrorism expert about his lack of recognition of colonial terrorism: "Why had he chosen to focus on the 1970s as the start of terrorist violence? ... An exchange began between us, where I attempted to explain that he is an actor in the construction of this knowledge, and so he cannot simply say that he arbitrarily chose to start there, without justifying his decision. Ultimately, I was driving him towards accepting that he was wilfully blind in refusing to include colonial violence against Māori within his construction of terroristic violence within the history of New Zealand" (Qureshi, 2019, para. 6). Just as Pākehā have dominated the historiography of Aotearoa New Zealand and definitions of what constitutes terrorism, so too, in the aftermath of the terrorist attack, Pākehā dominated spaces for voice across most public platforms, including news media commentaries, media interviews, and public talks. For the authors, having to watch and listen to Pākehā being afforded a public voice ahead of Muslims, Māori, and other peoples of color, epitomized white privilege. For example, the discourse of "They Are Us," which became a slogan of solidarity with Muslims after Prime Minister Jacinda Ardern first used it in a media conference following the terrorist attack (Reicher, Haslam, and Van Bavel, 2019), was itself a form of "Othering." As eloquently stated by Guled Mire, a Muslim community leader, "Who does the 'they' refer to, and who is the 'us'? And I think that's quite problematic because in times like this ... we should be reassuring Muslims belong here, this is their home" (*1 News Now*, 2019, para. 8).

In contrast to the dominant discursive spaces in Aotearoa New Zealand after the terrorist attack, the presence of Māori voices on social media offered anchors to resist racist structures, simultaneously situating the response to the terrorist attack in continuity with the racist infrastructures of settler colonialism. As Waitoki (2019), a Māori scholar, stated in response to Prime Minister Ardern's "They Are Us" catchphrase, "my colleagues hit back on social media saying that the attack was not unprecedented, and that we were never innocent. We argued that 'this is not us,' really meant, 'actually, yes it is'" (p. 140).

Social media provided a digital space for "Others," including Māori, to share their whakaaro (thoughts), to ponder, to empower, to vent, to rage, and to engage in dialogue about the terrorist attack. In doing so, social media articulations provided a mechanism to disrupt white supremacy as well as strategies that erase conversations on white supremacy under the pretense of dialogue. This paper is an analysis of Twitter messages, or tweets, by selected Māori social media influencers in the aftermath of the Christchurch terrorist attack. First, it is important to understand the context of racism in Aotearoa New Zealand.

Colonization and Racism in Aotearoa New Zealand

The British progressively settled in Aotearoa New Zealand from around the early 1800s (Keiha and Moon, 2008) after Captain James Cook "discovered New Zealand in October 1769" (Zhang, 2018, p. 96). The expansion into Aotearoa New Zealand was, as Māori scholar Walker (2004) stated, "predicated on assumptions of racial, religious, cultural and technological superiority" (p. 9). Māori scholar Mikaere (2011) argued that since the arrival of the British, Māori have "suffered and continue to suffer a great deal as a result of Pākehā racism" (p. 68). Furthermore, racism has killed Māori quickly but also insidiously and slowly (Waitoki, 2019). For example, Māori in Rangiaowhia were captured and burned alive by colonial forces in February 1864—the land was confiscated and turned over to Pākehā for settlement (Hargreaves, 1959); and it has been widely published that racism has produced disparities in health status between Māori and Pākehā (Kearns, Moewaka-Barnes, and McCreanor, 2009) resulting in lower life expectancy for Māori (Woodward and Blakely, 2014) as they have "the poorest health status of any ethnic group in New Zealand" (Ministry of Health, 2013, para. 1). The processes of colonization have meant that Māori are negatively overrepresented right across the health and social spectrum. As highlighted by Durie (2003), "There are no surprises. On almost any indicator, such as health, education, employment, offending, home ownership, or income levels, Māori performance is substantially worse" (p. 21).

One measure of racism is the media because they are reflective of wider society (Downing and Husband, 2005; Spoonley, 1990). Historically, the media in Aotearoa New Zealand were explicitly racist (Thompson, 1953, 1954; Will, 1973). More recently, analyses of media in Aotearoa New Zealand "have consistently shown that news about Māori is both relatively rare and that it prioritises violence and criminality" (Nairn et al., 2012, p. 38). With the advent of the internet, white supremacy has entered the digital era (Daniels, 2009), and Māori have not escaped online racism. For example, Elers (2014) found that Google's autocomplete (predictive text) function included the suggestions when typing "Maori are" into the Google search engine: (1) "Maori are scum," (2) "Maori are stupid," (3) "Maori are lazy"—this was later resolved by Google (Deane, 2014).

Racism online, of course, extends well into the social media sphere, with recent research showing that one in three Māori (32 percent) has endured online racial abuse in 2018 (*PeoplesHarassmentReport*, 2019), which gives meaning to why O'Connell-Rapira's (2019) opinion piece in *The Spinoff* was titled "Why Social Media Is Not a Safe Place for Indigenous People." With racism burgeoning in the digital era, it is unsurprising then that a discussion of the Christchurch terrorist attack can be found on the white supremacist website Stormfront (Quek, 2019). Facebook was the social media platform that Tarrant used to livestream killing fifty-one innocent Muslims using a helmet camera

(Haleem, 2019). Hence, racism and white supremacy are well and truly alive online, including on social media. On the other hand, Māori and other Indigenous peoples are using social media to "'reterritorialise' and 'Indigenise' the information and communication space" (Wilson et al., 2017, p. 1). So it is at this nexus of social media where Māori and other Indigenous peoples are still navigating the terrain, which includes the understanding and sharing of Indigenous knowledges, cultures, and customs as well as articulating Indigenous voices as a form of resistance.

Tensions in the Negotiation of Social Media as an Indigenous Space

There are tensions for Indigenous people in the negotiation of new dynamics and crucial challenges arising from social media, in protecting and sharing traditional knowledge systems (Smith, Burke, and Ward, 2000), maintaining autonomy and control of online media (Soriano, 2012; Waitoa, Scheyvens, and Warren, 2015), facilitating traditional social relations (Smith et al., 2000), and adapting to the assigned roles and responsibilities that accompany the aforementioned points. It seems that for many Indigenous peoples the internet is "an arena of struggle" (Soriano, 2012, p. 42) where they must balance between taking advantage of the benefits of being able to digitally articulate Indigenous voice and connect Indigenous peoples as the world becomes increasingly globalized and connected, while challenging forces that further risk Indigenous culture or way of being.

Social media can be a vehicle for agency in self-representation (Lumby, 2010), whereby users create their own narratives in a platform that supports visual, oral, and textual modes of presenting information. This can allow users to reclaim information or knowledge that has been lost through ongoing processes of urbanization and detribalization, such as through the revitalization of Indigenous languages (Bradley and Dyson, 2015; Greenwood, Te Aika, and Davis, 2011) and in relation to cultural heritage and values (O'Carroll, 2014). However, Waitoa et al. (2015) maintained that while social media can align with aspects of tikanga Māori (customs), such as through concepts of tino rangatiratanga (self-determination) and whanaungatanga (relationships), it conflicts with other tikanga Māori, such as potential cultural misappropriation. A broader issue is that there appears to be a divergence between Indigenous worldviews and the neoliberal ideologies underpinning the design of social media and the associated roles assigned to users. In contrast to a collectivist tikanga Māori practices (Mead, 2003), social media has been described as the branding of the self (Fuchs, 2017), whereby users engage in free labor in uploading content for presentation, driven by individualistic notions of competition in accumulating friends and followers as forms of cultural and social online capital. It is also important to consider who is likely to be excluded from electronic communication, highlighting the potential to reinforce offline socioeconomic disparities (Bodie and Dutta, 2008).

In spite of these challenges, one should take neither a techno-deterministic nor a techno-pessimistic view, as social media is both an enabling and a constraining medium that has a dialectical relationship with society with multidimensional effects (Fuchs, 2012). Social media has been a powerful tool in organizing activism among Indigenous (e.g., Preston, 2013; Soriano, 2012) and marginalized peoples (e.g., DeSouza and Dutta, 2008; Pal and Dutta, 2012), as other contributors to this text, such as Berglund and Moeke-Pickering et al., discuss. In doing so, there is a potential to evoke solidarity, such as a shared recognition of the impact of colonization and its continuity (Carlson et al., 2017). Yet social media does not necessarily ensure democratic networked organization structures, as often presented, but rather embedded into social media movements are hierarchies and internal power structures (Gerbaudo, 2012). The contradiction that activists face in utilizing social media to communicate among themselves and to the public is that by doing so, the platforms expose them to police surveillance, corporate control, corporate censorship, and the exploitation of digital labor (Fuchs, 2014).

A perhaps extreme example of the navigation of this tension is Māori activist Tāme Iti's Twitter use, relayed through his family, during his imprisonment as a way of dismantling the communication barriers of spatial confinement and using the master's tools to dismantle the master's house, given that the state used mobile technologies for surveillance, which led to Iti's incarceration (Elers and Elers, 2018). More recently, social media has been used as a tool to assist in the Ihumātao protest movement that drew in thousands of people to stop housing development on stolen Māori land. However, it can be difficult to challenge dominant narratives online, when one's voice is part of the minority. For example, many Indigenous Australians who respond to racism through social media do so with the knowledge that their opposition will bring about further racism (Carlson et al., 2017). A cursory search of some Māori "influencers" who regularly post messages about Māori concerns, issues, rights, sovereignty, social justice, politics, and health and well-being on the social media platform Twitter shows that they are often on the receiving end of racist online attacks.

Methodology

This chapter examines uses of social media, namely Twitter, as a communication tool by Māori for antiracist activism, to express their whakaaro (thoughts/opinions) of racism and white supremacy in Aotearoa New Zealand after the Christchurch terrorist attack. It is grounded in an Indigenous antioppressive approach, known as Kaupapa Māori, that seeks to shift and unravel the tangled

Table 4.1
Tweets retrieved by social media user

Name and Twitter handle	Background	Followers	Tweets
Morgan Godfery (@MorganGodfery)	Writer and trade unionist	12,200	83
Tau Henare (@tauhenare)	Former member of Parliament and former minister of Māori affairs	8,534	141
Leonie Pihama (@kaupapamaori)	Professor of Māori research at Ngā Wai a Te Tūī, Māori and Indigenous Research Centre, Unitec	5,335	71
Tina Ngata (@nonplasticmaori)	Lecturer at Te Wānanga o Aotearoa	4,031	73
Rangi Kemara (@Te_Taipo)	Activist and communications security specialist	3,027	218
		Total	717

colonial relations of power and privilege, being concerned with struggles for autonomy over cultural well-being (Smith, 1999). Core to Kaupapa Māori and other decolonizing methodologies is ensuring that the research is beneficial, not harmful, for Indigenous communities (Groh, 2018; Kovach, 2005). Kaupapa Māori has guided research in examining and challenging dominant representations of Indigenous peoples in mainstream media outlets (e.g., Elers and Elers, 2017, 2018).

We initially sought to capture Twitter messages based on relevant hashtags, but this returned millions of results. Also, it was difficult to determine Māori social media users; for instance, some Twitter handles using Māori names were not Māori, and sometimes not from Aotearoa New Zealand. Eventually, we sought social media users that are active participators in discussing Māori social and political issues online to a wide audience (with at least three thousand followers). While they needed a significant number of followers, we excluded individuals who do not focus primarily on Māori social and political issues; hence, we chose not to include Taika Waititi, a Hollywood director who is Māori and probably has the most Twitter followers among all Māori social media users. Eventually, we retrieved Twitter messages posted between March 14 and March 21, 2019, from five social media users. This allowed for time zone differences in Twitter's search function and for the collection of messages in the immediate aftermath of the attack. An inherent limitation in researching Twitter posts is that messages that have been deleted can no longer be recovered using software due to Twitter's policies (Twitter, 2015). Nevertheless, in total this returned 717 tweets, as outlined in table 4.1. There has been some debate about ethical practices in analyzing internet-based content (Convery and Cox, 2012; Eastham, 2011; Lafferty and Manca, 2015). The authors deemed the analysis to be ethical, as the content retrieved was not set to private, despite the potential to do so within Twitter, and, on inspection, the messages appeared to target a wide audience and did not contain "clues" (Eastham, 2011, p. 355) regarding intended private writing, such as through the use of pseudonyms. Moreover, the influencers in our study are vocal actors relating to Māori issues.

Their Twitter messages were considered as text and were analyzed using a methodology known as textual analysis (Bainbridge, 2015; McKee, 2003). Within the domain of cultural studies / media studies / communication studies the text is something that "generates meaning through signifying practices" (Barker, 2004, p. 199). A textual analysis is essentially a "close reading" of the text and is comprised of three stages: (1) breaking down a text into its various components, (2) framing a text (becoming aware of how the text is presented to us and where we find the text), and (3) looking at the relationship between texts (Bainbridge, 2015). The next section is our analysis of the texts.

Twitter in the Aftermath of the Terrorist Attack

The pervading theme from our analysis of Twitter messages was the recognition that racism is embedded in historical and cultural contexts of Aotearoa New Zealand. Hence, Twitter became a platform to vocalize the colonial terrorism inflicted upon Māori and to show that this colonial nation was founded on white supremacy and terrorism. Leonie Pihama tweeted, "And we will remember this hatred is embedded within 200 years of colonisation and is intensified through white supremacist hatred. And the combination of that kills, it murders people in prayer who came here with a promise of safety Māori have experienced all forms of terrorism since 1642" (@kaupapamaori). The connection drawn between the racist history of colonization and the Christchurch terror attack worked to disrupt the hegemonic structure of "This is not us." The message also functioned to remember the very roots of racism and the anchoring of the colonial project in Aotearoa New Zealand, as Rangi Kemara tweeted: "'We hear talk that there's too many Chinese or too many Africans. That's how we felt (when Europeans came to New Zealand) but we didn't go and shoot them. It was the other way around.'—Tame Iti" (@Te_Taipo). The remembering of Māori responses to the colonial invasion interrupts the racist discourse that marks the "Other" to catalyze fear. The remembering of the ways in which Māori communities were attacked by colonial forces interrupts the white supremacist articulation of the outsider as the basis of the violence. The messages were explicit that the terrorist attack was not unprecedented, standing in as reminders of racist violence that formed the very basis of settler colonialism. Tina Ngata wrote: "It's. Not. Unprecedented. Stop erasing Indigenous slaughters" (@nonplasticmaori).

The discursive framing by political leaders and the news media that the terrorist attack was "unprecedented" was a stimulus for the influencers to correct the inaccurate myths of colonial histories and media discourse and to dismantle whitewashed historiographies. Witnessing the attacks as a reflection of racism in the colonizing process of Aotearoa New Zealand disrupted the mainstream coverage of the event, inviting publics to see the connections. "This is not 'unprecedented.' This is not a crazed individual. This is the direct outcome of the legacy of colonising white supremacy racist hatred. I read the documents that this racist murdered wrote and we must see its roots in global colonial imperialism & entrenched racism" (@kaupapamaori). This Twitter message countered the white discursive tactic of attributing blame to mental illness when a terrorist act is committed by a white person and challenged audiences to consider this act as part of ongoing violent colonial practices. Particularly salient was the link drawn with everyday forms of racism that forms the basis of the settler colonial ideology. Twitter messages underlined the racist policies of the government that form the broader infrastructures of hate. As Tina Ngata tweeted, "Until the govt (whose policies shape our communities), recognise, acknowledge and address their own inherent racism (which means constitutional reformation) we won't see much change" (@nonplasticmaori). The call for change in this instance is situated amid the recognition of the ways in which government policies embody racism. The influencers seized the opportunity to draw attention to it. Rather than perceiving the terrorist attack as an anomaly, these messages offer invitations to witness the attack as a reflection of the overarching racism in society. Further connecting instances of racism and white supremacy, other racist events were also mentioned. "A Māori man, speaking a welcome to community gathering, gets shouted down for speaking in NZs only indigenous language. #ThisIsNZ" (@tauhenare).

Twitter became the medium to recognize and draw attention to the daily injustices and struggles that Māori face merely by existing. The hashtag #ThisIsNZ was a reminder of the lived realities of Māori in Aotearoa New Zealand. Also, the message invited the audience to think about tolerance, not for Pākehā to tolerate Māori by allowing Māori to speak their own language, but that Māori shouldn't tolerate racist abuse any further. The hashtag #ThisIsNZ was also used to highlight the experiences of racism against Muslims in Aotearoa New Zealand: "A mosque in NZ, sent a Pigs Head, not once, but several times. #ThisIsNZ" (@tauhenare).

The hashtag can also be interpreted as a form of disruption against how the country is represented to ourselves and to the global community. For example, Aotearoa New Zealand is often described as being "diverse, isolated, breathtaking, friendly, unusual, green, dynamic, desolate, majestic, warm, fresh, and independent" (Brownhill, 2014, p. 128). However, the hashtag #ThisIsNZ functioned to change the ways in which Aotearoa New Zealand was conceptualized by articulating the cultural realities of Māori and other peoples of color. The Twitter messages were not just storytelling—they were revealing truth. "People talk about Friday as the end of our innocence. No, it was the end of our shameful secret" (@nonplasticmaori). Seeing the attack as a revelation of the infrastructure of hate in Aotearoa New Zealand society invited an alternative discursive opening. Simultaneously, the Twitter messages narrated the racist structures of silence that targeted Māori communities instead of registering white supremacist hate. This critique of the surveillance apparatus once again drew attention to the racist structure of the state, as the following two tweets highlight:

> One of the Auckland "Euro" groups sent out a google invite recently for a retreat where they'd do things like pagan rites and *firearms* training. But of course the cops had probably dedicated all their resources to watching the snail activists on the West Coast instead. (@MorganGodfery)

> Christchurch mosque shootings: Too busy worrying about gangs and Māori radicals: "We were too complacent" @nzherald, No sir, you were too #Racist. Its been going on for years. You cant see, if you dont look. (@Te_Taipo)

The above message used a headline from the *New Zealand Herald* as an entry point to critically interrogate the government's incompetence for failing to register an actual threat because resources were diverted to monitoring gangs and Māori activists. Similar messages were posted as the Māori social media influencers worked to destabilize stereotypical notions of "gang members," "Māori," "Muslims," and other peoples of color, while reconfiguring the outward gaze of the security agencies to look at themselves. "Our security services werent looking, they were looking at Muslims, Māori and others of colour, gangs etc. This guy was an unassuming white guy that looked and breathed like the majority" (@tauhenare). Tau Henare's (@tauhenare) comments were insightful given that he is a former member of parliament and former government minister. His messages expressed regret for his own involvement in the expansion project of state power: "How much more power do you need to watch white fanatics/terrorists. FFS, I voted to increase their powers but they failed to watch because they were blind to the threat thats been with us for decades. And we send Tame Iti to jail on firearms charges. #EnoughIsEnough" (@tauhenare). He acknowledged giving the state more powers to surveil for terrorists, and there was a sense of anger about the incompetence of the authorities, who were oblivious to the real threat of white supremacy. The state, however, was not the only power to be critiqued, as media personalities and conservative leaders also come under scrutiny. For example, in response to the Twitter message, "And the neo nationalist right are the result of the virtue signalling exclusionary left," by broadcast journalist Sean Plunket, Godfery stated, "Sean, you are a hate-monger who plays to the alt-right and white nationalists. You should be taken off air" (@MorganGodfery). Only a month before the attack Plunket stated he did not want the history of colonization to be taught in schools (Palmer, 2019). In that sense the terrorist attack functioned as a release valve as the influencers demonstrated a deep commitment to holding racist ideologies to account. Controversial right-wing speakers who had recently visited Aotearoa New Zealand were also in the line of sight. "You get now why we protested against Southern and Molyneux. Because YOUR ideology of race hate and Islamophobia stimulates extreme violence" (@Te_Taipo). The reference to Lauren Southern and Stefan Molyneux acted as a "told you so" to mainstream society and proponents of "free speech" who campaigned to allow Southern and Molyneux the "right" to speak. The use of "You" ("You get now why we protested") and "YOUR" ("Because YOUR ideology of race hate") worked to "Other" dominant voices.

Discussion

This chapter analyzed Twitter messages by several Māori social media influencers in the aftermath of the terrorist attack. In responding to the terrorist attack, Twitter was utilized as a way to highlight the historical and ongoing systemic racism against Māori. On the one hand, this systemic racism founded in colonialism is reproduced through mainstream media outlets (van Dijk, 1999), which can be observed in the long-standing negative representation of Māori in media outlets (e.g., Rubie-Davies, Liu, and Lee, 2013). However, on the other hand, systemic racism is erased through the media's coverage from a dominant Pākehā perspective, whereby the selection of "newsworthy" stories works to silence Māori experiences, histories, and worldviews (Moewaka Barnes et al., 2013). Thus, Twitter was utilized as a vehicle in self-representation that is advocatory for Māori through the dissemination of their stories and lived realities into the public sphere.

Furthermore, the content that drew a connection between racism toward immigrants and refugees and racism toward Indigenous peoples both disrupts the claims about the "diverse," "friendly," "warm" (Brownhill, 2014, p. 128) and naturally harmonious character of Aotearoa New Zealand and simultaneously offers an anchor for solidarity. The linkage between various forms of racism offers a wider framework for situating racism. In the broader context of the state response to the attack and the overarching discursive space, Māori articulations foreground the history of racism in Aotearoa New Zealand. Twitter messages documented the various forms of racist violence that are normalized in mainstream society in Aotearoa New Zealand, witnessing these forms of violence in continuity with the terrorist attack. For the Māori social media influencers, Twitter was a space for resistance against racism that was expressed in various forms and media following the terrorist attack. Individuals and media expressing or complicit in racist rhetoric were named or "outed" as strategic acts of resistance. Furthermore, as the influencers clearly expressed, the terrorism attack was not "unprecedented" or a "random act," but it was rather situated within a broader context of racism and any attempted erasure of this context was inherently racist. Thus, Twitter was a space to challenge dominant representations for the influencers and a medium to make themselves seen and heard.

Located within the interplay of culture and communication was the expression of Indigeneity and Māori cultural identity that was enacted through the influencers' Twitter messages, which strengthened their narratives of resistance against racism and white supremacy. Corresponding with Lee's (2018) observations, social media was utilized in a way that was reflective of cultural aspirations and Indigenous ways of being, including the use of Māori language. Moreover, although the influencers were using their own private Twitter accounts, we believe that their voices aligned with what many Māori were thinking and saying offline; for example, the reference to the surveillance of Tāme Iti and others instead of white supremacists was a topical point of discussion among Māori whānau (family) and friends. In that regard, the influencers took on the role of articulating Māori voice and, by doing so, took on not only leadership roles but also activism.

Their activism carved out a digital path for other Māori to venture and reproduce disruptive narratives on social media that dismantle racism and white supremacy in Aotearoa New Zealand. The top-down imposition of the state apparatuses that privilege the colonial hierarchical order limits voice, and direct action through the use of social media is now a viable form of countering the dominant hegemonic narratives. From a scholarly perspective, the influencers offered new ways to critically think about Indigenous activism and resistance in the online sphere. Their articulations have provided entry points to understand and conceptualize racism and white supremacy as well as how to challenge them. Spatially located within the digital context, Māori and Indigenous activism on social media offers a base to theorize communicative infrastructures as a mechanism for voices that have been systematically silenced through colonial practices and the historical conditions of racism and white supremacy in Aotearoa New Zealand. However, there is more work to be done in both theory and practice.

References

1 News Now. (2019, March 22). "They are us" well-intentioned but feeds "othering" says Muslim community leader. https://www.tvnz.co.nz/one-news/new-zealand/they-us-well-intentioned-but-feeds-othering-says-muslim-community-leader.

Bainbridge, J. (2015). Media texts. In J. Bainbridge, N. Goc, and L. Tynan (Eds.), *Media and journalism: New approaches to theory and practice* (3rd ed., pp. 194–213). Oxford: University of Oxford Press.

Barker, C. (2004). *The Sage dictionary of cultural studies*. Thousand Oaks, CA: Sage.

Bodie, G. D., and Dutta, M. J. (2008). Understanding health literacy for strategic health marketing: eHealth literacy, health disparities, and the digital divide. *Health Marketing Quarterly, 25*(1–2), 175–203. https://doi.org/10.1080 /07359680802126301.

Bradley, F., and Dyson, L. E. (2015). Why mobile? Indigenous people and mobile technologies at the edge. In L. E. Dyson, S. Grant, and M. Hendriks (Eds.), *Indigenous people and mobile technologies*. New York: Routledge. https://doi.org/10 .4324/9781315759364.

Brownhill, S. (2014). Education in Australia and New Zealand. In M. A. Brown and J. White (Eds.), *Exploring childhood in a comparative context* (pp. 128–143). New York: Routledge.

Carlson, B. L., Jones, L. V., Harris, M., Quezada, N., and Frazer, R. (2017). Trauma, shared recognition and Indigenous resistance on social media. *Australasian Journal of Information Systems, 21*. https://doi.org/10.3127/ajis.v21i0.1570.

Convery, I., and Cox, D. (2012). A review of research ethics in internet-based research. *Practitioner Research in Higher Education, 6*(1), 50–57. http://ojs.cumbria.ac.uk /index.php/prhe/article/view/100.

Daniels, J. (2009). *Cyber racism: White supremacy online and the new attack on civil rights*. Lanham, MD: Rowman & Littlefield.

Deane, S. (2014, March 8). Insults to Māori taken off search engine. *New Zealand Herald*. https://www.nzherald.co.nz/nz/news/article.cfm?c_id=1&objectid =11216009.

DeSouza, R., and Dutta, M. J. (2008). Global and local networking for HIV/AIDS prevention: The case of the Saathii E-forum. *Journal of Health Communication, 13*(4), 326–344. https://doi.org/10.1080/10810730802063363.

Downing, J., and Husband, C. (2005). *Representing "race": Racisms, ethnicity, and the media*. Thousand Oaks, CA: Sage.

Durie, M. (2003). *Ngā kāhui pou: Launching Māori futures*. Wellington: Huia.

Eastham, L. A. (2011). Research using blogs for data: Public documents or private musings? *Research in Nursing and Health, 34*(4), 353–361. https://doi.org/10.1002 /nur.20443.

Elers, S. (2014). Māori are scum, stupid, lazy: Māori according to Google. *Te Kaharoa, 7*(1), 16–24. https://doi.org/10.24135/tekaharoa.v7i1.45.

Elers, S., and Elers, P. (2017). Myth, Māori and two cartoons: A semiotic analysis. *Ethical Space: The International Journal of Communication Ethics, 14*(2/3), 42–51.

Elers, S., and Elers, P. (2018). Tame Iti and Twitter: A case study of a Māori activist's use of Twitter from prison. *Media International Australia, 169*(1), 74–83. https:// doi.org/10.1177/1329878X18803380.

Fuchs, C. (2012). Social media, riots, and revolutions. *Capital and Class, 36*(3), 383–391. https://doi.org/10.1177/0309816812453613.

Fuchs, C. (2014). *Digital labour and Karl Marx*. London: Routledge.

Fuchs, C. (2017). *Social media: A critical introduction* (2nd ed.). Thousand Oaks, CA: Sage.

Gerbaudo, P. (2012). *Tweets and the streets*. Thousand Oaks, CA: Sage.

Greenwood, J., Te Aika, L. H., and Davis, N. (2011). Creating virtual marae: An examination of how digital technologies have been adopted by Māori in Aotearoa

New Zealand. In P. R. Leigh (Ed.), *International exploration of technology equity and the digital divide: Critical, historical and social perspectives* (pp. 58–79). Hershey, PA: Information Science Reference.

Groh, A. (2018). *Research methods in Indigenous contexts.* Amsterdam: Springer.

Haleem, I. (2019). Carnage in Christchurch: The logic of live-streaming slaughter (RSIS commentaries, No. 048). *RSIS commentaries.* Singapore: Nanyang Technological University. http://hdl.handle.net/10220/47938.

Hargreaves, R. P. (1959). The Māori agriculture of the Auckland province in the mid-nineteenth century. *Journal of the Polynesian Society, 68*(2), 61–79. https://www.jstor.org/stable/20703721.

Kearns, R., Moewaka-Barnes, H., and McCreanor, T. (2009). Placing racism in public health: A perspective from Aotearoa/New Zealand. *GeoJournal, 74*(2), 123–129. https://doi.org/10.1007/s10708-009-9261-1.

Keiha, P., and Moon, P. (2008). The emergence and evolution of Urban Māori Authorities: A response to Māori urbanisation. *Te Kaharoa, 1*(1). https://doi.org/10.24135/tekaharoa.v1i1.132.

Kovach, M. (2005). Emerging from the margins: Indigenous methodologies. In L. Brown and S. Strega (Eds.), *Research as resistance: Revisiting critical, Indigenous, and anti-oppressive approaches* (pp. 19–36). Toronto: Canadian Scholars' Press.

Lafferty, N. T., and Manca, A. (2015). Perspectives on social media in and as research: A synthetic review. *International Review of Psychiatry, 27*(2), 85–96. https://doi.org/10.3109/09540261.2015.1009419.

Lee, M. (2018). Navigating the social media space for Māori and Indigenous communities. In I. Piven, R. Gandell, M. Lee, and A. M. Simpson (Eds.), *Global perspectives on social media in tertiary learning and teaching: Emerging research and opportunities* (pp. 51–71). Hershey, PA: IGI Global.

Lumby, B. (2010). Cyber-indigeneity: urban Indigenous identity on Facebook. *The Australian Journal of Indigenous Education, 39*(S1), 68–75. https://doi.org/10.1375/S1326011100001150.

McKee, A. (2003). *Textual analysis: A beginner's guide.* Thousand Oaks, CA: Sage.

Mead, S. M. (2003). *Tikanga Māori: Living by Māori values.* Wellington: Huia.

Mikaere, A. (2011). *Colonising myths Māori realities: He rukuruku whakaaro.* Wellington: Huia.

Ministry of Health. (2013). Māori health. http://www.health.govt.nz/our-work/populations/Māori-health.

Moewaka Barnes, A. M., Taiapa, K., Borell, B., and McCreanor, T. (2013). Maori experiences and responses to racism in Aotearoa New Zealand. *MAI Journal, 2*(2), 63–77.

Nairn, R., Moewaka Barnes, A., Borell, B., Rankine, J., Gregory, A., and McCreanor, T. (2012). Māori news is bad news: That's certainly so on television. *MAI Journal, 1*(1), 38–49.

O'Carroll, A. D. (2014). Kanohi ki te kanohi—a thing of the past? Examining the notion of "virtual" ahikā and the implications for kanohi ki te kanohi. *Pimatisiwin: A Journal of Aboriginal and Indigenous Community Health, 11*(3), 441–455.

O'Connell-Rapira, L. (2019, March 7). Why social media is not a safe place for Indigenous people. *The Spin Off.* https://thespinoff.co.nz/atea/07-03-2019/why-social-media-is-not-a-safe-place-for-indigenous-people/.

Office of Film and Literature Classification. (2019). Christchurch attacks classification information. https://www.classificationoffice.govt.nz/news/latest-news/christchurch-attacks-press-releases/.

Pal, M., and Dutta, M. J. (2012). Organizing resistance on the internet: The case of the international campaign for justice in Bhopal. *Communication, Culture & Critique*, 5(2), 230–251. https://doi.org/10.1111/j.1753-9137.2012.01129.x.

Palmer, S. (2019, February 2). "Propaganda": Sean Plunket slams "biased" compulsory Māori history calls. *Newshub*. https://www.newshub.co.nz/home/new-zealand /2019/02/propaganda-sean-plunket-slams-biased-compulsory-maori-history-calls .html.

PeoplesHarassmentReport. (2019). Online hate is common and widespread, but it's worse for people of colour, young people, LGBT folk and women. https:// peoplesharassmentreport.com/online-hate.

Preston, J. (2013). Neoliberal settler colonialism: Canada and the tar sands. *Race & Class*, 55(2), 42–59. https://doi.org/10.1177/0306396813497877.

Quek, N. (2019). Bloodbath in Christchurch: The rise of far-right terrorism (RSIS commentaries, no. 047). *RSIS Commentaries*. Singapore: Nanyang Technological University. http://hdl.handle.net/10220/47937.

Qureshi, A. (2019, March 20). New Zealand cannot erase colonial terrorism from its history. *The Spinoff*. https://thespinoff.co.nz/atea/20-03-2019/new-zealand-cannot -erase-colonial-terrorism-from-its-history/.

Reicher, S., Haslam, A., and Van Bavel, J. (2019). The road to Christchurch: A tale of two leaderships. *New Zealand Journal of Psycholog*, 48(1), 13–15.

Rubie-Davies, C. M., Liu, S., and Lee, K. K (2013). Watching each other: Portrayals of gender and ethnicity in television advertisements. *Journal of Social Psychology*, 153(2), 175–195. https://doi.org/10.1080/00224545.2012.717974.

Small, S. (2005). Racist ideologies. In A. Tibbles (Ed.), *Translating slavery: Against human dignity* (pp. 107–112). Liverpool: National Museums Liverpool.

Smith, C., Burke, H., and Ward, G. K. (2000). Globalisation and Indigenous peoples: Threat or empowerment? In C. Smith and G. Ward (Eds.), *Indigenous cultures in an interconnected world* (pp. 1–26). Vancouver: UBC Press.

Smith, L. (1999). *Decolonizing methodologies: Research and Indigenous peoples*. London: Zed Books.

Soriano, C. R. (2012). The arts of Indigenous online dissent: Negotiating technology, Indigeneity, and activism in the Cordillera. *Telematics and Informatics*, 29(1), 33–44. https://doi.org/10.1016/j.tele.2011.04.004.

Spoonley, P. (1990). Racism, race relations and the media. In P. Spoonley and W. Hirsh (Eds.), *Between the lines: Racism and the New Zealand media* (pp. 26–37). London: Heinemann Reed.

Thompson, R. H. T. (1953). Māori affairs and the New Zealand press. *Journal of the Polynesian Society*, 62(4), 366–383. https://www.jstor.org/stable/20703395.

Thompson, R. H. (1954). Maori affairs and the New Zealand press: II. *Journal of the Polynesian Society*, 63(1), 1–16.

Twitter. (2015). Developer agreement and policy. https://dev.twitter.com/overview /terms/agreement-and-policy.

van Dijk, T. A. (1999). Discourse and racism. *Discourse and Society*, 10(2), 147–148. https://doi.org/10.1177/0957926599010002001.

Waitoa, J., Scheyvens, R., and Warren, T. R. (2015). E-whanaungatanga: The role of social media in Māori political empowerment. *AlterNative: An International Journal of Indigenous Peoples*, 11(1), 45–58. https://doi.org/10.1177 /117718011501100104.

Waitoki, W. (2019). "This is not us": But actually, it is. Talking about when to raise the issue of colonisation. *New Zealand Journal of Psychology*, 48(1), 140–145.

Walker, R. (2004). *Ka whawhai tonu matou: Struggle without end*. London: Penguin.

Will, D. G. (1973). Stereotypes of Māoris held by Europeans: A study based on four newspapers of the liberal period. Master's thesis, Massey University. http://mro.massey.ac.nz/handle/10179/7295.

Wilson, A., Carlson, B. L., and Sciascia, A. (2017). Reterritorialising social media: Indigenous people rise up. *Australasian Journal of Information Systems, 21*. https://doi.org/10.3127/ajis.v21i0.1591.

Woodward, A., and Blakely, T. (2014). *The healthy country? A history of life and death in New Zealand*. Auckland: Auckland University Press.

Zhang, J. (2018). The bioregional park: Commemorating the visit of Captain Cook. Master's thesis, UNITEC Institute of Technology. https://unitec.researchbank.ac.nz/bitstream/handle/10652/4380/MLA_2018_Jie%20Zhang_1440695.pdf.

5

ⵉⵎⴰⵣⵉⵖⵏ ⵏ ⵍⵎⵖⵔⵉⴱ ⴷ ⵓⵣⵍⵓⵣⵣⵓ ⴳ ⵓⴼⴰⵢⵙⴱⵓⴽ: ⴰⵙⵉⴷⴷⵔ ⵉ ⵜⴷⵍⵙⴰ ⴷ ⵜⵓⵜⵍⴰⵢⵜ ⵉ ⵉⵎⵣⴷⴰⵖ ⵉⵥⵖⵓⵇⴰⵏ

The Imazighen of Morocco and the Diaspora on Facebook

Indigenous Cultural and Language Revitalization

MOUNIA MNOUER

I am a heterosexual Indigenous female who grew up in Morocco. My ethnicity is Amazigh, as both of my parents are Imazighen and their parents are Imazighen who lived in Amazigh lands in Morocco. The Imazighen are the Indigenous peoples of North Africa. I grew up speaking our language, Tamazight, only at home with my parents because Arabic and French were the dominant languages. Content at school was taught in Arabic, and then later French was introduced. Growing up, I did not learn the Tifinagh script (see chapter title), and I still am unable to write or speak the language fluently. I moved to the

United States at the age of twenty-seven for graduate school; most of my graduate studies reflected a Western framework. However, during this time, away from my family and Amazigh lands, I was able to start creating a community of Imazighen online through Facebook. Through these connections, I became more informed about Amazigh issues from non-Western perspectives and learned to better understand the situation of Imazighen through online communities.

Just as university associations can serve as a space for people from certain ethnic groups to unite and celebrate their cultural and linguistic identities, social media has also been used as a platform to reach larger crowds, especially for activism purposes (Poell and van Dijck, 2015). The use of social media can allow Indigenous people to communicate and connect on a global scale (Wilson, Carlson, and Sciascia, 2017). In Morocco, understanding the depth of the cultures of Imazighen was not a priority, as Amazigh cultures were reduced to folk festivals (Maddy-Weitzman, 2012) that are meant to provide only a surface image of such rich cultures and to marginalize Imazighen and force them to assimilate Arab and French cultures. In response, some Moroccan Amazigh associations have turned to Facebook as a social media space to connect with other Amazigh people in Morocco and in the diaspora.

My goal in this chapter is to shed light on the contributions that my Indigenous communities in Morocco and in the diaspora accomplish through Facebook. My goal is also to better understand the situation of Imazighen through online communities, given that I do not live in Morocco anymore. I focus my analysis on three different Facebook pages: two that emerged in Morocco and one in the diaspora, specifically in the United States. These associations have the shared goal of supporting the Amazigh cause by using their pages to connect with Amazigh communities, to support language revitalization, and to promote cultural traditions of the Amazigh people. In addition, these Facebook pages also inspire their users to become accountable for the status of Tamazight in present-day Morocco.

I begin my discussion with the National Federation of Amazigh Associations (FNAA) Facebook page. I chose it because this federation includes many Amazigh associations in Morocco. Therefore, it encompasses a larger number of activists who work on issues related to Imazighen. Although they also have a YouTube channel and a Twitter account, they are not up to date and there is no activity with audiences on these social media platforms. Additionally, these social media platforms have comparably few postings. I then turn to the Facebook page for La Voix de la Femme Amazighe (VFA), which means the Voice of the Amazigh Woman in English. I chose this Facebook page because it focuses on the matters of Amazigh women and their role in cultural heritage preservation and revitalization. This association has a Twitter account also, but it has not been updated for over a year. The last Facebook page I discuss is

Tamazgha Voice Media (TVM). This page was created by activists who live outside of Tamazgha (the native land of the Amazigh). I chose this page to gain insight into how Amazigh activism is done in the diaspora and how different it is, if at all, from activism in Morocco.

For all three Facebook pages, I coded the content to discover (1) which themes emerged as the most frequent, (2) how followers interact with the content, and (3) how their work contributes to Amazigh activism. In order to accurately represent the content, I had conversations with members of these three Facebook pages. My purpose was to strengthen my analysis and to share the voices of the activists in the Amazigh community. The names of the people I interviewed have been changed in this chapter; I've done this to maintain their confidentiality. The members of the three different pages all work toward defending the language and political and cultural rights of the Amazigh, and their work could put them in jeopardy.

Historical and Cultural Context

The Native people of North Africa are the Amazigh. They were once frequently referred to as "Berber." The Amazigh refer to the geography of their region as Tamazgha, reaching the Canary Islands on the west, Siwa in Egypt on the east, and Mali and Niger on the south (Kratochwil, 1999). The majority of the Amazigh are concentrated in Morocco, with 40 percent of the population; 20 percent in Algeria; about 8 to 9 percent in Libya; 1 to 2 percent in Tunisia; about 20,000 in Egypt, Siwa Oasis; and about a million Tuareg Amazigh in Mali and Niger (Maddy-Weitzman, 2012). The term "Berber" was not created by the Indigenous tribes themselves; it was derived from the word "Barbarians" and is argued to have been used by groups like the Greeks to refer to people who spoke a different tongue (Ouali, 2011). The term "Berber" can also refer to the language varieties of the Indigenous people in the Tamazgha region. As an Amazigh, like many of my fellow Amazigh people, I find the term derogatory because it fails to capture the identity and existence of the Amazigh, relegating us instead to something "savage" or "strange." Therefore, I use the term "Amazigh" in this chapter, which in the Tamazight language means "free" and Imazighen, the plural word in Tamazight, to refer to the Amazigh people.

The Amazigh people view their dialects as an important factor in preserving their ethnic identities. Indigenous language revitalization in the context of the United States could be conceptualized in terms of the efforts that members of Indigenous communities and grassroots organizations engage in to preserve and sustain their Indigenous languages and cultures (Hermes, 2012; Reyhner and Lockard, 2009). In the case of Morocco, revitalization efforts are also a response to the history of language colonization and dominance. After Morocco was recognized as an independent country from the French in 1956, Arabic became the official language of the country, and Morocco was declared an Islamic country as well (El Aissati, 2005). Tamazight, on the other hand, the term used to unify the dialects of the Indigenous people in North Africa, was not valued or officially recognized. After Morocco became independent, Arabic and French continued to be the dominant languages in the country. Recognizing the marginalization of Tamazight, some university associations defending the Amazigh and Tamazight started to emerge. However, most were viewed as attempts to disrupt the unity of the country (Lehtinen, 2003). The Amazigh movement has been active since the late 1960s, when the Imazighen began to demand their rights as a nation with its own linguistic and cultural identity (Collado, 2013). Eventually, the constitution reforms that came from the Moroccan parliament recognized Tamazight as an official language in 2011, and Tifinagh, the script used to write Tamazight, is considered a national alphabet in Morocco (El Kessab et al., 2015). Even though Tifinagh allows Tamazight to gain power, as the language has both the written and the spoken varieties now (Boukous, 2014), the language continues to face some difficulties. First, there is a lack of teacher training for primary schools (El Aissati, Karsmakers, and Kurvers, 2011); moreover, Tamazight language has yet to gain full status, as it is not taught in all schools in Morocco and the cultures associated with it are still not fully a part of the daily life in Morocco. To ensure the continuity of Tamazight, many Imazighen committed to preserving Amazigh cultural heritage and to making it an integral part of the Moroccan national identity.

FNAA Facebook Page and Cultural and Language Revitalization

The Federation Nationale des Associations Amazighes (FNAA) is a nongovernmental organization, based in the capital of Morocco, Rabat, that works towards "the promotion of Tamazight, defending the linguistic, cultural, political, economic and social rights of Amazigh citizens in Morocco in all sectors of public life" (FNAA, Facebook page). The organization is constituted of 105 Moroccan associations engaged in the Amazigh cause. The FNAA Facebook page has 1,031 followers and 1,017 likes and includes short written comments, articles, and photos. The languages used on the Facebook page include Tamazight, Arabic, French, and, very occasionally, English. However, the dominant language used is Arabic.

The content of FNAA's page demonstrates an active effort to revitalize and defend Tamazight and Amazigh cultural heritage. The linguistic revitalization and defense are seen in the page promoting training sessions that FNAA organized in Rabat, Morocco, to develop and promote the linguistic rights of the Amazigh. Others train journalists in Morocco's capital to support the rules of Tamazight grammar in different media in an effort to protect multilingual diversity. Other posts defend Tifinagh against the claims that the script is hard to learn by children in schools. This defense of Tifinagh was made by the former president of the National Council of Human Rights in Morocco and rejects the language's dismissal and its properties. Other FNAA posts demand answers from the parliament about the delay in integrating Tamazight language in public life, as the law has been inactive since the government passed it in 2011. FNAA posts should be understood as linguistic activism, as they hold everyone accountable for improving the status of Tamazight and Imazighen in Morocco.

The FNAA page also emphasizes themes of cultural revitalization and a defense of the Amazigh heritage. The page shares articles from online and the electronic press that promote the Amazigh heritage, such as the celebration of the Amazigh New Year. Not only does the page promote the celebration of the Indigenous peoples' New Year, it also shares articles from different activists including the president of FNAA that critique the government spokesman's refusal to recognize the Amazigh New Year as a holiday in Morocco. When the Moroccan government rejected Amazigh names people chose for their children, the FNAA page drew attention to this racial discrimination against the Amazigh and condemned it. Although at first glance the focus of FNAA seems to be primarily the promotion of cultural rights and heritage of Imazighen, the page enacts a sort of cultural and political activism to make sure everyone is accountable for the protection of the Amazigh and their cultural and language heritage.

I interviewed a member of FNAA about the types of activism their federation does and how they believe Facebook helps or hinders their activism. I asked Moha about how the posts are received by the community and how Facebook influences the community. Moha is an Amazigh born of the Rif region in Morocco who majored in Amazigh studies at college in Oujda. Moha stated that since Tamazight became official in the constitution in 2011, the role of FNAA has followed up on officializing the law and making sure the language is integrated in public life. Moha stated that FNAA supports Amazigh issues through club meetings, workshops, and activism through strikes, addressing different organizations about the needs of the Amazigh cause. Moha joined FNAA in 2013 as an activist and now works in the administration of FNAA. Moha shared that the FNAA member in charge of posting articles, training sessions, and material on Facebook makes recommendations and the members agree on what should be posted; other times, associations in FNAA send their material to the manager to post. After this, there is an evaluation with all members to discuss errors or strategic and respectful responses to the comments. This is necessary in case members responded in a way that caused them to be critiqued by the public for being "too defensive." Moha also states that Facebook is an important space for credibility and accountability for FNAA. For instance,

Moha states here how FNAA needs to be vigilant about the timing of when something is posted: "If the activity is organized by FNAA, it cannot go to journalists until it is posted on the Facebook pages in order to ensure other sources do not provide false information. There are enemies of the Amazigh cause, especially in electronic journalism."

I asked Moha whether they consider using Facebook an act of resistance. He prefers to use the word "plea" and not "resistance," as FNAA thinks of the case of Amazigh as a *mismanagement* and the role of the activists is to manage the case well. He explains, "When we defend and evaluate the cause of the Amazigh, we elevate the government." Moha considers their Facebook page as a way of correcting any misinformation about the Amazigh and a way to educate and increase the network of the Amazigh people and those defending the cause. I also asked Moha why the dominant language on their Facebook page was Arabic. His response was that if their federation writes in Tamazight exclusively, only the Amazigh who understand and speak the language will understand. Since Tamazight is still not taught in schools across the country, Arabic is just a means to reach the goal. He added that they use Arabic and are obliged to use it for now because FNAA would like to reach larger numbers of people in the community. While language revitalization on the FNAA page is not done through writing in the Indigenous language, they do so in defending the language and working toward ensuring the language is taught across all schools in Morocco and gains a similar status to Arabic.

When I read the comments and saw the likes on the material FNAA posted in Facebook, I noticed that there are generally positive responses from Facebook users and a few shares of the articles posted on the FNAA Facebook page. The likes and supportive comments mean that people are interacting with the material. I have not seen debates or internet trolling. It is safe to say that Facebook is used as a platform to inform and educate the community of Imazighen and non-Imazighen alike about the rights of the Indigenous people of Morocco. Even though the page has only a little over a thousand followers, it connects the community of Imazighen activists who work toward defending the linguistic and cultural rights of the Amazigh people of Morocco. Importantly, it makes people aware of the situation of Tamazight and Imazighen in Morocco through making sure the language and cultures of the Amazigh are accounted for by people in Morocco.

La Voix de la Femme Amazighe (VFA) and Cultural Revitalization

The VFA Facebook page, created in 2009, has a little over six thousand followers. According to their website, the VFA promotes the rights of Amazigh women in terms of human rights, education, and literacy (La Voix de la Femme Amazighe, n.d.-b). In addition to their website and Facebook page, they also have a Twitter account, but it is not active. Posts on the VFA Facebook page emphasize cultural revitalization of Amazigh heritage, especially as it relates to Amazigh women. This is accomplished through posts that show Amazigh products sold by Amazigh women and posts about a call to their Facebook followers to promote Amazigh products to elevate and preserve the culture of the Amazigh. Cultural revitalization as a theme is also seen in the pictures of the workshops that the association organized for Amazigh women entrepreneurs in order to train them on how they could use the internet to promote and preserve their cultural heritage through their Amazigh products and Indigenous resources.

The theme of cultural revitalization was also demonstrated through the activism of the VFA in terms of reviving an Amazigh custom that existed three thousand years ago. This custom ensures the right of economic equality between men and women after marriage, and in case of divorce. This custom has become a law in Morocco under article 49 of the family code, and it aims at requiring that all judges who marry people let the spouses know about their rights. The VFA Facebook disseminated the results of field research that the association conducted in the south of Morocco for eight months that shows how some divorced women are still not aware of this law and that it is neither completely activated nor consistently used throughout Morocco. To address this situation, VFA posted information about two different conferences and training workshops to equip other Amazigh associations with strategies to defend the rights of Amazigh women in Amazigh towns such as Azrou, Khenifra, and the Tinghir regions. Announcements publicizing these conferences have fifteen shares on Facebook. The activism of VFA through Facebook in this regard shows efforts to make this law visible to all women in Morocco and specifically Amazigh women by bringing to life the Amazigh custom that allows a woman to have her economic rights recognized in the case of divorce.

In terms of the audience interaction with the Facebook page content, there seems to be positive feedback shown through many likes and shares of information about training workshops. There were also shares of local Amazigh products from the Facebook audience to revitalize the cultural heritage of the Amazigh. The comments on Facebook are positive. The positivity is seen in expressing pride in the Amazigh identity and wishing the association success. However, there was one comment about posting a postcard about the Amazigh New Year where Arabic was used first, then Tamazight second. The comment critiqued the association for not writing in Tifinagh first, as a part of preserving the language identity. One member of the association replied respectfully by stating that the important thing is for the message to be accessible to the community. This demonstrates the strategy of the page in its desire to bring the community together through revitalizing the culture and the customs of the Imazighen to the Amazigh and non-Amazigh. In addition, the comment also shows how there is still no consensus in the community about how Tamazight can be used to preserve the Amazigh identity. Tifinagh script is not dominant on the page; this could be due to the fact that the page focuses more on cultural revitalization of the Amazigh people, specifically Amazigh women.

Yamna, one of the members of VFA, lived in the south of Morocco before settling in the capital. Yamna's parents are both Amazigh from Khenifra. Growing up there, Yamna heard Tamazight in her home and saw the culture in wedding ceremonies, celebrations, and clothing. Her mother used to make Amazigh rugs. Although Yamna does not speak Tamazight fluently, she understands the language and can respond in short sentences. According to Yamna, she did not speak Tamazight fluently because Arabic was the dominant language and her parents insisted that she speak proper Arabic so that she would not be bullied at school for speaking Tamazight or "improper" Arabic. When I asked Yamna about her association's work through Facebook, she responded by saying that the association had a website and a Twitter account. However, the association became even more visible after they started using Facebook. Because of their visibility on Facebook, many young people started contacting the association to ask more questions about their work and to express interest in attending some of the association's events and workshops. Yamna confirmed that their Facebook posts promote their activities and workshops, raise awareness about older Amazigh customs, and empower Amazigh businesswomen through promoting their cultural heritage and products and making them visible to Moroccan people.

Many people, according to Yamna, were able to join their workshops because they saw information about it on Facebook. The presence of VFA through Facebook demonstrates how it can bring the community together through workshops and information that have the goal of revitalizing the cultural heritage of Imazighen and supporting Amazigh women, which contributes to the political and economic rights of the Amazigh in Morocco. Just like FNAA, VFA is also using Facebook as an accountability tool to make sure the Indigenous people are aware of their rights and to publish any violations against Amazigh people. Because the association is understaffed, VFA members reply to only some comments on Facebook. However, according to Yamna, many associations and people who have come across their page have contacted them to gain more information about the association and their activities. With their six thousand followers, VFA contributes to the activism of the Imazighen in Morocco. Like FNAA, the VFA is also holding people responsible for the activation and/or implementation of laws.

Tamazgha Voice Media (TVM) between Revitalization and Political Resistance

TVM is a Facebook page that was created by Amazigh members in the diaspora in 2018. The page has a little over 9,300 followers. The languages used on the page are primarily Arabic and English, then Tamazight. The page shows Indigenous cultural and language revitalization. It also demonstrates education and information about the Imazighen's political situation. Posts include articles from *Amazigh World News*, which aims at sharing information about Amazigh people, languages, and cultures. One repost, for example, focuses on the right to fly the Amazigh flag, while others focus on cultural revitalization efforts such as songs that Amazigh activists and artists sing in Tamazight about the heritage of the Amazigh lands and ancestors. The format of the posts is through pictures and videos that aim to bring the community together; this seems to be successful, if the positive comments on the videos and pictures are any indication. In addition to sharing songs of different Amazigh artists about the land, TVM broadcasts live video about the politics of land in Tamazgha with an Amazigh professor. The live video lasted about an hour, and the conversation was in Tamazight and Arabic. At the time I drafted this chapter, the video had an astounding 38,000 views and 891 shares, with positive live comments and questions for more clarification. The video revolves around the politics of Akhal, which means land in Tamazight, and how the Imazighen's lands and resources have been wrested from the Imazighen. The video also tackles the politics of silencing people especially in the Sous area in Morocco by the government. This sharing of a live video on the TVM page demonstrates the power of social media to foster political conversations (Carlson and Frazer, 2016).

In addition to cultural revitalization and expressing Amazigh voices in terms of the right to land, waving the Amazigh flag, and sharing songs of ethnic identity and belonging, TVM also demonstrates efforts in revitalizing the language of Imazighen. This can be seen in the writing of some posts in the Tifinagh script, sharing videos of two children who read and perform theater in the Tamazight language, which received positive responses from the page followers such as pride in the Tamazight language and hope in the future generation of Imazighen to preserve the Indigenous heritage. TVM's team also posted pictures of one of the members participating in a conference in New York at the United Nations headquarters on August 9, 2019. The theme of the conference was International Indigenous Language Day. Even though the member was representing an Amazigh association in Morocco, posting of live videos from the conference on the TVM's page still received very positive comments and pride from the community. Therefore, TVM exhibits efforts in bringing the Amazigh people together.

As a follower, I contacted the administrator and received a response immediately. Fatima is from Ihahane, a region near Essawira in Morocco. She is
Amazigh and learned the language in Tamaynout's Amazigh association as a
teenager in Morocco. Fatima did not speak Tamazight as a child, but she
started learning it when she visited her grandparents. Fatima has been an
Amazigh activist since 1998. Currently, she lives in the United States, where
her activism persists. Therefore, she decided to take the initiative and use
Facebook to create an audience so that people could follow the Amazigh cause
in Tamazgha and in the diaspora and discuss it via Facebook. I asked Fatima
how their page is connecting the community. She replied by saying that they
monitor people who like the content they post, and they send them invitations to follow their page. Fatima added that they also receive messages from
people requiring that they write in Tamazight and Tifinagh. When I asked
Fatima why TVM chose to write in Arabic and English more than in Tamazight,
she responded by saying that they are receiving more volunteers to write in
Tamazight because they would like to reinforce language identity of the Imazighen. However, TVM also would like the information on the Amazigh
cause to reach non-Amazigh communities that support the Amazigh as well.
From what I saw on the page, there was no call-out culture or disruptions from
internet trolls. In terms of posts and rules of conversation on the page, the
administrator engages with the material, responds to comments, or likes them.
When I asked Fatima about rules of sharing and commenting on the page, she
stated that because the goal of their page is to educate, they often try to correct
any misconceptions about the Amazigh. Users who disrespect the Amazigh
are banned from the page.

Unlike the FNAA and VFA pages, TVM calls their activism "resistance
against extermination and discrimination of the Amazigh people." The strategy of revitalizing the language and the cultures of the Amazigh takes the form
of direct critiques of governments that do not support the Amazigh heritage
in North Africa and highlights the struggle of the Amazigh people in terms
of language rights. The TVM Facebook page also sustains cultural pride by
publicly celebrating the Amazigh year and by posting about the rights of the
Amazigh to wave our flag. The flag has four colors: blue for the ocean, green
for the mountains, yellow for the Sahara, and red for the blood shed for Amazigh
freedom and the Tifinagh letter ⵣ in the middle as a symbol of the free people
(figure 5.1). TVM publicizes and cultivates cultural pride in the Amazigh identity through the members' participation in seemingly simple yet profound
actions such as the Amazigh community waving the Amazigh flag in the United
States. TVM's goal is clearly to educate and inform the community of Imazighen and all people throughout the world about the latest news and struggles of Imazighen in Morocco and in the diaspora.

FIG. 5.1 Amazigh flag created by Agraw Imazighen in the 1970s. The flag was adopted in 1998 as the flag of the Amazigh people by the Amazigh World Congress. (Credit: Painting of Amazigh flag by Monica Brown, photo by Mounia Mnouer.)

Conclusion

In conclusion, Facebook serves as a platform for cultural and language revitalization by Amazigh activists in Morocco and in the diaspora. In the context of social media emanating from within Morocco, FNAA and VFA show how this revitalization occurs through sharing video, photos, posts, articles and through workshop sessions that aim at defending the linguistic and cultural rights of Imazighen and the promotion of Tamazight in Morocco. In addition, the pages also show activism in terms of training the community about their ethnic, cultural, and linguistic rights. The strategies used by the FNAA and VFA pages also hold the Moroccan people accountable for the improvement of the status of the Amazigh. For example, their posts remind people that since Tamazight became an official language in Morocco in 2011, procedures on integrating the language in public life need to follow. The activists' efforts on Facebook demonstrate a movement toward integrating Tamazight and the cultures associated with it as part of a broader Moroccan national identity (Ennaji, 2019). FNAA and VFA page members call their activism on the page a plea for the Amazigh cause where linguistic and cultural rights must be defended, preserved, and protected.

TVM, based outside of Tamazgha, on the other hand, takes on a strategy of resistance against discrimination and extermination of Amazigh people in the world through educating people about the language through postings in Tamazight and about Tamazight. Their page also educates the public through presenting live videos on the meaning and culture of Akhal (land), along with the political history that allowed for exploitation of Amazigh lands and resources. This way of informing the community carries with it a theme of resistance. Because TVM functions in the diaspora, its page is critical in the defense of Amazigh rights through educating and critiquing of the governments. While the page receives positive feedback from its followers, TVM stated that there are political ramifications to their online activism, as they received email threats from Moroccan authorities who aim to silence their activism. However, TVM continues to resist by defending the Amazigh on Facebook.

Facebook has proven to be a powerful tool used by Amazigh activists in Morocco and in the diaspora to revitalize Amazigh cultural heritage and Tamazight language. Although the pages in Morocco and in the diaspora undertake different strategies, they share the theme of connecting the community of Amazigh and educating the non-Amazigh in the world. The three pages I've focused on here are still active and keep receiving positive comments, clearly demonstrating how Facebook can serve as a vital platform for Indigenous people to rise against settlers' mentalities (Wilson et al., 2017).

References

Boukous, A. (2014). The planning of standardizing Amazigh language: The Moroccan experience. *Iles d imesli, 6*, 7–23.

Carlson, B., and Frazer, R. (2016). Indigenous activism and social media: A global response to #SOSBLAKAUSTRALIA. In A. McCosker, S. Vivienne, and A. Johns (Eds.), *Negotiating digital citizenship: Control, contest and culture* (pp. 115–130). Lanham, MD: Rowman and Littlefield.

Collado, Á. S. (2013). The Amazigh movement in Morocco: New generations, new references of mobilization and new forms of opposition. *Middle East Journal of Culture and Communication, 6*(1), 55–74.

El Aissati, A. (2005). A socio-historical perspective on the Amazigh (Berber) cultural movement in North Africa. *Afrika Focus, 18*(1/2), 59–72.

El Aissati, A., Karsmakers, S., and Kurvers, J. (2011). "We are all beginners": Amazigh in language policy and educational practice in Morocco. *Compare: A Journal of Comparative and International Education, 41*(2), 211–222.

El Kessab, B., Daoui, C., Bouikhalene, B., and Salouan, R. (2015). Handwriting Moroccan regions recognition using Tifinagh character. *Data in Brief, 4*, 534–543.

Ennaji, M. (2019). The Berber cultural movement in the Maghreb: Contemporary issues in transnationalism. In A. De Toro and J. Tauchnitz (Eds.), *The world in movement* (pp. 238–251). Leiden: Brill.

FNAA Facebook page. https://www.facebook.com/FNAA.ONG/about/?ref=page _internal.

Hermes, M. (2012). Indigenous language revitalization and documentation in the United States: Collaboration despite colonialism. *Language and Linguistics Compass, 6*(3), 131–142.

Kratochwil, G. (1999). Some observations on the First Amazigh World Congress (August 27–30, 1997, Tafira, Canary Islands). *Die welt des Islams, 39*(2), 149–158.

La Federation Nationale des Associations Amazighes. (n.d.). A propos. http://fnaa.ma /a-propos/.

La Voix de la Femme Amazighe. (n.d.-a). A propos. https://www.imsli.org.ma/?fbclid =IwAR15VfX3WmwqDdloHOR6e6DtpQkE4NMi34U9wW99HizAfKZyJbm7v aVq5xo.

La Voix de la Femme Amazighe. (n.d.-b). Facebook. https://www.facebook.com /voixfemmeamazighe/.

Lehtinen, T. (2003). Nation à la marge de l'Etat: La construction identaire du Mouvement Culturel Amazigh dans l'espace national marocain et au-delà des frontières étatiques. Doctoral dissertation, EHESS.

Maddy-Weitzman, B. (2012). Arabization and its discontents: The rise of the Amazigh movement in North Africa. *Journal of the Middle East and Africa, 3*(2), 109–135.

Ouali, H. (2011). *Agreement, pronominal clitics and negation in Tamazight Berber: A unified analysis.* New York: Continuum.

Poell, T., and van Dijck, J. (2015). Social media and activist communication. In C. Atton (Ed.), *The Routledge companion to alternative and community media* (pp. 527–537). London: Routledge.

Reyhner, J. A., and Lockard, L. (Eds.). (2009). *Indigenous language revitalization: Encouragement, guidance and lessons learned.* Flagstaff: Northern Arizona University Press.

Tafideraliyt Imazighen Fnaa. (n.d.). Facebook. https://www.facebook.com/tafide rlayetimazighen.fnaa.

Tamazgha Voice Media-TVM. (n.d.). Facebook. https://www.facebook.com/Tamazgha VoiceMedia/.

Wilson, A., Carlson, B. L., and Sciascia, A. (2017). Reterritorializing social media: Indigenous people rise up. *Australasian Journal of Information Systems, 21,* 1–4.

6

How We Connect

■■■■■■■■■■■■■■■■■■■■■■■

An Indigenous Feminist
Approach to Digital Methods

MARISA ELENA DUARTE AND

MORGAN VIGIL-HAYES

Feminist technologists have documented and established the contours of sexism and misogyny shaping global tech culture. Indeed, scholarly journals, industry associations, and scholarly associations now designate space for feminist technoscientific research and commentary; feminism represents a space of technoscientific innovation, advocacy, and inventiveness. This, however, does not indicate an end to misogynistic practices shaping the global diffusion and uses of information and communication technologies (ICTs). Rather, it indicates a proportionally limited scholarly awareness of how ideologies of heteropatriarchal white supremacy shape fields such as computer science, information science and informatics, information systems, digital studies, and internet studies, in addition to the range of social and technical phenomena associated researchers choose to investigate. With regard to Indigenous studies, ideologies of white male supremacy are deeply embedded in colonial and imperial institutions in which ICTs play an integral structural role. Thus an Indigenous feminist approach to digital methods is about leveraging a decolonial or anticolonial critique of ICTs toward creating alternative structures—both tangible and intangible—that allow for the rapid and secure dissemination of information and knowledge for the benefit of marginalized peoples, centering the goals of Indigenous women and girls. There is a growing area of scholarship around feminist digital approaches, particularly as pertains to analysis of digital usage patterns as well as to the actual practice of collecting and analyzing digital data (Adam, 2000; Karusala et al., 2017; Meng, DiSalvo, and Zegura, 2019; Wong-Villacres, Velasquez, and Kumar, 2017). However, Indigenous feminist viewpoints and methodologies have yet to be well integrated into this burgeoning subfield. In this chapter we articulate dimensions of these viewpoints and approaches and also forward an approach to digital methods that relates our experiences as women with complicated mixed-race and Indigenous family histories and advanced degrees in information science and computer science, respectively, to the kinds of structural changes we advance in our work: improved internet access for Native and Indigenous communities for the purpose of disseminating actionable information and knowledge about Native and Indigenous issues. Our approach is reflexive. By describing how we connect—that is, how through relational scholarship we improve internet connectivity toward Indigenous connective action—we characterize the interrelatedness of Indigenous science, technology, activism, and gender and belonging in digital studies.

Literature Review

In 2006, feminist philosopher Maria Lugones asserted the need for spaces to host "complex conversations," that is, dialogues that, through a range of modes of delivery, could broach the philosophical and experiential differences that characterize epistemic injustice, including colonial injustice against women and Indigenous peoples. As researchers of ICTs, we recognize that the medium is also the message. Our investigations are designed to create communicative channels for not only the profound relational insights of what Archibald (2008) terms Indigenous storywork, but also the lighthearted and rapid-fire messaging of tweets, the digital tactics of social movement collectives, the reliable information diffusion of tribal governments, and the memory work of Indigenous digital archives (Duarte, 2015, 2017a, 2017b; Duarte and Vigil-Hayes, 2017; Vigil-Hayes et al., 2017; Vigil-Hayes, Parkhurst, and Duarte, 2019). Indeed, as misogyny against Indigenous women and girls is pervasive through symbolic, physical, legislative, interpersonal, and technological acts of violence, there is a greater need to, as Allard and Ferris (2015) eloquently state, "create and mobiliz[e], via multiple forms of digital media, knowledge that contests and re-envisions conceptions of violence against certain people as normal" (p. 361).

The labor to accomplish such tasks is enormous, in particular when we consider the sociotechnical complexity of multiple forms of digital media, especially as these relate to the layers of trust needed to substantiate messaging through vulnerable social movements, the hard-wired architecture of digital systems, platforms, and interfaces, and the material realities that define Indigeneity: relational ways of being within Indigenous homelands. Indeed, Anishinaabe scholar Leanne Simpson (2017) contemplates the relationship between interpersonal trust and the connective power of social media in Indigenous feminist organizing, and ultimately is skeptical of the idealization of social media as a means for Indigenous feminist political mobilization. She is skeptical of "simulations that serve to only amplify capitalism, misogyny, transphobia, anti-queerness, and white supremacy and create further dependencies on settler colonialism in the physical world . . . [and] further alienation from oneself, from Indigenous thought and practices, and from the Indigenous material world" (p. 221). This kind of skepticism is not unwarranted. In 2016 Bailey and Shayan presented an analysis of the technological dimensions of the ongoing murders and disappearances of Indigenous women and girls in Canada. Their framework identifies cyberstalking as a predicate to the physical assaults of Indigenous women and girls. Social networking sites represent locations wherein predators groom and track women and girls, and where traumatized communities enact lateral violence, amplifying the colonial mentality that requires systematic destruction of Indigenous women and matrilineal practices, values, and beliefs.

Nevertheless, social networking sites as well as digital archives also clearly represent locations through which Indigenous women activists and allies organize to disseminate information and knowledge about disparate Indigenous peoples movements, the sum of which forms one aspect of what Simpson (2017) refers to as a timeless, continual "constellated intelligence." Indeed, in an analysis of Indigenous women's rhetorical presentations through grassroots #NoDAPL digital archives, ally scholar Meredith Privott (2019) identifies how the discursive dissemination of the Indigenous feminist ethos shaping the visionary work at Oceti Sakowin and other camps around the Standing Rock Sioux Tribe reflects the early modern intelligence networks that Brooks (2008) identifies among Indigenous thinkers and writers circulating through the burgeoning northeastern United States. However, it is not the network that drives the circulation of Indigenous intelligence, but rather the epistemic knowing among various Indigenous peoples that, fundamentally, water is life.

Thus contemporary Indigenous reliance on social and political mobilization through digital means is not due to a fascination with the networks—what Munster (2013) calls an "aesthesia of networks"—but rather how the relational responsibilities of diverse Indigenous peoples to each other (1) as peoples and as kin, (2) as relatives of the biomes in which they reside, (3) as kin of nonhuman relatives including four-legged beings, winged beings, rock nations, plant nations, and so forth, and (4) as comrades in what Subcomandante Marcos calls the colonial "war against forgetting" require that Indigenous feminists circulate intergenerational knowledge about their oppressed and liberationist status by whatever means necessary. In 1978, Vine Deloria Jr. identified libraries and archives as the institutional means to preserve Indigenous peoples' right to know the causes of their oppression. In the 1990s, Subcomandante Marcos called on Indigenous peoples to create technological "networks from below" to aid in the neoliberal colonial wars that promise to alienate autonomous Indigenous peoples from their homelands and ways of life. Network theorist Manual Castells observed the rise of the EZLN movement as evidence of the pervasiveness of networked ICTs and their usefulness in identity-based social movements (Castells, 1997). More specifically, in 2005, ally scholar Ronald Niezen identified how the rise of a global Indigenous political identity, a kind of digital Indigenous selfhood, was related to the worldwide spread of internet protocol and its use as a tool to communicate and exercise inherently sovereign Indigenous rights from elders in their homelands all the way to representatives operating within the United Nations (Niezen, 2005). The malleability and availability of various internet-ready systems and platforms make the internet and social networking sites a reasonable means through which Indigenous peoples can maintain a literal physical foothold in the territories they must protect from colonial encroachment while also sustaining the trustworthy interpersonal networks of kin that characterize Indigenous peoples' manners of relating with one another.

Indeed, the manner of constructing and sustaining interpersonal relationships, inclusive of their technological artifacts, distinguishes Indigenous feminist approaches to digital infrastructures. As Allard and Ferris (2015) attest in their analysis of a participatory archive centered around Missing and Murdered Indigenous Women—a digital infrastructure designed to provide access to "reflective, meaningful, and representative content that resonates with community ways of seeing and understanding the world"—Indigenous knowledge must be at the center of infrastructural designs (p. 366). Furthermore, in her analysis of the history of tribal librarianship in the United States, Diné and Eastern Shoshone scholar Sandy Littletree (2019) finds that relationality—the interpersonal connections that define Indigenous peoplehood—is the driver and design requirement, so to speak, for the instantiation of Indigenous ways of knowing and their attendant knowledge artifacts including datasets, documents, bodies of information, and digital systems and devices. Recognizing the implications of "digital standpoints," intersectional feminists Jackson and Banaszczyk (2016) have likewise written about the integral nature of computational methods that incorporate the viewpoints of marginalized women in investigations about gender oppression. Luka and Millette (2018) find that the inclusion of marginalized women in the design of social media studies shapes the analysis of big data, as they rely on a feminist ethics of care to "critically rethink the ongoing intersectional networks of relations, values, and ethical commitments that undergird our research and those of others" (4).

Thus an Indigenous feminist approach to digital methods is not simply about applying computational methods or design-based methods to raise awareness of injustice against Indigenous women and peoples; rather, it is about developing the networks of kin that enliven technicized practices toward Indigenous autonomy and sovereignty and that in so doing divest the authority of settler patriarchy over Indigenous airwaves, airspace, knowledge institutions, and media networks. The process is the purpose. Where a feminist decolonial approach articulates digital infrastructures to divest the settler patriarchy, an Indigenous feminist ethics of care is considerate of the need for Indigenous women and queer and trans folk to analyze and interrogate patterns and trends in datasets relevant to their lived experience, as well as the need for Indigenous women to be advanced to positions of structural power in the pluriverse of networked societies. As researchers, their lived experience forms the basis of their domain knowledge, which is at once both analytically powerful as well as socially and politically empowering.

What Motivates Us

This deeply relational understanding of the structural potency of ICTs has shaped our work as researchers and colleagues for over ten years. We first met as doctoral students at the University of Washington in Seattle. At the time, we were both affiliated with a research cluster focused on information and communication technologies for development (ICTD) and had agreed to meet at a cafe in the U-District so we could share notes about a common interest: the communicative potential of sovereign Native American tribes constructing internet network backbones. As women researchers trained in, respectively, information science and computer science, we could discern the sociotechnical novelty of this phenomena, but more fundamentally, we were interested in supporting the installation of material technological infrastructures that could potentially shape socially just futures for Native and Indigenous peoples.

Over time we found that as a team we were savvy about the colonial implications of technological infrastructures, as well as the settler misogyny that pervades the tech industry and academia. Both of us hail from families with lineages, political belonging, and psychosocial aspects shaped by colonial legacies. The colonial and nation building wars shaping Spain, the United States, and Mexico shape our Indigenous belonging as women of, respectively, Yaqui and Ute heritage. Our families are mixed: we are also responsive to lineages from the era of Mexican Independence in Sonora, the settlements and acéquia families of New Spain, and the various waves of U.S. women's liberation movements, and are cognizant of our rights and status as educated American women with degrees from American R1 universities. We persist through academia due to our political and social lucidity. We design our research based on moral principles of equity and justice for women and girls broadly, but more specifically, as we imagine healthier futures for Indigenous women and girls, inclusive of the social textures and material infrastructures shaping their everyday lives. Thus we combine our devotion to science and research with our love for our families and with profound respect for others who have endured as our families have, resulting in work based in a praxis of compassion.

Attending to the Network: Features of a Digital Indigenous Feminist Analytic

To practice technoscience with compassion is to be attentive to the multiple social, political, psychological, and emotional implications of the tangible and intangible infrastructures we create. As feminist practitioners of ICTD, our understanding of sociality is attentive to the inequities shaped by racism/sexism. As decolonial thinkers, our understanding of the political is attentive to the inequities shaped by governmentality under nationalism/colonialism.

Colonization and racism/sexism have psychological and emotional effects for both the oppressed and the oppressor, and media have the capacity to boost or exacerbate these relational effects across multiple dimensions of Indigenous peoplehood, including kinship, language, homelands, ceremonial cycles, and histories of belonging. Many scholars have written about the relational aspects of social media in broad strokes. From our vantage point in computer science and information science, we operationalize social media as platforms that users interact with as though through a cloud, uploading data to profiles that propagate permutations of that data for the purpose of attracting more interactions. Social media platforms are constructed through the pervasive accessibility of servers and data centers; cellular towers, fiberoptic cables, and wireless connectivity (2G–5G); affordable devices such as tablets, smartphones, and laptops; and a vigorous application development ecology (apps) (Duarte, 2017c; Vigil, Rantanen, and Belding, 2015; Vigil-Hayes et al., 2017). In combination with users—humans who create social networks through the means of social media interfaces—these abet the flow of data that cohere around topics meaningful to self-defining social groups. For example, in our work discerning the Twitter messaging associated with the political candidacy of 108 Native Americans in the 2018 U.S. midterm elections, we observed different self-organizing social groups promulgate #sherepresents and #maga through the Twittersphere in response to the increasing effectiveness of Native American women's political representation (Vigil-Hayes et al., 2019). Where #sherepresents—a hashtag created by *Indian Country Today* editor Mark Trahant—was tweeted by supporters of the women leaders and by groups advocating gender equity, civil rights, and racial diversity, #maga, or Make America Great Again, was fomented by advocates of the white supremacist and misogynistic rhetoric of President Donald Trump and Republican Party candidates seeking to capitalize on this racism. On a psychological level, #maga is a colonizing fear-based rhetoric seeking the removal of women, Native Americans, and people of color from positions of power in favor of leadership by white men, regardless of their moral character or leadership skill. The phrasing and its placement are designed to intimidate and silence its opponents. #sherepresents, on the other hand, is not designed as a tool of psychological warfare. It is a phrase intended to honor the leadership of the Native American women running for office that year and was created to inspire and empower them and others like them. Thus, on a relational level, both #maga and #sherepresents have an effect through the dimensions of Indigenous peoplehood. However, where #maga evokes colonial trauma with regard to loss of Indigenous languages and ceremonial cycles, forced removal from homelands, and broken families, #sherepresents evokes the strength of Native American women who proudly belong to and represent their peoples, and who are willing to take on a role in the U.S. government as an advocate for issues that are meaningful to Indian Country and Americans with related experiences of marginalization. For our purposes, as a team that practices full-stack development toward feminist Indigenous goals, we seek to understand the finer details about how hashtags like #sherepresents relate to the accessibility of ICTs in Indian Country. This is because we need to be able to design the hardware, software, training, policies, and practices that shape the uptake of social media in Indian Country so that Indigenous peoples can keep creating empowering social media campaigns like #sherepresents as they engage in structural and political change.

To do this, we study issue networks. When social groups frequently circulate social media messaging around select topics, they form issue groups, which, when we statistically render relevant datasets into graphs, are observable to us as heterogenous clusters of networks that we call issue networks. We describe the methodological process of generating issue networks in figure 6.1, where we demonstrate how we are able to create a network projection on all the hashtags observed in a Twitter dataset based on the Jaccard similarity of sets of common users that have tweeted those hashtags (Jaccard, 1912).

We then use the Louvain community detection algorithm on the network projection to identify the issue networks that exist within the larger network projection (Blondel et al., 2008). The visual result of positioning the nodes in community clusters resembles dense constellations of stars or nests of anemones, and we interpret them statistically by evaluating the betweenness centrality of nodes, and socially by the sociological meaning and historical context of pervasive and persistent topics churning through the networks.[1] By examining the issue networks of Indigenous peoples, it is possible for us to capture

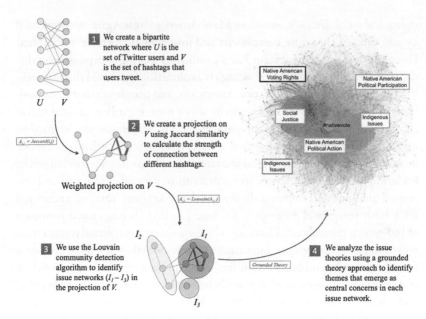

FIG. 6.1 Diagram stepping through the phases of our iterative, interdisciplinary process of attending to the network. (Credit: Chapter authors.)

instances of Indigenous political and social goals and to statistically represent these as evidence of the social power of Indigenous justice. As an example, phase 4 of figure 6.1 illustrates the issue network that was generated using the hashtags that appeared in Twitter traces surrounding #nativevote during the 2018 U.S. midterm elections, where our analysis found that issue groups revealed a strong connection between Indigenous issues (e.g., missing and murdered Indigenous women) and Native American political action. Thus our work contributes to the visibility of Indigenous causes in scientific and scholarly forums, while also allowing us to quantitatively gauge the bandwidth needed to allow for vigorous Indigenous political engagement through the infrastructures undergirding social media: wireless infrastructures, spectrum, connectivity, and devices (Vigil-Hayes et al., 2017).

While our specific methods consist of a toolkit of approaches that are well known and in use by researchers in associated fields, we outline here those that are most pertinent to the foundations of our overarching methodology. Specifically, to uphold the relational aspects of working with "big data" means working with domain experts through the question formation, data gathering, and analytic process. Moreover, we never simply "gather data," but rather we conscientiously construct datasets through careful curation. To honor the intellectual lineage and disciplinary training of each member of our research teams means that we cocreate a complementary suite of methods for each research project, allowing the methodological know-how of each team member to shape our focus and interpretation of results. To that end, as we continuously focus and adjust our analytical lenses, we also learn our ways of doing science and research with each other, expand our understanding of Indian Country and relevant issues, and enliven the networks we research by being with each other as thinkers. Our trust in each other gives us the intellectual courage to collectively dive deep into complex datasets, asking questions that are technically, socially, and philosophically challenging. Being aware of the distinctiveness of our approaches also gives us the know-how to prepare our findings for scholarly and scientific conferences and publications; we design paper discussions to Indigenize the spaces of our collegial engagement. Finally, we treat the publication review process as an opportunity to engage in critical reflection about how our work as a team relates to broader commitments in Indian Country, to current events, and to our work as individuals and, mostly, within our lives as women scientists of conscience.

Working with Domain Experts

Critical to our methodology is understanding the junctures between knowledge domains, particularly how one might be in service to another. When we seek to analyze a complex sociotechnical system, we identify and partner with experts who draw on their life experience and domain knowledge to explain the subtler aspects—boundaries, terminologies, discourses, subjugated histories, key actors—shaping the system we seek to understand. In our study of how Native American advocates used Twitter during the 2016 U.S. presidential primary election season, we reached out to colleagues who were themselves involved in Native American advocacy and asked them to list all of the keywords, hashtags, and user accounts they followed on Twitter to sustain their awareness of Native American political discourse (Duarte, 2017a; Vigil-Hayes et al., 2017). Similarly, in our study of the 2018 U.S. midterm elections, we reached out to Mark Trahant, the editor of the Indian Country Today Media Network, who had curated a list of all Native American, Native Alaskan, and Native Hawaiian candidates running for office in November 2018 (Vigil-Hayes et al., 2019). These domain experts provided insight into the complex systems we hoped to explore, enabling us to challenge and expand our own preconceived notions of relevant query terms that might be used for data inputs. Importantly, we do not consider those with whom we partner to be research participants or informants in a field site, but rather we recognize them as our knowledgeable and respected colleagues, friends, leaders, elders, and relatives in the intellectual landscape of Indian Country. We recognize their expertise because it is has been sanctioned and authorized by many others who are actively involved in sustaining the political, social, and intellectual life of Indian Country. In other words, before statistically analyzing the data-driven social networks of a sociotechnical system like Twitter, we reach into our own social network, one that we have constructed over decades of conscientious engagement and trust building within Indian Country. Thus our methodology also strengthens, broadens, and enlivens our personal social networks as we share ideas, insights, knowledge, and contacts through the process of interpersonal collaboration.

Curating Data Inputs

"Garbage in, garbage out" is a saying that computer scientists use to describe the truism that if one inputs nonsensical data into a computing process, it can output only nonsensical data. The truth behind this glib statement has been something we have grappled with time and time again in our work. While the statement is logically true, we have found that it must be carefully applied when working with complex and complicated datasets. When high-quality, accurate, and precise data about an entire people are notoriously scarce—as is the case with Native American and Indigenous peoples—computational scholars must be cautious when evaluating the value of data points that do exist. In the absence of clearly labeled datasets, questions must be answered with inferences from the datasets that are of integrity and that do exist.

One of the first times we experienced this was during the early research stages of a study of Native American advocacy through Twitter. We initially thought that if we collected data from the Twitter accounts of prominent social and political leaders in Indian Country we would find evidence of the impact of the Hillary Clinton, Bernie Sanders, and Donald Trump presidential campaigns in our dataset. Instead, we found nothing of the sort. In place of messaging about campaign politics, we found a significant quantity of messaging that indicated political issues that were not campaign staples of any of the 2016 U.S. presidential candidates. This caused us to reframe our understanding of political participation in Indian Country; the datasets revealed that Native American rights advocates were more likely to tweet about environmental degradation, police brutality, Indigenous identity, and violence against Indigenous women and girls than about U.S. presidential politics. When we submitted our findings to the double-blind peer review process, our reviewers required that we compare the Native American rights advocates dataset to a "mainstream" American population, which to us, at the time, did not make methodological sense. In a way, it seemed as if our reviewers either were doubtful of the distinctiveness and robustness of our method of curating tweets signifying Native American political engagement or needed additional evidence that Native American rights advocates were tweeting about these types of issues at greater rates than a general (read "non-Native") population. In any case, we abided by their recommendation and compared our dataset to a general stream of tweets relating to the U.S. presidential campaigns. The results only compounded our initial realization, which was that in 2016, shortly before the worst of the state, county, and private security company violence against #NoDAPL Water Protectors in North Dakota, Native American advocates were tweeting about many of the issues that emerged in the standoff against the illegally constructed Dakota Access Pipeline whereas the general mainstream American public were mostly tweeting about entertainment news and the interpersonal jibing surrounding the 2016 U.S. presidential candidates. The lesson here is that if we had not relied on domain experts to curate data, we would likely have made the mistake of attempting to identify issues we thought that Native and Indigenous people might find interesting about the 2016 presidential candidates rather than surfacing what Native and Indigenous people at the time were actually most often retweeting and reposting through the Native Twittersphere. We had to quantitatively discern and prove what we know to be true—where scientific truth was for us reflective of the social reality of Indigenous peoples in the United States in the spring of 2016—through conscientious data curation amid a rigorous methodology.

To this end, we employ a process of curating data inputs that relies on the wisdom of domain experts and iterative cycles of collection, observation, and revision. We ask domain experts to provide the keywords, hashtags, and user names that will compose an initial filter that allows us to capture potentially useful data from the deluge of content generated on social media. With these expertly curated starting points, we begin a sample collection knowing that we are capturing data that reflect the heart of the communities we seek to understand. As we sift through the initial content captured by our filter, mixed-methods analysis by our multitalented research teams allows us to understand additional parameters that might need to be added to the filter or filter parameters that may capture content too generally and thus must be further specified. We refer to the content that is generated from this carefully identified set of filters as curated content.

Creating a Complementary Suite of Methods

Conducting a meaningful analysis requires us to develop a complementary suite of methods that combines the large-scale efficiency of quantitative approaches with the precision of qualitative approaches. After our filters have been finalized, we allow data collection to proceed for an extended period of time. For our studies, we typically collect between nine and twenty-five gigabytes of data per month; a typical study usually involves at least two months' worth of data, and some have involved four months' worth. During that time, we work as a team to develop epistemic, conceptual, and policy-minded vantage points from whence we can approach the impending datasets from a just and historically informed perspective. We frontload the work of boundary spanning by discussing matters such as the following: What are the implications of our proposed work for current events in Indian Country? What are the implications of our proposed work regarding contemporary debates in the field of Indigenous approaches to information and computer science? What are the methodological challenges here, in terms of operationalizing disparate or convergent terminologies, feminist citation practices, and ontological stakes? We often use this time to review known published literature with fresh eyes, to revisit our methods toolkits, and to update our understanding of our shared knowledge domains.

When we initially analyze data, we use a MapReduce paradigm to gain a "big picture" perspective on the data, answering questions such as these: What were the top hashtags used in this dataset? Who were the most prolific content creators? Which user tags get mentioned the most? Which hashtags tend to be most pervasive in this dataset over time? By using quantitative methods to answer these high-level questions about the data, we are able to hone in on a smaller subset of our data that would be most interesting for qualitative inspection by a human analyst, who can more efficiently focus on answering these questions: How are these top hashtags being used? What are the political contexts surrounding the usage of a particular word or phrase?

Of course, methodically answering these questions takes time and effort. We first attend to the network we investigate by creating a visual representation of it. This involves the application of advanced social network modeling through the creation of heat maps, Jaccardian similarity indices, social graphs developed through the Louvain community detection method, and color-coded bipartite networks (Blondel et al., 2008). We then attend to the visual representation of the networks through a combination of qualitative and quantitative means. We identify and analyze the structures that appear in the networks, which are statistical representations of influence, and then interpret their relative influence in light of the social and political significance of the various subtopics represented by issue networks. Once we identify subtopics and qualitatively characterize issue networks, we decide which of our qualitative methods we will use to sustain our "deep dive." Our toolkit includes analytic approaches such as grounded theoretical thematic analysis, content analysis, and discourse analysis; reflexive approaches such as dialogue and storywork; and archival analysis including critical review of relevant websites, news articles, policy papers, primary and secondary source historical documents, and government documents.

The "Deep Dive": Adjusting Our Analytic Lenses, Evaluating Findings in Light of Indigenous Histories

By the time we are ready for a "deep dive," as a team we inevitably realize how our labor is detailed, contextual, in situ, and sociotechnical. Discerning issue networks is methodological, with each research decision bearing social and political implications, and with each decision shaped by the life experience and domain knowledge that our research team members bring to bear. Accordingly, our approach is iterative. Our social graphs and qualitative analyses consist of multiple compelling structures and patterns, and as a team we have to decide which ones are most revealing given our lines of inquiry. We liken the predive process to that of a hawk scanning a lush and vast landscape, circling in an ever tightening gyre until focusing on a single point of prey or respite. Similarly, as a team, we adjust our data-collection queries and statistical community detection methods to acquire and visualize distinctively useful ranges of datasets, noting large and small structures in a topography of issue networks, and focusing on the patterns that are both statistically significant and qualitatively meaningful. We refine our queries—narrowing or broadening the noun phrases we collect from the Twitter streaming API, for example—to create and examine particularly interesting network structures at more granular levels, often interpreting the meaning of individual social media posts in terms of rhetoric, historicity, race/gender, geography, and current events and in relation to their rate of circulation in an ecology of posts. We call this the "deep dive," and just as swimmers who must surface for air after a deep dive, as researchers we find we are part of a flow of movement, with ours comprising a rigorous pace of creative scholarly insight that requires maintenance: we triangulate, document, analyze, narrate, diagram, periodize, and reconsider in light of the findings from multiple relevant deep dives. By repeating this exercise multiple times, as a team we surface findings, some of which we decide to publish and present, and some of which we strategically retain in the intellectual domain of our research teams, allowing unpublished insights to grow in meaning over time, waiting for the social or historical moment to arrive when as a team we are prepared to once again establish a research site in the digital overlay circulating through Indian Country. The deep dive requires such a simultaneous orchestration of higher order thinking skills and specialized knowledge across various team members such that, for us, it represents a culmination of Indigenous feminist intelligence work: reasonable and diplomatic analysis of information toward the promotion and enforcement of Indigenous peoplehood and tribal sovereignty.

Designing Discussions to Indigenize the Scholarly Forum

As an interdisciplinary team, we present our work in a range of forums, including computer science conferences, Indigenous studies conferences, the press, and policy makers, journalists, activists, and other scientists. Indigenous feminist scholarship requires preparing findings for multiple audiences: impactful results need to be expressed in ways that are meaningful to those who can apply them toward structural change.

As researchers in computer science and information science, our goal is to Indigenize the scholarly forums we participate in. However, the multifaceted nature of our methodologies always entails a carefully designed discussion of findings that simultaneously explains colonial perspectives embedded in the common practices of our fields and that defends the methodological rigor of network analysis with an Indigenous feminist framework. One of the challenges we face in crafting discussions for computer science audiences is justifying the validity of our findings when the calculation of that validity depends on the life experience and domain expertise of the scholars analyzing the social graphs we cocreate. The accusation is of bias, and it is based in a Western European philosophy of scientific objectivity that demands that the investigator maintain a relational distance from the investigated as a matter of rigor. We consistently find it difficult to defend our relational approach as scientifically rigorous, even though Indigenous scholars and scientists have determined that the dictates of relational accountability actually require and yield an extra level of rigor in the design and production of research.

Another challenge we experience has to do with racist and colonizing logics in our peer reviews. Some racist reviews emerge out of settler ignorance of Indigenous peoples and issues and include requests to cite settler theorists as opposed to the Indigenous, antiracist, feminist, decolonial, and Black studies scholars whose conceptual frameworks more accurately and precisely elucidate the social contexts and phenomena we study. Other reviews are plainly discriminatory. For example, we once received a review critiquing our choice of Native American rights advocates as a sample study population; the reviewer insisted that since Indigenous languages represented only a minor fraction of the world's languages and since most Indigenous people were dead, they were not a population worthy of study. We have also received critiques suggesting that descriptive research that fuses social theory and quantitative approaches cannot be predictive or generalizable and is therefore a poor fit for technically oriented social computing and computer science venues. There is an assumption that scientific documentation of the messiness of marginalized human groups is not efficient or practical in the technical system design process and is therefore not integral to the industrial tendency of the field of human-computer interaction, a field that is heavily subsidized by the neoliberal and heteropatriarchal ideologies of multinational tech corporations.

Because of the nature of the peer-review process, it is our responsibility as decolonial scholars and a matter of collegial respect to productively engage with our reviews, even those that, from our perspective, are narrow-minded, settler-colonial in orientation, anti-Indigenous, and arrogant. Responding to these kinds of reviews is an intellectual, ethical, and emotional challenge: it requires that we tease apart the arrogant and narrow-minded remarks from the constructive insights that help us more effectively present our work. To do this, as a team we deconstruct each review, using a spreadsheet that is divided into sections where we can "park" our responses, from our frustrated reactions, to our ideas on how to teach our reviewers about the validity and rigor of Indigenous methodologies and Native science. We put on our "privilege goggles," that is, the lenses we have all learned to wear as we walk through the delusion of White heteropatriarchy in academia. As a team, each member has, at one point or another, had to put on their "privilege goggles" from the vantage point of their field of expertise and has deconstructed reviewer comments by rapidly assessing the criticisms and viewpoints they have heard from professors, colleagues, graduate students, and industry professionals who have also happened to embrace settler-colonial or antifeminist ideologies. In effect, we read our reviews through a kind of, to quote African American sociologist W.E.B. Du Bois, "double consciousness," wherein we must activate our knowledge of the way the heteronormative white settler computer and information scientists think and believe and combine it with our knowledge of Indigenous realities in order to produce decolonial responses that reinforce the scientific merit of our work.

This exercise advances a shared understanding of how racism/arrogance works in our fields and how we can rhetorically and pedagogically turn it on its head through the peer-review process. In so doing we support each other in moving beyond the crazy-making effects of narrow-mindedness in Western science. We also cultivate what feminist philosopher Jose Medina (2013) calls "subversive lucidity": the ability to predict racist/sexist postures and attacks and to speak to them in ways that compassionately educate, defend, and protect the moral truth value of virtuous and just creative tension. Subversive lucidity is what gives us the know-how to be able to more strategically design the discussion sections of each paper we coauthor. For us, the discussion sections are not only where we answer our research questions and present the conceptual and design implications of our findings but also where we Indigenize the minds of our readers by crafting sentences and logics that assert the rights of Indigenous peoples, especially women and girls, to be heard, represented, and empowered, especially through the social power of technoscience.

Conclusion: Designing Healthy Indigenous Futures

Every manuscript we have submitted to technical publication venues has been met with wildly mixed reviews that require us to explain and defend the usage of Indigenous feminist frameworks as an integral part of a meaningful computational analysis of online communities. In considering the logical presentation of our work, we must always consider how settler-colonial scholars will perceive the validity of our findings given that they may not have been able to replicate the results. Through our defense of our science, we defend our right to contribute to the conceptual shaping of technoscientific fields. It is an emotional labor. We perceive and address the emotional tensions embedded in our reviews and in the ways our settler colleagues respond to our practice of science. The emotional labor affects us, as we live with the traces of historical trauma and the structural violence of sexism in our bodies, psyches, families, and communities. We decompress with each other, tapping into our collegial support systems to touch base with Indigenous, feminist, and people of color allies, learning their tactics for responsiveness, defense, and self-care. We mentor each other, and we mentor our graduate students. It is an unpaid and unacknowledged emotional labor that we append to every publication. The more we do this labor, the more we advocate for women, queer and trans scholars, Indigenous people, and people of color with feminist, antiracist and anticolonial values working in STEM fields.

We want our datasets, findings, frameworks, and methodologies to depict a reality that is recognizable to us. One of the unique strengths of an Indigenous feminist approach to network analysis is the ability to simultaneously plumb new levels of understanding while being aware of the limitations imposed by the availability of data. For instance, we always maintain awareness that data are merely a model representing reality and not reality itself (Duarte and Vigil-Hayes, 2017). There are many people who do not participate in the process of data generation (by choice or omission), and the method by which a measurable trace (i.e., data) is generated significantly impacts what can be known from that trace. However, there is so much that can be learned from the data and knowledge we have. Just as a tracker might follow a herd of elk across a landscape, we follow the signals of reality. While not every individual in a herd leaves footprints, droppings, or tufts of fur that a tracker can observe, there are signs all around that show her where the herd is going and where they have been. The tracker follows the signs of the elk, but she also follows her knowledge of the land; she knows where to locate water and grazing land and whether a storm is approaching. She is able to use her contextual knowledge about the land, how elk behave, and the observable traces of the elk to follow them and find them. Similarly, while any given digital data point may provide only faint signals toward reality, when we compile many data points of many types and integrate these datasets with relational knowledge of the communities and places we seek to understand, our impression of reality is clarified and the faint signals are verified and amplified. Clearly distinguishing between datasets and reality helps us avoid becoming fascinated with the simulations and simulacra that Simpson (2017) identifies in her critique of connective action networks. It is true that connective action networks are qualitatively distinct from face-to-face trust-based activist collectives, but as social media researchers, we also know that contemporary lived experience consists of a layering of social textures shaped by ranges of digital connectivity and access through biomes: one is never entirely offline or online but instead acts through the awareness of a datafied existence and, if Indigenous, of the responsibilities to living landscapes.

Thus, as we deepen our understanding of Indigenous peoples' uses of social media, we can begin to envision Indigenous futures. With these visions, we are able to design the technologies that make them possible. Our work understanding Indigenous social media has motivated a technical partnership with RED-INet, a middle-mile fiber optic network in northern New Mexico governed by a joint powers agreement between Rio Arriba County, Ohkay Owingeh Pueblo, Pojoaque Pueblo, Santa Clara Pueblo, and Tesuque Pueblo. Our findings of how social media politically and technically empowers Indigenous communities is informing the design and build-out of novel "first-mile" network infrastructures and applications that will help connect more homes and community centers in the four Pueblos served by REDINet. Critically, our findings have helped technologists realize the importance of designing information technologies and systems that are for specific groups of people in specific places. We are Indigenizing technical infrastructures and design processes.

Despite the challenges of publishing work using an Indigenous feminist approach in mainstream human-computer interaction (HCI) venues, we have been making an impact in these scholarly communities. It has been literally rewarding. A few established and respected HCI scholars have championed our methodological approach and have connected us with venues and opportunities through which we can share and discuss the values of taking an Indigenous feminist approach to understanding digital media. We are increasingly called upon to consult with other scholars on how to use this approach in their own domains of interest within digital media studies. Our impact in the HCI research community is also evident through more tangible outcomes. Despite reviewers' skepticism, our first publication using an Indigenous feminist approach was awarded an Honorable Mention for Best Paper (top 10 percent of papers) in the Proceedings of the Association of Computing Machinery International Conference on Computer-Supported Cooperative Work and Social Computing, and our second publication was recognized with the Diversity and Inclusion award (2 percent of papers) in the same venue.

For us, though, the true reward has been in forging creative relationships with powerfully situated intersectional and Indigenous feminists, devoted and generous community partners, and rights advocates who find ways to implement savvy structural changes. We laugh together, we think together, we write together, we see the world together, and we speak back to injustice together. We show our care for our loved ones by coconstructing the invisible networks through which they can thrive.

Acknowledgments

We would like to honor the talent and thoughtfulness of our colleagues with whom we have partnered over the years through this particular body of work:

Nicholet Deschine Parkhurst, Mark Trahant, Sandy Littletree, Miranda Belarde-Lewis, Elizabeth Belding, Ellen Zegura, and Jennifer Case Nevarez.

Note

1   Betweenness centrality is a scientific network metric that is used to measure the connective power of a particular node in a network (Barthelemy, 2004).

References

Adam, A. (2000). Gender and computer ethics. *ACM SIGCAS Computers and Society*, *30*(4), 17–24.
Allard, D., and Ferris, S. (2015). Antiviolence and marginalized communities: Knowledge creation, community mobilization, and social justice through a participatory archiving approach. *Library Trends, 64*(2), 360–383.
Archibald, J. (2008). *Indigenous storywork: Educating the heart, mind, body, and spirit.* Vancouver: UBC Press.
Bailey, J., and Shayan, S. (2016). Missing and murdered Indigenous women crisis: Technological dimensions. *Canadian Journal of Women and the Law, 28*(2), 321–341.
Barthelemy, M. (2004). Betweenness centrality in large complex networks. *European Physical Journal, 38*(2), 163–168.
Blondel, V. D., Guillaume, J. L., Lambiotte, R., and Lefebvre, E. (2008). Fast unfolding of communities in large networks. *Journal of Statistical Mechanics: Theory and Experiment, 2008*(10), P10008.
Brooks, L. (2008). *The common pot: The recovery of Native space in the Northeast.* Minneapolis: University of Minnesota Press.
Castells, M. (1997). *The power of identity: The information age: Economy, society, and culture* (Vol. 2). Cambridge, MA: Blackwell.
Deloria, V., Jr. (1978). *The right to know: A paper.* Washington, DC: United States Department of the Interior, Office of Library and Information Services.
Duarte, M. E. (2015). Knowledge, technology, and self-determination. In M. Woons (Ed.), *Restoring Indigenous self-determination: theoretical and practical approaches.* E-International Relations.
Duarte, M. E. (2017a). Connected activism: Indigenous uses of social media for shaping political change. *Australasian Journal of Information Systems, 21*, 1–21.
Duarte, M. E. (2017b, June 25). Integrating relationality with interface design in the digitization of Native American literature. Conference presentation, Native American and Indigenous Studies Association, Vancouver.
Duarte, M. E. (2017c). *Network sovereignty: Building the internet across Indian country.* Seattle: University of Washington Press.
Duarte, M. E., and Vigil-Hayes, M. (2017). #Indigenous: A technical and decolonial analysis of activist uses of hashtags across social movements. *Mediatropes, 7*(1), 166–184.
Jaccard, P. (1912). The distribution of the flora in the alpine zone. *New Phytologist, 11*(2), 37–50.
Jackson, S. J., and Banaszczyk, S. (2016). Digital standpoints: Debating gendered violence and racial exclusions in the feminist counterpublic. *Journal of Communication Inquiry, 40*(4), 391–407.

Karusala, N., Vishwanath, A., Kumar, A., Mangal, A., and Kumar, N. (2017). Care as a resource in underserved learning environments. *Proceedings of the ACM on Human-Computer Interaction, 1*(104), 1–22.

Littletree, S. (2019, May 28). Honoring relationality: Centering Indigenous perspectives in library services. Invited lecture, Mount Royal University Library, Calgary.

Lugones, M. (2006). On complex conversation. *Hypatia, 21*(3), 75–85.

Luka, M. E., and Millette, M. (2018). (Re) framing big data: Activating situated knowledges and a feminist ethics of care in social media research. *Social Media+ Society, 4*(2).

Medina, J. (2013). *Epistemology of resistance: Gender and racial oppression, epistemic injustice, and the social imagination.* Oxford: Oxford University Press.

Meng, A., DiSalvo, C., and Zegura, E. (2019). Collaborative data work towards a caring democracy. *Proceedings of the ACM on Human-Computer Interaction, 3*(42), 1–23.

Munster, A. (2013). *An aesthesia of networks: Conjunctive experience in art and technology.* Cambridge, MA: MIT Press.

Niezen, R. (2005). Digital Indigeneity: The construction of virtual selfhood in the Indigenous Peoples' Movement. *Comparative Studies in Society and History, 47*(3), 532–551.

Privott, M. (2019). An ethos of responsibility and Indigenous women water protectors in the #NoDAPL movement. *American Indian Quarterly, 43*(1), 74–100.

Simpson, L. B. (2017). *As we have always done: Indigenous freedom through radical resistance.* Minneapolis: University of Minnesota Press.

Vigil, M., Rantanen, M., and Belding, E. (2015). A first look at tribal web traffic. In *Proceedings of the 24th International Conference on World Wide Web* (pp. 1155–1165). New York: ACM.

Vigil-Hayes, M., Duarte, M. E., Parkhurst, N. D., and Belding, E. (2017). #Indigenous: Tracking the connective actions of Native American advocates on Twitter. In *Proceedings of the 20th ACM Conference on Computer Supported Cooperative Work and Social Computing* (pp. 1387–1399). New York: ACM.

Vigil-Hayes, M., Parkhurst, N. D., and Duarte, M. E. (2019). Complex, contemporary and unconventional: Characterizing the tweets of the #NativeVote Movement and Native American candidates through the 2018 US midterm elections. *Proceedings of the 22nd ACM Conference in Computer Supported Cooperative Work and Social Computing, 3*(103), 1–27.

Wong-Villacres, M., Velasquez, C. M., and Kumar, N. (2017). Social media for earthquake response: Unpacking its limitations with care. *Proceedings of the ACM on Human-Computer Interaction, 1*(112), 1–22.

7

Indigenous Social Activism Using Twitter

■■■■■■■■■■■■■■■■■■■■■

Amplifying Voices
Using #MMIWG

TAIMA MOEKE-PICKERING,

JULIA ROWAT, SHEILA COTE-MEEK,

AND ANN PEGORARO

Social media has become a site for amplifying Indigenous voices. Individuals who actively engage in political protest behavior tend to be more frequent users of social media (Earl and Kimport, 2011; Valenzuela, 2013), and those with large social networks are more likely to be civically engaged than those with smaller networks (Gil de Zúñiga and Valenzuela, 2010; Son and Lin, 2008). The correlation of these two phenomena promotes individuals' positive association with their group identity, allowing social media platforms to reach a large-scale audience (Lovejoy and Saxton, 2012).

Since Twitter launched just over a decade ago, the platform has become known as a place to disseminate information quickly. Perhaps the most obvious aspect of Twitter is the platform's ability to facilitate connections between followers, resulting in the formation of collaborations across groups, sectors, and countries. Seizing an opportunity to disseminate news and information, users have found Twitter to be a powerful forum to reach like-minded individuals and potential followers. Given the success of marginalized groups, such as @mmiw, @idlenomore, @nodapl, @blacklivesmatter, @metoo, and @womensmarch, who have used social media to mobilize their followers and bring their issues to the public, Twitter has become a critical outlet for conveying their viewpoints and logistics with their movements. Twitter likes and retweets confirm impact and reach and serve as a means to attract attention, educate, and mobilize followers. To further denote the impact and reach of Twitter, Moeke-Pickering, Cote-Meek, and Pegoraro (2018) found that from August 2016 to June 18, 2017, the hashtag #nodapl (Dakota Access Pipeline protest movement) had a reach of 13.3 billion and 23.5 billion impressions by way of 4.5 million users, indicating the power of Twitter activism by Indigenous groups (p. 58).

Unfortunately, the anonymity of Twitter simultaneously creates a space where cyberbullying and cyberharassment are rampant, especially from those whose views or politics differ. Indigenous users can also be the target of racism and harassment for their views on issues important to Indigenous peoples. Racism is, in itself, a traumatic experience for Indigenous and racialized peoples (Cote-Meek, 2014; Dei, Karumancery, and Karumancery-Luik, 2004). This is only compounded on social media as ideas are public and can be viewed, shared, and retweeted by anyone all over the world in a matter of minutes. It is important that users of social media platforms who are Indigenous have an awareness of the racism that operates on sites such as Twitter since it can impact one's health and safety. Carlson et al. (2017) use the term "shared recognition" to describe the collective anger and frustration experienced by Indigenous Australians when traumatic events happened to them in the public domain, acting as a reminder of ongoing, enduring colonial violence (p. 1). A shared recognition, as a form of social activism, is particularly useful as it assists users to reframe racist tweets rather than internalize them personally. While cyberbullying and/or harassment persists, Indigenous Twitter users persevere as the overall message of Indigenous activism has a sense of greater good for the communities they are serving.

In this chapter, we share research about social media, namely Twitter, usage associated with Missing and Murdered Indigenous Women and Girls (MMIWG) in Canada and why this type of activism is useful and important for Indigenous communities, families, and the public. We also discuss how mainstream media, specifically newspapers, handled the MMIWG inquiry and how Indigenous Twitter users confront the truth about sexual violence against MMIWG.

National Inquiry on Missing and Murdered
Indigenous Women and Girls (MMIWG)

On June 3, 2019, the National Inquiry on MMIWG released to the public, including the families and friends of the women, the report "Reclaiming Power and Place: The Final Report of the National Inquiry into Missing and Murdered Indigenous Women and Girls." The families and friends of MMIWG had been waiting anxiously for the recommendations from the two-volume report that comprised the truths of more than 2,380 family members, survivors of violence, experts, and knowledge keepers shared over two years of public hearings (National Inquiry Committee into Missing and Murdered Indigenous Women and Girls, 2019, p. 1). Evidence for this report was gathered from 1,484 family members and survivors, 819 individuals who shared through artistic expressions, and 83 experts, knowledge keepers, and officials at fifteen community hearings and nine institutional hearings. In the main, the report painted a grim picture of the high rates of violence inflicted on Indigenous women and girls and the poor tracking of homicide cases and the discrepancies of statistics on MMIWG. Government-enacted processes of colonization, such as the Indian Act, revealed Canada's systematic oppression and discrimination toward Indigenous women (Collins, 2017), which have enabled this national crisis to continue.

To set the context, on December 8, 2015, Prime Minister Justin Trudeau launched an inquiry into the systemic problem of MMIWG. By August 3, 2016, the inquiry commissioners were named and began their national inquiry on September 1, 2016. The first public hearings were carried out on May 29, 2017. Shortly after the inquiry launch in 2015, Moeke-Pickering et al. (2018) conducted a literature review of research on MMIWG in Canada. At that time, they found scant research carried out by few researchers (Beniuk, 2012; Boyce, 2016; Brennan, 2011; Eberts, 2014; Gilchrist, 2010; Pearce, 2013) all alluding to the grim facts that Indigenous women were overrepresented as victims of sexual and physical violence and homicide. Martin-Hill (2003) reported that Indigenous women were stigmatized; they were viewed as prostitutes, street people, and addicts. Sex workers, street people, and addicts do not deserve to be murdered, no matter what the stereotypes or stigmatizations are. Cote-Meek (2014), Razack (2000), and Kuokkanen (2008) have all written about the impact of ongoing colonialism on Indigenous peoples. Further, Cote-Meek (2014) contends that colonialism required a specific ideology rooted in racism that reduced and dehumanized Indigenous women and girls. Jiwani and Young (2006) also claimed that racialized stereotypes about MMIWG informed societal constructions (p. 902), rendering Indigenous women as prostitutes who belong "in the lower echelon of the moral order" (p. 903). Studies by Bailey and Shayan (2016) and Felt (2016), who drew data from social media users, both

identified that subversive texts about Indigenous women perpetuated a racialized and sexist discourse. The media portrayal of MMIWG as living a risky lifestyle enabled the negative profiling of victims to continue (Strega et al., 2014).
The numbers of MMIWG have also been difficult to determine. For example,
in 2015, the Native Women's Association of Canada reported that they had
gathered information on 582 cases, and the Royal Canadian Mounted Police
had found 1,200 MMIWG in their files. The differing versions of statistics have
been confusing and distracting. As Gilchrist (2010) reported, half of MMIWG
murder cases remain unsolved, creating a serious matter that warranted immediate attention. Media reports of MMIWG have obscured the seriousness of
crimes against Indigenous peoples, of their victimization, which sends the
wrong message to the public that crimes against Indigenous people do not
matter (Gilchrist, 2010, p. 376). While the literature does provide some insight
into MMIWG, it was the national inquiry into MMIWG that was deemed
necessary to bring attention to understanding more about the high rates of
MMIWG in Canada. It was promising that the MMIWG commissioners'
inquiry team encouraged the public to provide input by using the hashtags
#mmiw and #ourinquiry. Our research demonstrates that this was the turn of
the tide for social media users. This was an affirmation that their opinions could
matter.

To set a context for understanding how mainstream media reacted to the
national inquiry, the authors conducted a LexisNexis search of Canadian newspaper articles using the terms "MMIW" and/or "inquiry" during the period
December 8, 2015, to June 13, 2017. This was done to get a sense of how the media
represented MMIWG in the lead-up to and during the inquiry. Sherene
Razack's (2002) research on violence against women revealed how traditional
forms of media skew the struggles of Indigenous women in order to position
the colonial violence they face as a result of their own wrongdoings. Razack
noted, "Newspaper records in Canada's nineteenth century reveal there was a
conflation of Aboriginal woman and prostitute and an accompanying belief
that when they encountered violence, Aboriginal women simply got what they
deserved. Police seldom intervened, even when the victims' cries could be clearly
heard" (p. 130).

The association with Indigenous women and prostitution is a devaluation
and dehumanization tactic. Unfortunately, it feeds the public's sentiments
about the victims, creating a tendency to believe false information that can lead
to a lack of motivation to resolve the crisis. We have no doubt that conflating
Indigenous women's bodies with prostitution further perpetuated colonial bias
and violence against Indigenous women and girls. We also wanted to take
another look at how the media were portraying MMIWG stories in light of
the inquiry announcement. A total of sixty-six Canadian newspapers were
reviewed, including but not limited to the *Canadian Press*, the *Times and*

Transcript, the *Prince George Citizen*, the *Vancouver Province*, the *Calgary Herald*, the *Toronto Star*, the *Star Phoenix*, the *Sault Star*, the *Regina Leader-Post*, and the *National Post*. In the main, we noticed three trends: there was more attention about how the inquiry should be conducted (e.g., whether the inquiry should be Indigenous-centered, more examination of police processes, whether commissioners should have a feminist approach, etc.), there was more effort to interview families about their experiences, and there were more women journalists reporting on MMIWG. Kerry Benjoe of the *Leader-Post* reported on December 9, 2015, that the mother of Kelly Goforth (one of the MMIWG) cried tears of joy over the rollout of the MMIWG inquiry: "The families, the people who are closest to those we have already lost, are those ones who can provide some really good insight on that front, on how systems have responded. In order to have a better, more efficient, more timely response then we need to have that." She said the plan to engage the public through social media is also good. Gloria Galloway of the *Globe and Mail* reported on August 3, 2016, that the inquiry should also probe into the Indian Act and systemic causes. "Although the inquiry will not have the authority to make findings of police misconduct or to compel law-enforcement agencies to reopen cold cases, the government says the commissioners will have the power to look at police practices and conduct. Families of victims have complained that police do not investigate the disappearances of indigenous women with the same diligence that is applied when Caucasian women go missing, and they say suspicious deaths are too often attributed to natural causes." Likewise, Steve Lambert reported in the *Canadian Press* on March 7, 2017, that there were many unanswered questions about how many communities the Inquiry Commission would visit. "For people in other communities, will there be subsidies for travel costs, therapy or emotional supports for people who face the trauma of retelling their stories, as well as access to traditional First Nation ceremonies?" Looking at the key trends from the Canadian newspaper reviews alongside the Twitter ones, Moeke-Pickering et al. (2018) took a snapshot of the hashtags #mmiw and #inquiry from September 1, 2016, to July 29, 2017. They found that during that eleven-month period, Twitter users created 107,800 tweets for #MMIW and #MMIWG, which produced 156.1 million impressions (Moeke-Pickering et al., 2018, p. 59). Importantly, they found that for this period the top five Twitter users who gained a large number of retweets for their MMIWG content were Indigenous women.

To summarize, we noticed that the trend by mainstream media and social media users during the lead-up and first few months of the inquiry gave more airtime to the stories of the loved ones of MMIWG and that there was an increase in women being interviewed. Importantly, we noticed an increased analysis of the systemic causes of violence against Indigenous women and girls and why the inquiry should be more Indigenous and centered on women in their processes.

The 2019 National Inquiry report (released on June 3, 2019) received a mixed response. The report both confirmed the breadth and scope of MMIWG across Canada and challenged Canadians' notions of the pervasiveness of injustices against Indigenous women and girls. There were scathing attacks that questioned whether the numbers in the report were accurate and the severity of the word "genocide" used by the authors to describe the ongoing colonial actions of Canada. The statement read, "This report is about deliberate race, identity and gender-based genocide" (National Inquiry Committee into Missing and Murdered Indigenous Women and Girls, 2019, p. 5). The term gender-based genocide is a harsh reality for Canadians to face. The authors rightly use the term to situate genocide as an ongoing sexualized violence that Indigenous women and girls experience, a truth that Indigenous peoples no longer will ignore.

Sadly, the debate over the use of the word "genocide" became the major media focus and drew attention away from the sexualized violence experienced by Indigenous women and girls in Canada and how to address the way the police handled homicide processes. What was interesting to watch was the keyboard social media warriors who reacted to the debate on "genocide," adding more Indigenous contexts as well as a more informed intersectional analysis of the impact of genocide on women and girls.

Joan Bryden, a journalist for the *National Post*, reported that the Leger Poll taken from June 7 to 10, 2019 (Association for Canadian Studies) showed 34 percent of Canadians disagreed with the terminology of "genocide" being used to describe the violations and abuses on MMIWG and 2SLGBTQQIA (two-spirit, lesbian, gay, bisexual, transgender, queer, questioning, intersex, and asexual peoples). Further, a poll of 1,528 Canadians (Leger for the Association for Canadian Studies) found that 53 percent of Canadians agreed that the systemic murders and disappearances of Indigenous women amounts to genocide (Bryden, 2019). Indigenous peoples themselves also used social media to express their endorsement of the term "genocide" as well as acknowledging that ongoing colonial policies are a major factor in MMIWG. Below are three key Indigenous social media leaders who used Twitter to inform, amplify, challenge, and bring awareness to the MMIWG Inquiry report recommendations and key issues especially in support of the term "genocide."

Cindy Blackstock (@cblackst—an Aboriginal child, youth, and family researcher and educator who has a following of 34,200) created the hashtag #isitgenocide to shine a light on MMIWG and genocide by launching a Twitter learning series to historically trace colonial polices, acts, and resources to show how the Canadian government systematically and deceitfully contributed to the act of genocide against MMIWG and 2SLGBTQQIA

Cindy Blackstock ✔
@cblackst

I launched a learning series for Canadians on "#isitgenocide?" in honour of the MMIW. Some have asked that I tag the entries so they are easier to follow so I am reposting prior entries with the #isitgenocide and will post a new learning resource daily with that hashtag. #1

> **Cindy Blackstock** ✔ @cblackst
>
> Learning for those wondering if "genocide" is the right term, I am launching a learning series today. Here is the first resource. The "great dying" of Indigenous peoples in the Americas may be linked to climate change: sciencedirect.com/science/articl...

4:59 AM · Jun 12, 2019   ⓘ

♡ 718   💬 453 people are Tweeting abo...

FIG. 7.1 Tweet from Cindy Blackstock, @cblackst. (Credit: Screenshot by chapter authors.)

(figure 7.1). @TanyaTalaga is an author, Atkinson Fellow in Public Policy, and journalist who has a following of 18,200 and noted that the death of women by the thousands is a "persistent and deliberate pattern" and noted that "genocide" is the right word (Tanya Talaga, Indigenous issues columnist, June 3, 2019, thestar.com).

@Pam_Palmater a Native lawyer, professor, author, blogger, and advocate for Native rights and social justice who has a following of 38,700 on her Twitter account. She was active on social media and television, bringing awareness to the report and to keep the focus on the recommendations. Palmater stated, "One of the root causes of why we have this genocide in Canada is because Canada not only fails to uphold the basic human rights of Indigenous women and girls, but they purposely breach it so state actors—like police officials who engage in sexualized violence against Indigenous women and girls, or participate in human trafficking, child porn rings, all of those things. State actors involved in it, haven't been held to account" (Palmater, 2019).

The debate on whether genocide is the appropriate terminology grossly takes away from the truth shared by friends and family of MMIWG and members of the 2SLGBTQQIA community. It is important to highlight at this juncture that Indigenous women are at the forefront of leading Indigenous and women-centered debates. The media, both newspapers and television, are selecting them as spokespersons for their viewpoints on key issues. This provides viewers with a broader and in-depth perspective on how to better understand the patterns that caused MMIWG to go undetected and unreported. Social media unequivocally is a platform for individuals to provide a raw voice and a personal, if not cultural, insight into how Indigenous peoples voice their opinions and their hurt across the generations. Social media activism by Blackstock, Palmater, and Talaga demonstrate the power of influence that a few can make to educate their followers and the general public about racial and sexual intersectional analysis. Importantly, they set the record straight by calling the government, and its state actors, to account in doing their necessary part in decolonizing Canada's systems and practices.

Twitter Activism and #MMIWG

As a social media platform, Twitter is a space that has been utilized by Indigenous peoples and non-Indigenous allies to mobilize and engage in dialogue about Canada's complicit actions in the process of colonization, while raising awareness about MMIWG by using the hashtag #MMIWG. The use of hashtags, as a tool in online advocacy efforts, allows movements and ideas to spread organically to like-minded individuals (Saxton et al., 2015), thereby mobilizing groups and individuals together toward a collective goal. The use of the #MMIWG hashtag simultaneously calls out the colonial bodies who are responsible for keeping communities safe, by making sure they are held accountable (Brewer, 2018). Social media can provide a space that honors the lives and stories of MMIWG through amplifying the truth about violence against Indigenous women and girls. The effective use of #MMIWG engages a wide range of individuals in necessary conversations about the national crisis and gives individuals the power to engage and change the political landscape of media (Moeke-Pickering et al., 2018).

Social media can help to create a unified space where activists are supported in solidarity by a network of individuals who may be affiliated only through social media but mobilize together toward a common political goal (see Berglund, this volume; Vigil-Hayes et al., 2017). In a colonial state, it is important to create safe spaces through social media without boundaries wherein Indigenous peoples can mobilize and effectively communicate their political goals to enact change. Bennett (2012) argues that social media's "individual-ised collective action" allows "large numbers of people [to] join in loosely coor-dinated activities centered on more personal emotional identifications and rationale" (as cited in Saramo, 2016, p. 210). Although these organizations are loose in structure, their fixture in the political landscape challenges ongoing cultural regimes of colonialism and racism (Saramo, 2016). Using this type of connective action in combination with the hashtag #MMIWG helps to amplify voices and expand the reach of these tweets (Felt, 2016). By using the hashtag #MMIWG, Twitter users are able to effectively raise awareness to the national crisis of missing and murdered Indigenous women and girls and stir the col-lective political consciousness regarding the crisis, while respectfully acknowl-edging stories and narratives of Indigenous women and girls that have been hidden to a broader society (Moeke-Pickering et al., 2018; Saramo, 2016). Main-stream newspapers and television are also using social media sites to select Indigenous peoples for their viewpoints on certain issues. This creates a plat-form for Indigenous voices and experiences to be heard. Importantly social media balances the way that Indigenous issues are conveyed. As highlighted earlier, Blackstock, Palmater, and Talaga countered negative statements about the MMIWG inquiry report by informing intersectional contexts thereby becoming powerful allies in the media for MMIWG analyses.

What social media in effect allows for is a broader representation of view-points; thus the public is no longer dominated by one-sided mainstream nega-tive messages that are controlled by mainstream media. This is great news for Indigenous social media users (see Berglund, this volume). Typically, the more mainstream media tend to rely on sensationalist voices, key experts, research-ers, and politicians. The swiftness of social media means that the public has access to Twitter feeds daily. This is fortuitous for researchers especially to assist with formulating data sources including saving tweets to bookmarks. Social media is a space that amplifies Indigenous activism (Carlson, 2013; Carlson et al., 2017; Duarte, 2017; Duarte and Vigil-Hayes, 2017; Moeke-Pickering et al., 2018; Molyneaux et al., 2014; Saramo, 2016).

Unfortunately, there is a downside to social media. For example, Carlson et al. (2017) found that social media can also be a bullying space against Indige-nous and racialized peoples. While we are attempting to situate social media as a site for activism, we recognize that it is also a site where Indigenous peoples become targets of hate, bullying, and other forms of harassment. The theory of the "contact zone" is used by scholars as a trope for visualizing social spaces where cultures clash (Pratt, 1991). Regardless of the platform one chooses for social activism, there will always be implications and consequences for making a political statement. Whether one stands with a placard on the street or engages in a controversial conversation with another person, these are still forms of social activism, and there are implications and consequences for the statements one makes. It is important to note that there are bullying tactics used on sites like Twitter, where one's identity is hidden or protected by social media policies. There are the same extremist behaviors on social media as there are in the physical world. Typically, on Twitter, a person can receive positive feedback or be blocked. How do these bullying techniques prevent us from moving forward?

Imagine if social media users were all blocked from saying things that are vital and important. Would the MMIWG inquiry report be different if it relied on only mainstream media or a few sources as opposed to canvassing ideas from social media users? How would Indigenous peoples uncover the deep-rooted causes of systemic sexual violence against Indigenous women and girls if they were stopped from using or listening to women voices? Social media allows for the courageous voices of Indigenous users to rise. It also provides a platform for those being complicit to be challenged.

Conclusion

Practices of collective action and social activism have been changed by contemporary, technology-driven media. With the rise of social media, individuals now have the ability to connect and communicate with other individuals in ways that were previously restricted to more formalized organizations such as mainstream media. Emerging social media platforms allow for the communication of ideas and information among an informalized group of individuals without the burdens of costs, difficulties, and time constraints (Bimber, Flanagin, and Stohl, 2005) associated with traditional media sources. This change in the ways political information can be mobilized has caused a shift in acts of political action as well as the ever-changing landscape of social media particularly for Indigenous users (Berglund, this volume; Carlson et al., 2017; Duarte, 2017; Duarte and Vigil-Hayes, 2017; Moeke-Pickering et al., 2018). Social media's ability to connect individuals to each other more easily than traditional media outlets allows it to be a natural site of active political communication. This act of community building (Gil de Zúñiga and Valenzuela, 2010) results in social media users having positive associations with their participation, thus continuing to use social media for its ability to provide positive spaces and network building.

Creating a sense of group identity through social media enables users to be actively engaged with like-minded individuals online and offline (Valenzuela, 2013), thus translating conversations online into the offline public sphere. An example of this transformative action can be seen in the responses to the lead-up and the period following the commission's inquiry into MMIWG. Social media as a form of activism helped to counter narratives to discredit and/or minimize MMIWG. Social media is a platform that gives voice to the stories of MMIWG who deserve truth, respect, and honor.

References

Bailey, J., and Shayan, S. (2016). Missing and murdered Indigenous women crisis: Technological dimensions. *Canadian Journal of Women and the Law, 28*(2), 321–341.

Beniuk, J. (2012). Indigenous women as the other: An analysis of the missing Women's Commission of Inquiry. *Arbutus Review, 3*(2), 80–97.

Benjoe, K. (2015, December 9). MMIW inquiry met with optimism in Saskatchewan. *Regina Leader-Post.* https://leaderpost.com/news/local-news/regina-mother-cries-tears-of-joy-over-announcement-of-inquiry.

Bennett, W. L. (2012). The personalization of politics: Political identity, social media, and changing patterns of participation. *Annals of the American Academy, 644,* 20–39.

Bimber, B., Flanagin, A. J., and Stohl, C. (2005). Reconceptualizing collective action in the contemporary media environment. *Communication Theory, 15*(4), 365–388.

Boyce, J. (2016). Victimization of Aboriginal people in Canada. Juristat: Canadian Centre for Justice Statistics. https://search.proquest.com/docview/1806172353?accountid=12005.

Brennan, S. (2011). Violent victimization of aboriginal women in the Canadian provinces, 2009 (Catalogue no. 85-002-x). Juristat: Canadian Centre for Justice Statistics. http://www.statcan.gc.ca/pub/85-002-x/2011001/article/11439-eng.pdf.

Brewer, G. L. (2018, January 26). Where #Metoo meets #MMIW: The national conversation should include murdered and missing Indigenous women. *High Country News.* https://www.hcn.org/articles/indian-country-news-where-metoo-meets-mmiw.

Bryden, J. (2019, June 16). Half of Canadians say Indigenous women victims were part of "genocide" but the Leger poll also suggests there's disagreement about when it occurred and who is responsible. *National Post.* https://nationalpost.com/news/canada/majority-agrees-indigenous-women-victims-of-genocide-but-not-on-how-or-by-whom.

Carlson, B. (2013). The "new frontier": Emergent Indigenous identities and social media. In M. Harris, M., Nakata, M., and Carlson, B. (Eds.), *The politics of identity: Emerging Indigeneity* (pp. 147–168). Sydney: University of Technology Sydney E-Press.

Carlson, B., Jones, L. V., Harris, M., Quezada, N., and Frazer, R. (2017). Trauma, shared recognition and Indigenous resistance on social media. *Australasian Journal of Information Systems, 21,* 1–18.

Collins, A. (2017). The colonial legacy: The legal oppression of Indigenous women and girls in Canada. *Glendon Journal of International Studies, 10.* https://gjis.journals.yorku.ca/index.php/gjis/article/view/40252.

Cote-Meek, S. (2014). *Colonized classrooms: Racism, trauma and resistance in post-secondary education.* Halifax: Fernwood.

Dei, G. J., Karumancery, L. L., and Karumancery-Luik, N. (2004). *Playing the race card: Exposing white power and privilege.* New York: Peter Lang.

Duarte, M. (2017). Connected activism: Indigenous uses of social media for shaping political change. *Australasian Journal of Information Systems, 21,* 1–12.

Duarte, M. E., and Vigil-Hayes, M. (2017). #Indigenous: A technical and decolonial analysis of activist uses of hashtags across social movements. *Media Tropes e-Journal, 7,* 166–184.

Earl, J., and Kimport, K. (2011). *Digitally enabled social change: Activism in the internet age.* Acting with Technology. Cambridge, MA: MIT Press.

Eberts, M. (2014). Knowing and unknowing: Settler reflections on missing and murdered Indigenous women. *Saskatchewan Law Review, 77,* 69–104.

Felt, M. (2016). Mobilizing affective political networks: The role of affect in calls for a national inquiry to murdered and missing Indigenous women during the 2015 Canadian Federal election. Presented at the 7th International Conference on Social Media and Society, London.

Galloway, G. (2016, August 3). Missing, murdered Indigenous women inquiry could target Indian Act. *Globe and Mail.* https://www.theglobeandmail.com/news /politics/missing-and-murdered-women-inquiry-could-target-indian-act /article31238356/.

Gilchrist, K. (2010). "Newsworthy" victims? *Feminist Media Studies, 10*(4), 373–390.

Gil de Zúñiga, H., and Valenzuela, S. (2010). The mediating path to a stronger citizenship: Online and offline networks, weak ties, and civic engagement. *Communication Research,* 38, 397–421.

Harding, R. (2005). The media, aboriginal people and common sense. *Canadian Journal of Native Studies, 25*(1), 311–335.

Jiwani, Y., & Young, M.L. (2006). Missing and murdered women: Reproducing marginality in news discourse. *Canadian Journal of Communication, 31,* 895–917.

Kuokkanen, R. (2008). Globalization as racialized, sexualized violence. *International Feminist Journal of Politics, 10,* 216–233.

Lambert, S. (2017, March 7). Advocates say MMIW inquiry must support family participation: A coalition of Manitoba families says they're still in the dark about how many communities the inquiry commission will visit. *Maclean's.* https://www .macleans.ca/news/advocates-say-mmiw-inquiry-must-support-family-participation/.

Lovejoy, K., and Saxton, G. D. (2012). Engaging stakeholders through Twitter: How non-profit organizations are getting more out of 140 characters or less. *Public Relations Review, 38,* 313–318. https://doi.org/10.1016/j.pubrev.2012.01.005.

Martin-Hill, D. (2003). She no speaks and other colonial constructs of the traditional woman. In K. Anderson and B. Lawrence (Eds.), *Strong women stories: Native vision and community survival* (pp. 106–120). Toronto: Sumach.

Moeke-Pickering, T., Cote-Meek, S., and Pegoraro, A. (2018). Understanding the ways missing and murdered Indigenous women are framed and handled by social media users. *Media International Australia, 169*(1), 54–64. https://doi.org/10.1177 /1329878X18803730.

Molyneaux, H., O'Donnell, S., Kakekaspan, C., Walmark, B., Budka, P., and Gibson, K. (2014). Research in brief: Social media in remote First Nation communities. *Canadian Journal of Communication, 39,* 275–288.

National Inquiry Committee into Missing and Murdered Indigenous Women and Girls. (2019). Power and place: The final report of the National Inquiry into Missing and Murdered Indigenous Women and Girls. https://www.mmiwg-ffada .ca/final-report/.

Native Women's Association of Canada. (2015). Missing and murdered women and girls fact sheet North. https://nwac.ca/wp-content /uploads/2015/05/2010 -Fact-Sheet-North-MMAWG.pdf.

Palmater, P. (2019, June 4). Canadian inquiry demands justice for genocide of Indigenous women and girls. https://therealnews.com/stories/canadian-inquiry -demands-justice-for-genocide-of-indigenous-women-and-girls.

Pearce, M. (2013). An awkward silence: Missing and murdered vulnerable women and the Canadian justice system. Doctoral thesis, University of Ottawa.

Pratt, M. L. (1991). Arts of the contact zone. *Profession, 91*, 33–40.

Razack, S. (2000). Gendered racial violence and spatialized justice: The murder of Pamela George. *Canadian Journal of Law and Society, 15*, 91–130.

Razack, S. (2002). *Race, space, and the Law: Unmapping a white settler society.* Toronto: Between the Lines.

Saramo, S. (2016). Unsettling spaces: Grassroots responses to Canada's missing and murdered Indigenous woman during the Harper government years. *Comparative American Studies an International Journal, 14*, 204–220. https://doi.org/10.1080/14775700.2016.1267311.

Saxton, G. D., Niyirora, J. N., Guo, C., and Waters, R. D. (2015). #AdvocatingForChange: The strategic use of hashtags in social media advocacy. *Advances in Social Work, 16*(1). https://doi.org/10.18060/17952.

Son, J., and Lin, N. (2008). Social capital and civic action: A network-based approach. *Social Science Research, 37*, 330–349.

Strega, S., Janzen, C., Morgan, J., Brown, L., Thomas, R., and Carriére, J. (2014). Never innocent victims street sex workers in Canadian print media. *Violence against Women, 20*(1), 6–25.

Talaga, Tanya. (2019, June 3). Why can't we use the word genocide? *Toronto Star.* https://www.thestar.com.

Trudeau, J. (2015). Prime Minister Trudeau delivers a speech to the AFN Special Chiefs Assembly. https://pm.gc.ca/eng/video/2015/12/08/prime-minister-trudeau-delivers-speech-afn-special-chiefs -assembly.

Valenzuela, S. (2013). Unpacking the use of social media for protest behavior: The roles of information, opinion expression, and activism. *American Behavioral Scientist, 57*, 920–942.

Vigil-Hayes, M., Duarte, M., Parkhurst, N. D., and Belding, E. (2017). #Indigenous: Tracking the connective actions of Native American advocates on Twitter. Presentation at CSCW 2017, Portland, OR.

8

Radical Relationality in the Native Twitterverse

■ ■

Indigenous Women,
Indigenous Feminisms, and
(Re)writing/(Re)righting
Resistance on #NativeTwitter

CUTCHA RISLING BALDY

Toward the end of his second term President Barack Obama visited the country of Laos in what the media framed as a "historic visit." The purpose of the four-day visit was to see various cultural sites and to participate in a summit of Southeast Asian countries. This was the first time an American president had visited the country, which resulted in a large media presence. On September 7, 2016, at a town hall with young leaders held in Luang Prabang, a Malaysian woman named Alice stood up and took the microphone: "My question is in solidarity with the Indigenous people in, not my country, but America itself. I just heard recently that this group of people is fighting to protect their ancestral land against the Dakota Access Pipeline. In your capacity, what can you do to ensure the protection of the ancestral land, the supply of clean water and also environmental justice is upheld?" (Arnold, 2016). Obama seemed flustered by the question. Thousands of miles from the Oceti Sakowin homelands and the ongoing fight by Water Protectors to stop the Dakota Access Pipeline was one woman, who seemingly had no personal or community connection to the Indigenous peoples and nations so far away from her home, who claimed space for the ongoing #NoDAPL movement. Even though this town hall had not necessarily been framed as a space to challenge the President on his policies or approaches to tribes and tribal nations, the question from this woman (often unidentified in media stories) reverberated across nations and lands around the world: "I just heard recently that this group of people is fighting to protect their ancestral land against the Dakota Access Pipeline. In your capacity, what can you do to ensure the protection of the ancestral land, the supply of clean water and also environmental justice is upheld?"

As a researcher, scholar, and activist often stuck behind a computer far away from the epicenter of Indigenous movements, this moment further illustrated for me how social media outreach and activism could span across waterscapes and landscapes from those who were holding ground against the Dakota Access Pipeline all the way to the country of Laos. The stakes in the #NoDAPL resistance were huge like protection of water and wildlife and the future of Indigenous lands against large corporate and capitalist interests all supported by the supposed "rule of law." For months, many of us had watched as Water Protectors gathered to stop construction of the Dakota Access Pipeline (DAPL) where it was set to cross the Missouri River just upriver from the Fort Berthold Reservation. The #NoDAPL movement had sprung up from ongoing grassroots efforts by community members to call attention to how Energy Transfer Partners was ignoring the concerns of Native peoples about the potential threats to the water supply, sacred sites, and burial sites in order to build the DAPL. Bobbi Jean Three Legs and other members of the Standing Rock Youth Council had been working on these issues by writing and delivering a petition to the Army Corps of Engineers asking for a denial of permission for the DAPL to cross the Missouri River just north of the Standing Rock Sioux Reservation. The youth organized a run from their reservation all the way to the Army Corps. In a 2018 publication, Mary Rebecca Ferguson notes,

> The petition itself was written by thirteen-year-old Anna Lee Rain YellowHammer with the help of other youth from the Standing Rock Youth Council. . . .
> The run was a significant part of the #noDAPL movement because it united youth from many different Sioux reservations and gave them both a purpose and voice in this political debate. In addition, it greatly expanded the awareness and support for the movement, and the number of people at Sacred Stone Camp grew from fewer than twenty before the run to between seven and eight thousand people by the time runners returned to the encampment. (Ferguson, 2018, p. 80)

With the increase of people came an increase in police and state surveillance and also increased requests for assistance to quell the growing uprising. Nick

Estes (Lower Brule Sioux Tribe) writes, "After North Dakota Governor Jack Dalrymple declared a state of emergency on August 19, 2016—to safeguard the pipeline's final construction—the movement surged. Dalrymple deployed the National Guard and invoked powers under the Emergency Management Assistance Compact (EMAC) that are normally used only during natural disasters, such as floods, fires, and hurricanes. EMAC also allows for state, municipal, and federal law enforcement agencies to share equipment and personnel during what are declared community disorders, insurgency, or enemy attack" (2019, p. 2).

However, though corporate, state, and government interests attempted to control the narrative, it was often usurped and disrupted by the social media engagement of Water Protectors and independent media who were on the ground. Social media also helped people from around the world to engage with the #NoDAPL movement though they might not have been able to be physically present at the camps. Donations poured in from around the world, Amazon wish lists were created and quickly fulfilled, online fundraising campaigns were funded well over requested amounts, and videos, memes, and even counter–press releases were shared widely via social media to help clarify and often challenge the narrative that was being created by corporate strategists and professional public relations firms. Support for the movement grew online and was sustained despite mass media initially framing the movement as small or insignificant. Much of this framing changed on October 31, 2016, when over one million people "checked in" via Facebook to the Sacred Stone Camp. Facebook check-in allows users to publicly post where they are located. In this instance, over a million people reported that they were at the Sacred Stone camp, though at the time the numbers of people were estimated at closer to ten thousand. The message to check in on Facebook spread through social media circles because of the belief that this could help confuse the Morton County Sheriff's office, which at the time was thought to have been monitoring the social media posts, check-ins, and accounts of activists believed to be on the ground at the Sacred Stone Camp. Because of the over one million check-ins on Facebook the media quickly picked up on this viral moment with several stories and news reports (Meyer and Waddell, 2016). Following this, the #NoDAPL movement continued the momentum forward, buoyed by support from around the world. Tara Houska, (Couchiching First Nation), an activist and lawyer, was quoted in one *Time* article as saying, "It's nice to know folks out there understand. . . . There's incredible surveillance of the camps and we've seen the police response rapidly escalate to the now-militarized response to our protest" (Worland, 2016).

The growing social media presence and savvy of Water Protectors and their supporters effectively exploded the attempted narrative created by Energy Transfer Partners that framed Native people on the ground as violent aggressors or attempted insurgents. Estes explains how TigerSwan, a private security contractor that had been hired by the DAPL to assist in law enforcement "infiltrated the camps and planted false reports on social media and local news comparing Water Protectors to jihadist insurgents." According to TigerSwan, "The #NoDAPL movement was an ideologically driven insurgency with a strong religious component" (Estes, 2019, p. 3). However, social media posts, stories, blogs, and other independent media created in real time would prove otherwise. Disruption of these ongoing narratives that attempted to delegitimize Water Protectors work to defend the land, water, and the sacred was significantly highlighted by a relatively new feature of Facebook at the time—going "live"—which allowed users to broadcast video in real time and provided other Facebook users the ability to watch livestreamed content, engage with that content through comments and likes, and also share this content as it was being streamed. The videos were also archived and could be shared via Facebook after they had been recorded. Going live effectively allowed Water Protectors to stream content to the world, without the filter of major media or needing reporters or other media gatekeepers to be present at the event. For many at the #NoDAPL movement this also provided important opportunities for counternarratives and countermedia that could be broadcast at the same time as other media were being broadcast, which provided counterperspectives on events that were being framed by law enforcement agencies as violent or dangerous (Johnson, 2017). On November 20, 2016, law enforcement officers used "water cannons, teargas, and other 'less-than-lethal' weapons" on Water Protectors in below freezing temperatures (Wong, 2016). Live videos were shared around the world, with Water Protectors pleading for help, others sustaining injuries from rubber bullets, and even more requiring on-the-ground medical treatment. From behind their computer screens witnesses watched live footage of Water Protectors as they reported on the escalation of the incident. Drone footage of the event was also captured by Water Protectors and provided aerial shots confirming that law enforcement was separated from the Protectors by a barbed wire fence, casting doubt on early claims that there was an imminent threat or danger. Early reports of the incident framed it as a "clash" between protectors and police officers. The Morton County Sheriff's office attempted to control the narrative by describing the incident as an "ongoing riot" and Water Protectors as "very aggressive" (Wong, 2016). But the live footage was already demonstrating an important counternarrative to the official word of law enforcement agencies and public relations press releases. Live footage, drone footage, on-the-ground reporting, posts, tweets, photos, and memes all were deployed by the #NoDAPL movement to build an intervention that demonstrated worldwide support, to reclaim voices and spaces as Indigenized, and to demonstrate what Angel Hinzo (Ho-Chunk, enrolled Winnebago Tribe of Nebraska) and Lynn Clark call "digital survivance" (2019). As one Water Protector, E'sha Hoferer, explained in response to suggestions that protectors were carrying weapons, "We have our cameras and our prayers, that's all we have. . . . The world is watching" (Sottile, 2016).

The political and social interventions by Indigenous peoples in ongoing discourses and fights for social, political, and environmental justice have been built through storytelling and (re)storying the land and history with Indigenous voices. As Nick Estes explains, "Indigenous resistance draws from a long history, projecting itself backward and forward in time. While traditional historians merely interpret the past, radical Indigenous historians and Indigenous knowledge-keepers aim to change the colonial present, and to imagine a decolonial future by reconnecting to Indigenous places and histories. For this to occur, those suppressed practices must make a crack in history" (2019, p. 18). Estes draws necessary and needed connections between the Wounded Knee Massacre of 1890 and the Wounded Knee Occupation of 1973 with the ongoing resistance of the Oceti Sakowin peoples to this day. His book, *Our History Is the Future*, connects the #NoDAPL movement to ongoing histories of resistance by asserting that who stories our movements, our interventions, and our ongoing resistance to the occupation of our lands matters because without this intervention the state and/or ongoing colonial structures would continue to make us disappeared, removed, and misrepresented in order to justify dispossession of Indigenous lands and life. Our histories *are* the future and must be created, cared for, and built from our own voices, peoples, and resistance movements. How we center, analyze, and story these interweaving, interrelational narratives when we, as Māori scholar Linda T. Smith (2012) states, "(re)write" and "(re)right history" is how Indigenous theoretical interventions become community building praxis for Indigenous futures. Our movements, which often move like water with ebb and flow, are how we have always built, (re)built, and imagined our worlds. The mediums that we use to story our worlds, our histories, and our futures have ebbed and flowed as well, but as we engage more fully with the impact Indigenous voices can and should have on political and social interventions through social media we can also start to see how this has impacted Indigenous present and presence.

The chapters in this book speak to the power and importance of these stories across landscapes and waterscapes to (re)story our landscapes and waterscapes and "facilitate information flow." As Nicholet Deschine Parkhurst (Lakota of the Standing Rock Sioux Tribe and Diné of the Navajo Nation) discusses in chapter two, "From #Mniwiconi to #StandwithStandingRock," "communication technology to facilitate information flows has been happening since the late 1880s, when Lakota people sent messages, by way of train, to boarding school students about the Ghost Dance, an anticolonial resistance movement." Seeing this intergenerational connection as (re)centering Indigenous theory for Indigenous transformation, Parkhurst reminds us that success is ongoing and can be "transformative by raising consciousness of people and solidarity around the world, building virtual and physical communities, centering Indigenous voices and representations, disrupting public spheres, and creating communities of change." Bronwyn Carlson (Aboriginal born on D'harawal Country) and Ryan Frazer add to this discussion in chapter three by foregrounding how "the disruptive force of social media has provided powerful pathways through which Indigenous collectives can express and enact political agency, in a context where this agency has been violently suppressed."

Indigenous Women's Voices and Activism

I am primarily concerned in this chapter with exploring how Indigenous women's activism and voices have grounded frameworks of social justice in and through social media activism. Indigenous women's activism leads the way in (re)claiming land, life, history, and futures from early memoirs and autobiographies written by Indigenous women to the contemporary intervention of Indigenous women on social media. Some of the earliest writings that centered Indigenous perspectives and humanized Indigenous lives and stories were written by women. Sarah Winnemucca (Northern Paiute) and Lucy Thompson (Yurok) both wrote autobiographies in the late 1800s and early 1900s, respectively. Queen Liliuokalani (Kanaka Maoli) wrote political materials that asserted Hawaiian sovereignty while also demonstrating her ties to Hawaiian culture and history in the 1800s. Zitkala-Sa (Yankton Sioux) wrote autobiographical accounts with early publications in *Atlantic Monthly* beginning in 1900. These works would become foundational to early interventions by Indigenous writers and remain foundational to ongoing Indigenous writing and scholarship.

While there has been and continues to be an ongoing resurgence of Indigenous women's voices in writing, social media, and activist movements, this is not the case for most popular media, government representative bodies, law and policy institutes, task forces, or even agencies or organizations. The Native woman in the public imagination remains stuck in the past, voiceless, and seemingly representative of a conquered land and peoples. She is also heteronormative, attractive according to Western ideals and standards, and never representative of complex identities. Joanne Barker (Lenape, citizen of the Delaware Tribe of Indians) argues, "The insistent repetition of the racially gendered and sexualized image—of a particular kind of Indian woman/femininity and Indian man/masculinity—and its succession by contrite, defensive apologies laced with insult is neither a craze nor a gaffe. It is a racially gendered and sexed snapshot, a still image of a movingly malleable narrative of Indigenous womanhood/femininity and manhood/masculinity that reenacts Indigenous people's lack of knowledge and power over their own culture and identity in an inherently imperialist and colonialist world" (Barker, 2017, p. 2).

The imagined Native woman becomes the only acceptable Native woman, while actual Native women are rarely invited to represent themselves in national media and movies or as authors, writers, radio personalities, and so on. This can have dire effects for Native peoples as Barker points out: "Because international and state recognition of Indigenous rights as predicated on the cultural authenticity of a certain kind of Indigeneity, the costumed affiliations undermine the legitimacy of Indigenous claims to sovereignty and self-determination by rendering Indigenous culture and identity obsolete but for the costume" (2017, p. 3).

Settler identity can be created and is consistently re-created only through the settler imaginary, which "others" and "sexualizes" Indigenous and Black bodies. It is because of a settler colony built on gendered violence, as explained by Tiffany (Lethabo) King, that spatial processes are essential to settlement "which includes the clearing/genocide of Native bodies, the self-actualization of the Settler and the making of property taken up when theorizing Blackness in the 'New World'" (King, 2013, p. 2). Dehumanization of the "other" continues in order to justify ongoing occupation but also to create settler spaces, spaces that must erase Native present and presence. As King notes, "The inseparability of genocide and settlement force me to orient my examinations of the production of space in ways that always index the disappearance of the native. . . . In order to make space, people and their ways of existing are being erased" (2013, p. 8) This chapter explores Indigenous women's voices on Twitter and centers how Indigenous women use social media to dismantle and shift dominant narratives and settler-colonial claims to legitimacy through a type of storytelling that (re)claims and (re)stories land, life, and history to not only "make space" but also create new spaces of connection and "radial relationality." I explore how Indigenous women utilize social media to (re)center discourses of Indigenous presence and present and build connections to land and history.

Recentering Indigenous Presence, "Radical Relationality," and Twitter

How we connect Indigenous voices and stories to contemporary Indigenous issues is an important intervention into the imagined and also delimited spaces and geographies created and (re)created via mass media, social media, and online media and mediums. This (re)claiming of voice is an important intervention into ongoing issues that usually do not center Indigenous peoples' let alone Indigenous women's voices, yet many of these issues are clearly impacting Indigenous women. Rachel Flowers (Leeyq'sun) writes, "The story of the settler colony is founded on disappearing peoples, from terra nullius to missing and murdered Indigenous women. Colonialism operates as a form of structured dispossession and the current relationship between Indigenous peoples and the state is part of that continuum. Ongoing extractionist politics continue to inform our place-based arts of resistance and critiques in our struggles not only for land but also informed by the land" (2015, p. 42). Seneca scholar Mishuana Goeman explores how Indigenous writers "mediate and refute colonial organizing of land, bodies, and social and political landscapes" (2013, p. 3). I also explore how Indigenous women public figures are engaging in social media to mediate, refute, negotiate, and (re)assert Indigenous relationships, decolonization, and (re)indigenization. I am interested in approaching how Indigenous women on social media negotiate refusal and when or where they assert, as Audra Simpson (Kahnawake Mohawk) writes, "a political and ethical stance that stands in stark contrast to the desire to have one's distinctiveness as a culture, as a people, recognized" (Simpson, 2014, p. 11). I am conscious of and also grappling with Leanne Simpson's (Michi Saagiig Nishnaabeg) theorizing on how social media may disrupt or dispossess relationships and land as much as, if not more than, it connects and (re)asserts. How do we negotiate digital colonial spaces? And, as Simpson asks in her book *As We Have Always Done*, "How are we generating theory as praxis on the internet?" (2017, p. 223). My engagement with social media activism asks that we understand how we are advocates for decolonization who must refuse our positionality as "other" to social media, public discourse, and public engagement and instead center how we "open up space within our work to reflect upon and help shape the complex and contradictory cacophonies of these struggles, which abound with dynamic materialities and forces that exceed the internal locus of individual healing and the limited agenda of viewing academic research as a vocation for consciousness raising" (Yazzie and Baldy, 2018, p. 2).

I will begin here with some of my favorite tweets from the #DearNonNatives hashtag:

> Dear Non Natives—Don't compare me to Pocahontas. She was a child who endured rape & brainwashing—she shouldn't be the only Native you know.
> Dear Non Natives—U.S. Colonialism structurally destroys everyone through the imperial violences of race, class, gender.
> Dear Non Natives—Please don't dress up as "Indians" for Halloween. We are people, not costumes.
> Dear Non Natives—If you consider yourself an ally—do work—educate yourself. An ally requires knowledge of the people you are supporting.

At the end of summer 2015, this hashtag started trending on Twitter. #DearNonNatives would go on to bring a national spotlight to the contemporary voices and contemporary issues of Native peoples who would use this opportunity to tweet about stereotypes, historical inaccuracies, sovereignty, health care issues, and survivance. Brook Spotted Eagle (Oceti Sakonwin, Ihanktonwan D/Nakota), a graduate student in anthropology at the University of Washington, started this hashtag with an early afternoon tweet on July 31, 2015: "Dear non Natives," she wrote. "Natives are not extinct. We're still surviving genocide."

In 1987, when Vine Deloria Jr. (Standing Rock Sioux) wrote a follow-up preface for his 1969 seminal text *Custer Died for Your Sins: An Indian Manifesto*, he included a call to action for Native peoples to create a public discourse on Indian issues:

> The Indian task of keeping an informed public available to assist the tribes in their efforts to survive is never ending, and so the central message of this book, that Indians are alive, have certain dreams of their own, and are being overrun by the ignorance and mistaken, misdirected efforts of those who would help them, can never be repeated too often. Every generation of Indians will have to assume this burden which all divergent minorities bear, and many additional books on this subject will have to be written correcting misconceptions and calling attitudes to account. I hope this book can continue to make its contribution to the task of keeping American Indians before the American public and on the American domestic agenda. (p. xiii)

Building an "informed public," whether through writing, filmmaking, interviews, radio, art, public engagement, or other mediums, has continued not only through activist movements but also through websites, social media, and online media. Native people have continued to be generous with their time, energy, and labor, often engaging in things like curriculum development, easy-to-digest history lessons, public presentations and testimonies, or even websites and other resources for the general public to "learn more" about Native people or to "get the real history."

The education of settler subjects or even the intervention on settler narratives is part of how Indigenous women social media activists navigate public scholarship. Adrienne Keene (Cherokee, @nativeapprops), author of the popular blog Native Appropriations, has created numerous short articles that explore issues of Native representation and cultural appropriation. Keene began her blog in 2010 and has since become a leading voice on Twitter, often providing context to her many followers about issues affecting Native peoples that are currently making headlines. Her posts on Johnny Depp as Tonto, her analysis of mascots, and her attempts to educate through public scholarship about the disrespectful use of headdresses are well-known. Keene focuses on media representation and is currently the cohost of one of the most popular Indigenous-led podcasts, "All My Relations," which she hosts with Matika Wilbur, another well-known Native public figure. The podcast is an extension of Keene and Wilbur's work, focusing on important issues like food sovereignty, appropriation, and Columbus, but also engaging with the field of Native and Indigenous studies and building conversations that are specifically located in Indigenous epistemologies and frameworks. The podcast often invites scholars and community advocates to participate. It has built a large following and provides one example of a change in Keene's public facing scholarship, where many of these recorded conversations feel more directed toward Indigenous audiences with less focus on trying to educate or convince the "the general public" to care about Indigenous issues.

Keene has also been a key voice in building resources for use by the general public. She was an instrumental part of a collaboration with other Cherokee scholars Rebecca Nagle (@rebeccanagle) and Joseph M. Pierce (@pepepierce) to compose a "Syllabus: Elizabeth Warren, Cherokee Citizenship and DNA Testing." This syllabus was written "to frame the recent claims to Cherokee ancestry by US Senator Elizabeth Warren as part of a longer history of cultural appropriation, erasure, and settler colonialism. Warren's claims reveal the pervasive influence of biological essentialism—through the supposed certainty of DNA testing—in the globalized present" (Keene, Nagle, and Pierce, 2018). It was shared primarily via social media and became one very pointed response to the ongoing attempts by mass media to silence Indigenous critiques of Senator Elizabeth Warren as she began her campaign for the 2020 Democratic nomination for president. This may well be some of the most sustained critique of Warren and is being led primarily by Cherokee voices, with dignity and insight that continues despite the fact that mass media has yet to fully engage with these voices or critiques.

Along with this sustained critique and response to Warren is the centering of Indigenous voices that are dismantling discourses of "DNA testing" and Indigenous identity via social media. Access to a wider public audience and also pointed attacks on Indigenous peoples via social media platforms by many of Warren's own supporters resulted in numerous #NativeTwitter users providing research and scholarship that debunks DNA testing as a signifier of Indigenous identity. While this scholarship has been well-known and respected for several years in Indigenous studies, the engagement with this on a wider public scale has been built through Kim TallBear's ongoing presence on Twitter. TallBear (Sisseton Wahpeton Oyate, @KimTallBear) is a professor and also author of *Native American DNA: Tribal Belonging and the False Promise of Genetic Science.* Her expertise as an Indigenous scientist is often called upon and referred to by several Twitter users. She is quoted and approached via Twitter for clarification on issues of DNA testing. With the Warren controversy she intervenes on discourses that would frame critiques of DNA testing as "anti-science." TallBear is also a leading scholar and theorist, able to engage her current work in Indigenous sexualities and erotics through the social media platform. She challenges her audience, whether Indigenous or not, to expand their idea of what Indigenous studies is and can be. Her voice brings Indigenous science firmly into the present but also demands complex engagement from her audience.

Nagle is another example of an Indigenous woman who utilizes social media and online media to (re)write and (re)right history and to tell stories that center Indigenous peoples, land, and futures. Online, she is a consistent voice highlighting ongoing issues of Indigenous resistance. Her podcast "This Land" provides "an in depth look at how a cut and dry murder case opened an investigation into half the land in Oklahoma and the treaty rights of five tribes." It garnered national attention and reviews ("This Land" 2017). Just recently it was announced that Nagle was awarded the 2020 American Mosaic Journalism Prize (Schilling, 2020). Nagel also engages significantly with discourses surrounding Native mascots. The 2020 Super Bowl, which featured the San Francisco 49ers and the Kansas City Chiefs, was another illustration of how mass media would not engage with the impacts this representation and portrayal of Native peoples would have in Native communities. It has been well documented through studies that Native youth exposed to Native mascots reported depressed self-esteem, diminished community worth, and "fewer achievement-related possible selves" (Fryberg et al., 2008). It has also been documented that when people are exposed to Native stereotypes they often do not distinguish between their feelings about Native mascots and actual Native American people (Chaney, Burke, and Burkley, 2011). Yet the ignorance of a general public to many of these foundational studies is staggering. The past few years of social media activism have seen Native women like Amanda Blackhorse, Tara Houska, and Jacqueline Keeler engage with #HashtagActivism and #Twitterstorms to deliberately organize opportunities to get certain hashtags trending on Twitter. #NotYourMascot trended on Super Bowl Sunday in 2014 and was a finalist for "Digital Trend of the Year" in Utah State University's Digital Folklore Project, which tracks digital trends each year. It was on the heels of this activist work to get a national conversation started on Twitter about Native mascots that Comedy Central's popular satiric news show *The Daily Show* featured a story on the Washington (racial slur team name) football team, which included Blackhorse, Houska, several members of the 1491s, artist Gregg Deal, and Native journalist Simon Moya-Smith. This was a watershed moment for Native representation on *The Daily Show* and for late-night TV (Baldy, 2016, p. 97). Buoyed by the support, online activists continued to push for a cultural shift in how we talk about mascots and representation. The #NotYourMascot hashtag would become a leading example of the potential of collective organizing in a social media space like Twitter.

Houska continues her social media engagement utilizing her large following from her work on mascots and her features in various magazines, at invited lectures, and as part of the first Bernie Sanders campaign for president in 2016 to also call attention to other ongoing issues. Houska was a part of the Standing Rock resistance movement, posting updates and information from on the ground. Keene would also visit and post to her large following about the Sacred Stone camp and Water Protectors and participate in passing along to her many thousands of followers the "Standing Rock Syllabus," another important intervention created by Indigenous scholars and community activists to help educate the public about Standing Rock and the ongoing fights for return of ancestral lands and protection of our more-than-human relations.

Angela Starritt (Gitxsan Nation/Amsiwa, @AngelaSterritt) is an award-winning Canadian Broadcast Corporation journalist who utilizes her growing Twitter platform to call attention to stories about Indigenous peoples in order to gain support for direct actions. Her connections with CBC mean that she is often passing on stories that are already being covered by CBC, but her close following by several Indigenous peoples also ensures that these stories remain as leading reports across social media platforms. Starritt brings to the forefront Indigenous voices and stories that are meant to engage Indigenous peoples in dialogue with media and to bring attention to Indigenous issues that are immediate threats to community well-being. Starritt is reporting on stories but also helping to highlight voices of marginalized Indigenous peoples who may not otherwise have access to a worldwide audience.

Conclusion

This is only an introduction to a select group of Indigenous women who engage social media as a space of ongoing Indigenous resistance. Often on Twitter, users will create and share lists of Indigenous voices to follow in order to help grow this online community. It is made obvious by these growing lists that Indigenous voices around the world are engaging in active spatial survivance and intervening on public discourse as a means to disrupt and dismantle "popular narratives" that would continue to silence and dismiss Native peoples. These acts of survivance and representation are important as a global audience continues to grapple with how ongoing structures of settler colonialism and white supremacy inform not only media and pop culture but also policy, law, and political status.

How Indigenous women have engaged and also negotiated their presence and refusal via social media is an important illustration of how the ongoing work of understanding Indigenous resurgence is part of a contemporary landscape that includes digital, social, and online mediums. The interventions that we, as public intellectuals, produce must be conscious of how the negotiation of digital colonial spaces can be problematic and can further uphold the state as authority and arbiter of recognition and identity. I return here to Leanne

Simpson, who in her book *As We Have Always Done* reflects on the reliance of the Idle No More movement on social media engagement: "I wonder in hindsight if maybe we didn't build a movement, but rather we build a social media presence that privileged individuals over community, virtual validation over empathy, leadership without accountability and responsibility, and unchecked liberalism that has now left us more vulnerable to the superficial recognition of the neoliberal state?" (2017, p. 223). She cautions us, "There are no bodies on the Internet. There is no land. Insertion of Indigeneity in cyberspace is not insertion of Indigeneity in the physical world" (p. 221). She asks, "How are we generating theory as praxis on the internet?" (p. 223). Ongoing discussions among #NativeTwitter have included critiques about how building a popular following often leads toward "gatekeeping," where certain voices are elevated and centered while others are never invited to join this conversation. It is important that we consider the role of popular public Indigenous scholars and activists to build intersectional, interrelated movements that value the diversity of Indigenous voices. As I consider these and other important questions, I pause to recognize some of the Indigenous women's voices on Twitter who have inspired me by creating spaces of "radical relationality" via Twitter like Chelsea Vowell (Métis, @apihtawikosisan), Melanie Yazzie (Navajo, @melanie_yazzie), and Erica Violet Lee (Nēhiyaw, @EricaVioletLee). As Yazzie and Baldy assert, "Radical relationality is, after all, simply the ontology of keeping ourselves open to the possibility of making new relatives as one of the essential functions of life and, indeed, decolonization" (2018, p. 11). Vowell, Yazzie, and Lee, along with Zoe Todd (Métis, @ZoeSTodd) and others, have gestured toward spatial formations of decolonization via social media by centering voices and conversations that are primarily concerned with radical relationality, theory building, and radical imagination. Rather than focus on how Indigenous voices can "disrupt" and "interrupt" settler theories, actions, or even stereotypes and belief systems, Indigenous peoples across social media are (re)claiming presence and present for each other and finding ways to engage and sustain each other beyond the margins. In some cases we can see theory being built in and through relationships that are engaged across the Twitterverse. Some of these women I have never met in real life; others I have met only as a result of my reaching out to them via Twitter; stills others I have engaged with in deeply personal, often generative conversations through Twitter replies and messages. As we continue to build theory and praxis across these digital mediums, I hope that we can utilize our radical relationality to center the voices of some of our most marginalized Indigenous peoples and that our radical relationality includes a turn toward radical scholarship and radical decolonial praxis that not only spends our time "talking back" or "educating the general public" but instead creates generative theories of decolonization whether with social media or because of the connections we have started via social media.

In March 2015, Brook Spotted Eagle answered this call in her own way when she began tweeting with the hashtag #DearNativeYouth. #DearNativeYouth started as a rallying cry, to reach out through social media to say "we are here" and "we are everywhere" and we matter.

> Dear Native Youth—Let no one but yourself define who you are, where you
>   came from, or where you are headed. Your perseverance belongs to you.
> I have heard kids as young as 9 talk about suicide. Dear Native
>   Youth—We love you and appreciate you and want to support you.
>   #It takes a community.
> Dear Native Youth—Don't be swayed by what mainstream media
>   considered natives to be like. Be you and not anyone else. Let your
>   voice be heard.
> Dear Native Youth—You are loved beyond measure.

References

Arnold, J. (2016, September 7). User clip: Obama on Dakota Access Pipeline. C-Span. https://www.c-span.org/video/?c4619223/user-clip-obama-dakota-access-pipeline.

Baldy, C. R. (2016). The new Native intellectualism: #ElizabethCook-Lynn, social media movements, and the millennial Native American studies scholar. *Wicazo Sa Review, 31*(1), 90–110.

Barker, J. (Ed.). (2017). *Critically sovereign: Indigenous gender, sexuality, and feminist studies.* Durham, NC: Duke University Press.

Chaney, J., Burke, A., and Burkley, E. (2011). Do American Indian mascots = American Indian people? Examining implicit bias towards American Indian people and American Indian mascots. *American Indian and Alaska Native Mental Health Research, 18*(1), 42–62.

Deloria, V., Jr. (1969). *Custer died for your sins: An Indian manifesto.* Norman: University of Oklahoma Press.

Estes, N. (2019). *Our history is the future: Standing Rock versus the Dakota Access Pipeline, and the long tradition of Indigenous resistance.* New York: Verso.

Ferguson, M. R. (2018). Native youth contributions to Indigenous sovereignty and climate justice in the #noDAPL movement (Honors thesis, Bates College). https://scarab.bates.edu/honorstheses/256.

Flowers, R. (2015). Refusal to forgive: Indigenous women's love and rage. *Decolonization: Indigeneity, Education and Society, 4*(2), 32–49.

Fryberg, S. A., Markus, H. R., Oyserman, D., and Stone, J. M. (2008). Of warrior chiefs and Indian princesses: The psychological consequences of American Indian mascots. *Basic and Applied Social Psychology, 30*(3), 208–218.

Goeman, M. (2013). *Mark my words: Native women mapping our nations.* Minneapolis: University of Minnesota Press.

Hinzo, A. M., and Clark, L. S. (2019). Digital survivance and Trickster humor: Exploring visual and digital Indigenous epistemologies in the# NoDAPL movement. *Information, Communication and Society, 22*(6), 791–807.

Johnson, H. (2017). # NoDAPL: Social media, empowerment, and civic participation at Standing Rock. *Library Trends, 66*(2), 155–175.

Keeler, J. (2014, December 9). #NotYourMascot finalist for digital trend of the year. *Daily Kos.* https://www.dailykos.com/stories/2014/12/9/1350397/—NotYourMascot-Finalist-for-Digital-Trend-of-the-Year.

Keene, A., R. Nagle, and J. Pierce. (2018, December 19). "Syllabus: Elizabeth Warren, Cherokee citizenship, and DNA testing." Critical Ethnic Studies, University of Minnesota Press. http://www.criticalethnicstudiesjournal.org/blog/2018/12/19/syllabus-elizabeth-warren-cherokee-citizenship-and-dna-testing

King, T. J. (2013). In the clearing: Black female bodies, space and settler colonial landscapes. (Doctoral dissertation, University of Maryland.)

Meyer, M., and Waddell, K. (2016, October 31). Did the "check-in at Standing Rock" campaign start with protesters? *Atlantic.* https://www.theatlantic.com/technology/archive/2016/10/facebook-is-overtaken-with-check-ins-to-standing-rock/505988/.

Schilling, V. (2020, February 6). Cherokee author awarded $100,000 for journalism excellence. *Indian Country Today.* https://newsmaven.io/indiancountrytoday/news/cherokee-author-awarded-100-000-for-journalism-excellence-z-2FS1xSRkmE2HFP2cVH0A.

Simpson, A. (2014). *Mohawk interruptus: Political life across the borders of settler states.* Durham, NC: Duke University Press.

Simpson, L. B. (2017). *As we have always done: Indigenous freedom through radical resistance.* Minneapolis: University of Minnesota Press.

Smith, L. T. (2012 [1999]). *Decolonizing methodologies: Research and Indigenous peoples.* London: Zed Books.

Sottile, C. A. (2016, January 6). Dakota Access Pipeline fight watched on Facebook Live around world. *NBC News.* https://www.nbcnews.com/storyline/dakota-pipeline-protests/dakota-access-pipeline-fight-watched-facebook-live-around-world-n678366.

This Land. (2017). Crooked. https://crooked.com/podcast-series/this-land/.

Wong, J. C. (2016, November 21). Standing Rock protest: Hundreds clash with police over Dakota Access Pipeline. *Guardian.* https://www.theguardian.com/us-news/2016/nov/21/standing-rock-protest-hundreds-clash-with-police-over-dakota-access-pipeline.

Worland, J. (2016, October 31). Dakota Access Pipeline: Facebook check in supports protests. *Time.* https://time.com/4551866/facebook-dakota-access-pipeline-check-in/.

Yazzie, M. K., and Baldy, C. R. (2018). Introduction: Indigenous peoples and the politics of water. *Decolonization, Indigeneity, Education, and Society, 7*(1), 1–18.

9

The Rise of Black Rainbow

■■■■■■■■■■■■■■■■■■■■■

Queering and Indigenizing
Digital Media Strategies,
Resistance, and Change

ANDREW FARRELL

Indigenous LGBTIQ+ (lesbian, gay, bisexual, transgender, intersex, and queer) uses of social media cohere to the political demands of specific geopolitical locations (Duarte, 2017, p. 9). In Australia, Indigenous LGBTIQ+ peoples are working at the margins to identify and address significant social, cultural, and political disparities that ignore the community's existence and its complex and unique needs. In response, Indigenous LGBTIQ+ political activisms take a myriad of approaches that agitate for change under the conditions of a heterosexual, cisgendered, patriarchal settler-colonial society (Hodge, 2015, p. 264). This chapter explores the historical context that influences contemporary political mobilities of Indigenous LGBTIQ+ peoples, from protest to social media, from the 1970s onward. Shifting social, cultural, and political events have shaped our understanding of the status of LGBTIQ+ Aboriginal Torres Strait Islander peoples. This chapter explores Aboriginal and Torres Strait Islander LGBTIQ+ contributions to the Sydney Mardi Gras parade and festival from its grassroots beginnings and ongoing inclusion and exclusion in the event.

Across this history, the Aboriginal Torres Strait Islander LGBTIQ+ community also responded to the HIV+ AIDS crisis by forming a visible response to issues affecting First Nations peoples. I also discuss how these movements have been constituted through allied negotiations of place, space, and cultural autonomy. Finally, I discuss the new frontier of LGBTIQ+ political activism through social media including the activist group Queers for Reconciliation and the work of Black Rainbow, a Facebook group and emergent organization that identifies and provides a national advocacy platform and touchpoint for Aboriginal and Torres Strait Islander LGBTIQ+ peoples (blackrainbow .org.au). This chapter emphasizes the agency, equity, and justice sought by LGBTIQ+ Aboriginal and Torres Strait Islander peoples whose labor has often been underrepresented, fragmented, silenced, and forgotten. The continued prevalence of social media activism demonstrates the ongoing achievements of LGBTIQ+ Aboriginal and Torres Strait Islander peoples in broader social, cultural, and political developments.

History

To understand aspects of contemporary LGBTIQ+ Aboriginal and Torres Strait Islander activism we must recognize First Nations lesbian and gay activism and emergent transgender activism across social movements of the past fifty years. Indigenous involvement in urban gay and lesbian movements and the development of allied and autonomous social, political, and cultural organizing brings attention to the complex and intersecting relationships between Aboriginal and Torres Strait Islander, LGBTIQ+, and Aboriginal and Torres Strait Islander LGBTIQ+ histories.[1] These histories are challenging in the sense that there are many variables, silences, and limited primary historical records and detailed oral and written histories. Indigenous LGBTIQ+ histories are extrapolated from information made available by Aboriginal and Torres Strait Islander LGBTIQ+ peoples who have been persistently vocal, visible, and politically active. Aboriginal and Torres Strait Islander LGBTIQ+ histories are histories of flexible solidarity. As well as those on the front line, this is a history of communities who organized behind the scenes, on the "down low" and in closets, made creative and financial contributions, and undertook important familial and allied roles of support. These are unspoken yet vital components missing in the limited resources that inform how we may know the extent of this history.

Aboriginal and Torres Strait Islander gay and lesbian issues gained recognition through gay and lesbian activism from the late 1970s onward. Following race, feminist, and antiwar social movements, queer communities politically organized in mostly urban spaces where gay and lesbian communities were established. In the late 1970s, these communities conducted significant rallies and demonstrations that highlighted the experiences of gay peoples, notably the 1978 gay solidarity marches that led to the now nationally celebrated Sydney Gay and Lesbian Mardi Gras parade (Russell, 2017). These movements highlighted the violence and discrimination experienced by lesbian and gay people as well as organizing against issues such as the criminalization of homosexuality, which was a criminal offence up until 1984 in New South Wales. These local and national movements grew in response to LGBTIQ+ political movements abroad such as the Stonewall Riots of 1969. Through the platform of racial, sexual, and gendered equality, Indigenous issues were incorporated into the urban gay movements in Sydney from their early stages. The 1978 demonstration organized by Sydney's Gay Solidarity Group protested police brutality, chanting "stop police attacks on gays, women, and blacks" (Arrow, 2018, p. 496). This was led, in part, by Aboriginal women such as Chris Burke and Annie Pratten, who are named among the founding protestors now dubbed the '78ers (Russell, 2017). In the years to follow, the protests became an annual gay and lesbian pride march and evolved into a culturally significant parade and festival that displays Australia's LGBTIQ+ community. Aboriginal and Torres Strait Islander peoples did not have prominent visibility in Mardi Gras until the first Aboriginal marching group was included in 1980 and the first float, the Captain Cook float, appeared in its 1988 procession. Kalkatungu, Eastern Arrernte, and Alyawarre person Wilo Muwadda notes that the Captain Cook float "made a real statement about who we were and put us [Aboriginal peoples] into the gay community in a strong position" (Russell, 2017). The Captain Cook float was displayed in response to the 1988 bicentennial in which Australia marked two hundred years of occupation. Australia Day celebrations were met by one of the largest Indigenous protests in history, which challenged the celebration by highlighting that, for Aboriginal and Torres Strait Islander peoples, it has been two hundred years since invasion.

LGBTIQ+ Aboriginal and Torres Strait Islander participation in Mardi Gras became a common feature in the procession by the 1990s. During the time, various Indigenous entries emphasized and resonated with broader political issues while simultaneously injecting the parade with racial and cultural pride. The parade saw various floats and marching groups displaying topics such as identity, racism, treaty, inclusion, equality, freedom, and survival. Parade entries such as the First Nations: Freedom is Our Passion float celebrated the fiftieth anniversary of the NSW Freedom Rides movement, an Indigenous-led movement against racial segregation in regional and rural NSW in the 1960s that was also a response to African American protests of the same name (History of the First Peoples entries in the Sydney Mardi Gras Parade). Although Indigenous representation in Mardi Gras has expanded over time, it must be recognized that it took roughly a decade for the parade to host an Indigenous float. It wasn't until the early 2000s, over twenty years later, that the parade was led by an Aboriginal float entry as a Welcome to Country. Varying anecdotal evidence commends Mardi Gras for its role in inclusion, however Indigenous exclusion in ongoing LGBTIQ+ movements challenges the dominant narrative of progress, diversity, and acceptance. This is emphasized by the work of current Aboriginal LGBTIQ+ activists who argue that Aboriginal and Torres Strait Islander issues are deemed "too political" and outside of the agenda of current protests, which continue to fail racial minority experiences and concerns (Clark, 2017).

The exclusion of Aboriginal and Torres Strait Islander peoples in pride movements is reflected in the concerning acceptance of police, corporations, and the political right in the parade. The increasing presence of the police in pride marches is particularly concerning for Aboriginal and Torres Strait Islander peoples who face multiple forms of systematic discrimination and high rates of incarceration and deaths in custody. Transgender Aboriginal woman Veronica Baxter died in custody "three days after Mardi Gras. . . . [She] was arrested by Redfern police and held on remand at the all-male NSW Silverwater Metropolitan Reception and Remand Centre. Six days later, after a 14-hour break between checking her cell, she was found dead, hanging in her single cell" (J.D. 2011). There is still no justice for Baxter, her family, or her community. Only small factions of the community remembered her and mourned her loss and are still calling for answers. Indigenous queer activists have not forgotten and continue to highlight the complicity of pride organizations to the ongoing silence around justice for Indigenous transgender women and LGBTIQ+ peoples broadly. Unthinkably, the movement has chosen to encourage and allow authorities to march alongside community without considering the duty of care required for those statistically more vulnerable to police violence (Clark, 2017). Pride parades have become hostile and unsafe for sections of its communities. The political core of these movements has become increasingly commodified with major corporations sponsoring parade entries. The continued disparities faced by parts of our communities are ignored in favor of a façade of acceptance and less threatening political messages. Beyond this, community have self-determined and claimed space for Indigenous LGBTIQ+ peoples through events such as *Koorigras*—a stream of culturally centered events such as gallery openings, performances, and social events that continue to highlight Indigenous LGBTIQ+ pride.

The threat of HIV+ AIDS had a significant impact on Aboriginal and Torres Strait Islander LGBTIQ+ peoples across this time. Vital political solidarities among Indigenous gay and transgender peoples emerged out of the exclusionary suffering of racial and sexual discrimination of the time. Indigenous gay and transgender peoples from across the country came to Hamilton Downs Northern Territory, between October 31 and November 4, 1994, and formed the Anwernekenhe Conference, which challenged health organizations to recognize that "gay ATSI HIV+ men . . . are dying alone and in shame, often rejected by their families and communities and marginalised within the gay communities" (Koori Mail). Anwernekenhe campaigned around gay Aboriginal men's (and later on transgender and lesbian) issues, which included the recognition of racial and sexual discrimination, stigma, and exclusion within the already volatile and fearful social environment. This was compounded by taboos within Indigenous communities where the disease was articulated as the white man's disease (Gays and Lesbians Aboriginal Alliance, 1993; Hodge, 2015, p. 147). Gay Indigenous activists such as Narrunga and Kaurna man Rodney Junga-Williams came out as HIV-positive and rallied against early scare campaigns and reluctance within the Aboriginal community to get tested and to resist the deep shame associated with HIV+ AIDS (Hodge, 2015, pp. 138–143). He fought among the ranks of gay, lesbian, and transgender Aboriginal and Torres Strait Islander peoples across the nation to get Indigenous people on the agenda of relevant agencies, organizations, and groups responding to the HIV+ AIDS epidemic. Their labor mediated the unspoken spaces between community divides in order to survive against a disease that did not discriminate by race, class, or sexuality.

The Aboriginal and Torres Strait Islander response to HIV+ AIDS produced important texts that intervened in academic discourse on Indigenous identity. Indigenous gay and lesbian perspectives published the chapter "Peopling the Empty Mirror: The Prospects for Lesbian and Gay Aboriginal History" (Gays and Lesbians Aboriginal Alliance, 1993). It was the first published account of Aboriginal gay and lesbian people that outlined various contemporary social, political, and cultural concerns. Their approach to these conversations is framed by coalition building, as the authors are both Indigenous and non-Indigenous. Through a shared politics of reconciliation, the group developed a critique on the broader structural issues between Indigenous and non-Indigenous queers in particular (Hodge, 2015, p. 17). The text positions white LGBTIQ+ peoples as accountable to the microcosm of racial dominance in presumably shared and safe spaces where they perform their power and privilege against those without. This critique of whiteness within the LGBTIQ+ community is vital as it locates the many ways in which racialized violence occurs within the queer community. Riggs (2006) argues that white queers are not outside of oppression and suggests that in formulating discussions of advocacy in the Australian context we must interrogate and bring to account the existence of white privilege and an acknowledgment of the enactment of these privileges that persistently dominate LGBTIQ+ politics. These criticisms, when applied to early literature on LGBTIQ+ Aboriginal and Torres Strait Islander peoples, raise important questions about the role of non-Indigenous people in the emergence of Indigenous LGBTIQ+ politics, benevolent and otherwise. Riggs highlights that incommensurable racial and cultural differences between Indigenous and non-Indigenous peoples are an added obstacle that can overburden Indigenous LGBTIQ+ causes. This is to not entirely discount or discourage non-Indigenous allies but to suggest that they become aware, responsible, and accountable to the unnecessary strain they may contribute to the ongoing political advancement of Indigenous LGBTIQ+ peoples.

Beyond navigating relationships with non-Indigenous LGBTIQ+ communities, Indigenous LGBTIQ+ peoples have formed important transnational and translocal solidarities and shared cultural space (Harris and Prout-Quicke, 2019). Aboriginal and Torres Strait Islander LGBTIQ+ peoples have expressed their connection to movements of Indigenous LGBTIQ+ peoples elsewhere. The Gay and Lesbian Aboriginal Alliance identifies the important advocacy and scholarship of Two Spirit peoples on Turtle Island (United States) as inspiring and emboldening their cause (Gays and Lesbians Aboriginal Alliance, 1993, p. 11). Cross-cultural relationships between Indigenous LGBTIQ+ peoples form solidarities that potentially enable critical mass, visibility, and resistance. Morgensen (2011, p. 211) highlights the connection of transnational relationships between Indigenous LGBTIQ+ peoples, which have demonstrably improved the position of Indigenous LGBTIQ peoples, in particular the achievements of Indigenous queer health workers who secured important positions within health organizations across Turtle Island (United States and Canada), the Pacific, and Australia in response to HIV+ AIDS. These positions were utilized to undertake important forms of leadership and governance, facilitating geographically specific efforts to decolonize gender and sexuality. These roles continue to have relevance as positions that are used to advocate against homophobia and transphobia, and model acceptance within and across First Nations communities. Cherokee (noncitizen) scholar Qwo-Li Driskill (2010, p. 73) highlights that Two-Spirit and queer Native people are integrated into larger Indigenous worldviews and their roles within have the potential to mend and transform the relationship between Native communities and Two-Spirit and queer peoples under the shared spaces of settler-colonialism.

Australia is home to hundreds of sovereign Indigenous nations and territories. Across precolonial and postcontact periods, Indigenous people have produced and continue to contribute to unique genders and sexualities whose complex cultural interrelation spans tens of thousands of years. The reincorporation of sexually and gender diverse perspectives into Indigenous political activism means questioning and challenging Western heteropatriarchy, which is identified by Morgensen as a genocidal force that methodically attempts to isolate, disregard, and eliminate Native LGBTIQ+ peoples (2011, p. 23). Indigenous LGBTIQ+ people challenge a narrowing cis-heterosexist view of history by asserting that sexual and gender variations have always existed. These claims are reinforced by LGBTIQ+ Aboriginal and Torres Strait Islander peoples who argue that "Indigenous societies have, in some known cases, histories of acknowledging and celebrating gender diversity, recognising that people may not exist as one of two genders, rather, there is a multiplicity of gender identities" (Sullivan and Day, 2019, p. 2). Recognition of these diversities exists through terms such as "Sistergirl" and "Brotherboy," which culturally affirm Aboriginal and Torres Strait Islander trans and gender diverse experiences of gender.

Memory and Representation

Claims that validate Indigenous gender and sexual diversities demand significant and ongoing engagement and effort. From personal to group and community approaches, a sustained push toward a recognition of sexual and gender diversity of Indigenous peoples within Australia includes a continued investment in the politics of representation. Bundjalung queer scholar Maddee Clark argues that Indigenous queers are experiencing a crisis of "recognition" that has demanded that we, Indigenous LGBTIQ+ peoples, "articulate our identities within the colonial queer and trans communities in which we live and relate" (Clark, 2015, p. 2). Murri woman Wendy Dunn/Holland discusses these political tensions as they arise between Indigenous and non-Indigenous lesbians whose desires and aspirations diverge through cultural difference.[2] As an Aboriginal and lesbian-identified woman, Dunn's efforts to forge allegiances with non-Indigenous lesbians has resulted in her feeling like an outsider. She disagrees with various aspects of lesbian separatism that disregards Indigenous ways of knowing and being, particularly the distinct ways that Aboriginal and Torres Strait Islander peoples value and practice community and family. Dunn's observation and response rests in a politics that exists beyond the scope of white lesbian and feminist politics. While sympathetic to elements of lesbian politics, the reconciling of Indigenous political interests with them serves as a juncture in which she articulates the need to provide practical change to center First Nations politics (Gays and Lesbians Aboriginal Alliance, 1993, p. 7). This involves the employment of memory as a decolonial tool where Indigenous LGBTIQ+ politics recall and critique past policies and interventions that have had an impact on our gendered and sexual sovereignties, an impact that we have yet to fully uncover and recover.

Running parallel to the labor of LGBTIQ+ Indigenous peoples to recover our histories and critically engage in memory is the continued maintenance of amnesia about Indigenous experiences broadly. One of the ways that Indigenous LGBTIQ+ experiences are silenced and forgotten is through avenues in which knowledge about Indigenous peoples may be transmitted. Wiradjuri transgender/genderqueer-identified scholar Dr. Sandy O'Sullivan (2015) argues that Indigenous peoples operate within a "guest paradigm" in colonial institutions such as museums, which curate, govern, and dictate representations of

Indigenous peoples. First Nations LGBTIQ+ activists seek to push the boundaries of representation in search for justice against institutions that placate a centralizing ontology where colonial ideas about Indigenous peoples, genders, and sexualities are accepted and normalized. This includes the naturalizing of gender binaries, heterosexuality, and whiteness as social, cultural, and political defaults across settler-colonial contexts. The normalizing of identities through representational and symbolic avenues extends beyond physical public spaces such as museums and into the digital terrain. In the past decade, digital media platforms have taken to the topic of Indigenous gender and sexual diversities with great interest and in doing so have engaged in the discursive production and reproduction of Indigenous gender and sexuality. Media articles identifying, for example, Two-Spirit identity in Turtle Island (United States and Canada) have been circulated online. These texts have the potential to bring social momentum to the argument that Indigenous people globally had non-heterosexual, non-monogamous, and non-cisgender identities prior to colonization. The texts do this by re-presenting Indigenous practices of sexual and gender variations, which Baylis argues is a resistance of "the shackling forces of colonisation . . . imbuing new symbols through a language of Queer-Aboriginal expression" (2014).

Yawuru scholar Dodson (1994) points to the ways that non-Indigenous audiences filter Indigenous knowledge and experience for their own purposes. The public interest in Indigenous gender and sexual diversity has produced new challenges to community where depictions of Indigenous gender and sexuality are sometimes repackaged to convey new knowledge about Indigenous expressions of identity, culture, and history. For example, a radio segment titled "Native Americans Recognise Two Spirits and Five Genders" used a byline that reads "before European settlement, all Native American societies acknowledged three to five gender roles: Female, male, Two Spirit female, Two Spirit male and transgendered" (Lucy, 2017). At a glance, the text makes inaccurate claims that are vague and homogenizing, producing seemingly positive stereotypes of widespread acceptance of gender and sexual diversity. Texts often produce a homogeneous, consumable, and romanticized Indigenous genderfluid archetype while ignoring the potential of varied permutations of gender across time and space. While containing some valuable insight into some Indigenous articulations of gender and sexuality, public dissemination brings new challenges to Indigenous peoples. Dodson argues, "In making our self-representation public . . . we risk appropriation and abuse, and a danger that a selection of our representations will be used to once again fix Aboriginality into absolute and inflexible terms. . . . However, without our own voices, Aboriginality will continue to be a creation for and about us. This is all the more reason to insist that we have control over both the form and content of representation" (1994, p. 39).

Social Media

One of the first, if not the first, websites devoted to Indigenous LGBTIQ+ political activism was created by Queers for Reconciliation, an allied activist group of Indigenous and non-Indigenous queers in Sydney. It formed as a response to the *Wik* decision, a landmark legal claim to traditional lands by Aboriginal people in northern Queensland. The website is used to display the group's rationale and political motivation. It is also utilized as a space in which the group is able to promote and disseminate important materials relating to LGBTIQ+ Indigenous issues. Through glaringly loud rainbow text the home-page reads, "THIS SITE was developed to promote *Queers for Reconciliation*'s participation in Mardi Gras and will continue to be online as a contribution towards Reconciliation" (http://reconciliation.tripod.com). The site is a time capsule of a political movement largely organized offline. The group also uses the internet as a digital tactic to support groundwork such as collecting signatures for petitions (Duarte, 2017, p. 2). The site reproduces media articles, speeches, health reports, and various transcribed texts. What this group has created is a valuable representation that may be considered a digital "re-storying," the retelling of stories that interrupt dominant histories "in order to listen to Other stories . . . transform our collective futures . . . [and] contribute to movements for social justice" (Driskill, 2016, p. 3). The Queers for Reconciliation site demonstrates necessary changes in activist approaches as technology became available and accessible in Australia in the mid- to late 1990s. The website set the tone for future generations of online projects by demonstrating how technology can be useful in assisting and sustaining political movements, histories, and memories of LGBTIQ+ Aboriginal and Torres Strait Islander peoples so that "people [do not] forget those parts of history we have experienced, or are gone ourselves along with our memories and the yarns shared with us" (http://timbishop.com.au).

I have previously written on my personal involvement with the development of digital activism through Twitter, Facebook, and Wordpress as a queer-identified Aboriginal person (Farrell, 2017). Through conferences, events, and online activity, I acquired more incentive to work in the digital space both on- and offline. This is partially due to the possibilities of networking afforded on sites such as Facebook. As both Aboriginal and queer-identified, I still find it difficult to find safe, culturally affirming spaces, friendships, and community that are grounded in my physical location. Social media has enabled me to reach out, to connect with like-minded people who share similar but diverse cultural, sexual, and gendered experiences. Social media continues to have an impact in my life as I have invested time in the potential for social justice through my contribution to the group Black Rainbow. Within an increasingly tech-dependent and globalizing society, I value social media as a tool that has wide-reaching capacities. Through Black Rainbow, I have experienced the tangible ways that social media positively impacts Aboriginal and Torres Strait Islander LGBTIQ+ peoples.

Recent research on Indigenous uses of social media reflects the possibilities for embedding Indigenous subjectivities and transforming the digital landscape (Carlson, 2013). Current research on Indigenous peoples and social media demonstrates, particularly in the Australian context, that Aboriginal and Torres Strait Islander peoples are taking to social media platforms at a higher rate than the broader population (Carlson, 2013; Carlson and Frazer, 2018). The establishment of significant personal followings, social networking pages, and groups and a growing profile of Indigenous activists build a critical mass of Indigenous peoples online, a presence that is difficult to ignore. LGBTIQ+ Indigenous peoples are joining in the ranks of online social movements through social media profiles, pages, and groups. Autonomous and allied groups have surfaced online to accommodate advocacy, awareness, support, and social groups for LGBTIQ+ Aboriginal and Torres Strait Islander peoples including, but not limited to, Sistergirls and Brotherboys, Moolagoo Mob, Indigilez support group, First Nations Mardi Gras, BlaQ, and various closed and private groups (Farrell, 2017). These groups have enabled LGBTIQ+ Indigenous social media users to establish and perform social and cultural ties to people within and beyond communities where they live and relate. Online communities also provide new avenues for social and help-seeking behaviors and a platform to host services that encompass the range of health and well-being needs of Aboriginal and Torres Strait Islander LGBTIQ+ peoples. Publicly accessible groups such as Black Rainbow and recently formed groups such as BlaQ Aboriginal Corporation identify that they are "established as a collective response to the identified need for strengthened visibility of the Aboriginal and Torres Strait Islander LGBTQ+ community" (BlaQ). These social media and internet-based organizations continue a legacy of activism which addresses current concerns.

Black Rainbow

Black Rainbow's Facebook page was established in 2013 out of the need to put a spotlight on prevalent "limitations of participatory democracy" experienced by Indigenous LGBTIQ+ peoples within Australian society (Duarte, 2017, p. 6). Its founder, Dameyon Bonson, a Mangarayi and Torres Strait Islander gay man, notes that "Black Rainbow operates as a platform to highlight and positively reinforce the Aboriginal and Torres Strait Islander Community who identify as LGBTIQ+, that is it OK to be who they are and that they do have a place in the broader community" (Hill, 2017). Black Rainbow in its early iteration was created out of Bonson's advocacy, social work, and continued push toward the recognition of Aboriginal and Torres Strait Islander LGBTIQ+ people in policy

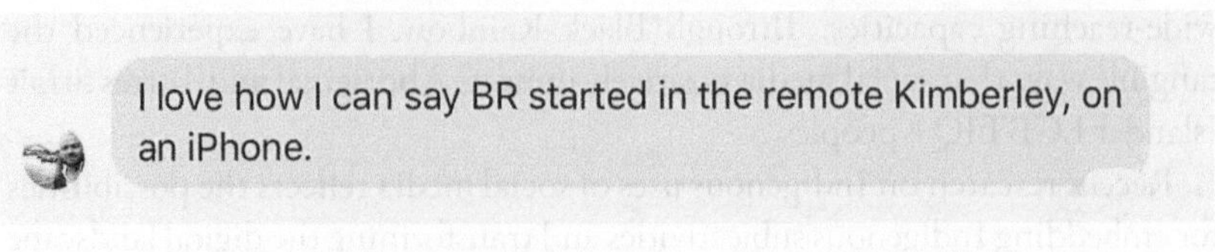

 I love how I can say BR started in the remote Kimberley, on an iPhone.

FIG. 9.1 Tweet from Black Rainbow. (Credit: Screenshot by chapter author with permission from Dameyon Bonson, Black Rainbow.)

around suicide, mental health, and the broader health and well-being frameworks that continue to marginalize and exclude Indigenous peoples. Bonson points to the lack of recognition of Aboriginal and Torres Strait Islander LGBTIQ+ peoples in health policy: "There was no representation of us ... [it] was like a light-bulb moment where I was just like; Hang on, there is no health promotion material that speaks directly to Aboriginal and Torres Strait Islander [people] who identify as LGBTI[Q+] outside of HIV. ... Despite all the literature and statistics about the instance of suicide (in both these communities) there was really no representation [of us]. Using the internet and Facebook seemed like the easiest way to connect other people to Black Rainbow" (Hill, 2017). Bonson continues to address these disparities through Twitter and various media articles that he has published around suicide and Indigenous LGBTIQ+ peoples. While maintaining an individual social media presence, Bonson sought community involvement, which led to the formation of a working group (figure 9.1).

The Black Rainbow working group, or leadership group, was formed out of professional and personal networking over a period of time. It is made up of Aboriginal and Torres Strait Islander LGBTIQ+-identified people whose work is situated across a diverse range of backgrounds and professions including contributions from those across education, health, disabilities, domestic violence, social work, mental health, and youth work. Black Rainbow has over time incorporated the valuable insight of community who both identify with and work for their communities in a number of capacities. Through the working group, Black Rainbow has adopted a range of social, cultural, and political approaches to Indigenous queer solidarities that rest in the rich diversities of Indigenous peoples found across the nation. It is a nonprofit group seeking organizational status that aims to sustain its integrity as a community-based group and its activism by leveraging the combined skills and determination of members. While diverse in culture, gender, sexuality, and ability, Black Rainbow does not account for all identities and experiences. There will always be room to grow. Black Rainbow is responsive to diversity and change in the ongoing period of recognition and change faced by our communities. Black Rainbow is also growing through community contributions and the allied support of individuals who have aligned with the core values of the organization.

The working group includes the work of youth ambassador Jake Gablonski, a gay-identified Wiradjuri man who has a "flourishing online presence, [and] worked with a variety of media platforms and networks and has collaborated with internationally recognised brands, charities and organisations to encourage social change . . . through mental health initiatives, identity and culture" (http://jakegablonski.com). Through his individual career achievements, Gablonski has become a public voice on a range of issues relating to identity, mental health, sexuality, and culture through online articles, interviews, and public speaking. Gablonski's activism is closely tied into his relationship with ongoing identity politics that underpin what it means to be Aboriginal and gay. He reveals his continued dismay with being questioned as Aboriginal: "After all of my involvement with suicide-prevention . . . and all other projects I've worked on as an Indigenous man, I still have my identity questioned with everything I do . . . some making misconceptions about whether I should even be allowed to identify as Aboriginal" (SBS, 2017). This is compounded by his experiences of homophobia when he realized that he was same-sex attracted. He highlights in an ABC radio interview that he has experienced a significant amount of social pressure and dissonance from inside and outside of his community. As a result, he felt that his identity was invalidated and that he could not be both Indigenous and LGBTIQ+ (ABC, 2019). Gablonski's work demonstrates the prevalence of ongoing fractures in Indigenous communities in relation to gender and sexuality as well as culture. His work challenges the continuance of centralizing ontologies that exclude Aboriginal and Torres Strait Islander LGBTIQ+ peoples within Aboriginal and Torres Strait Islander communities. Broadly, his story reflects that there continues to be widespread divisions between identity and acceptance that must continue to be challenged and transformed. The work of Gablonski in public visibility and media presence by various members of the Black Rainbow group is one of the ways that Black Rainbow engages in advocacy in the sense that it puts a spotlight on the absence of LGBTIQ+ Indigenous peoples by calling out social, cultural, and political disparities and calling for change.

Black Rainbow brings more than visibility through social media. The group continues to develop a range of initiatives that give back to community. One of the initiatives is a micro-grant for the purposes of providing small-scale funds to Indigenous LGBTIQ+ individuals and groups "to the value of $300 and include $200 to assist with hosting Indigenous LGBTIQ+ community events." They also provide LGBTIQ+-identified Indigenous people with phone data packages to those to seek help, "who may be homeless, leaving a domestic violent relationship or the justice system" (http://blackrainbow.org.au). These initiatives are designed to respond to the needs of Aboriginal and Torres Strait Islander LGBTIQ+ clients and mediate and mitigate help-seeking where services fail to be both inclusive and responsive to LGBTIQ+ Indigenous people as a distinct population (Carlson and Frazer, 2020).

As our public profile grew online, Black Rainbow has received donations from events and the broader community including festivals, businesses, and individuals, all of which are used toward our community initiatives. Black Rainbow's public profile has also reached the Australian public through being spotlighted by internationally famous drag performer Courtney Act, who chose Black Rainbow as her charity in the television dancing competition *Dancing with the Stars* in 2019 (OIP, 2019). Recently, the Facebook page has achieved over eleven thousand followers.

Black Rainbow has undertaken an important community consultation process around the specific needs of Aboriginal and Torres Strait Islander LGBTIQ+ peoples. These private consultations include communities across Australia including Melbourne, Darwin, and Canberra. This project is a response to the limited representation of Aboriginal and Torres Strait Islander LGBTIQ+ peoples in health policy and the stagnancy of actions taken towards recent recommendations including the recommendation that "Indigenous people identifying as LGBTQI should be represented on all Australian Government and other Indigenous mental health and suicide prevention advisory forums" (Aboriginal and Torres Strait Islander Suicide Prevention Evaluation Project Report, 2016). By adopting principles of equity and transformation, Black Rainbow shares a commitment to established goals set by LGBTIQ+ activists and movements, such as Anwernekenhe, which have achieved incremental changes for the recognition of sexual and gender diversity.

Generations on, First Nations LGBTIQ+ people have yet to see substantial structural outcomes. Bonson points to, and criticizes, the resilencing of the community in important documents as halting and unchanging, stating that "nationally and globally there has been limited investment in the social and emotional wellbeing of Indigenous LGBQTI people, outside of HIV+ which . . . carries with it significant stigma" (Bonson, 2019). The prevalence of stigma associated with past movements is seen as a barrier to ongoing resistance for those still working in health and well-being. As contemporary movements manage and aim to overcome ongoing stigmas, violence, and erasure, groups including Black Rainbow continue in the footsteps and fighting spirit of those before them. These groups also manage new challenges presented through social media including the risks and limitations of social media which: "We can not safely presume to achieve fair and just recognition" for our peoples (Duarte, 2017, p. 9). Digital spaces are experiments in social justice as we move toward more autonomous and self-determined paths that aim to overcome the limitations set upon us.

Social media plays a distinct role in recognition and acceptance as well as facilitating new approaches to help seeking. Carlson and Frazer argue that "through facilitating connections between billions of users, institutions, and knowledges, social media has become one of the primary pathways through which new, more distributed networks of care might be achieved" (Carlson et al., 2019, p. 90). The founder of Black Rainbow, Dameyon Bonson, has actively transformed social media connections into meaningful outcomes through his Black Rainbow workshops, which have been sought by health organizations around the country and delivered to the healthcare workforce. Titled Indigenous LGBQTI Inclusive Practices in Mental Health and Suicide Prevention, the workshop transforms the organizational culture of comprehensive healthcare settings, and its workforce, in order to increase their capacity to respond to the needs of Indigenous LGBTIQ+ people (https://inclusivepractices.com.au/). Health care professionals have responded positively to the workshop, with many participants reflecting on how mental health services can facilitate and encourage ethical and safer services to their LGBTIQ+ Aboriginal and Torres Strait Islander clients. A participant reflected, "I think I need to spend more time integrating the knowledge from today to really utilise it in my counselling work. In terms of the organisation where I work, it would be great to know more for the whole team." Another said, "We/I can always learn more about what can help our community. This training in itself has been amazing and it opens our eyes to the things we never knew about the LGBQTI community" (D. Bonson, personal communication, September 21, 2017). Responses to Bonson's workshop reveal that there needs to be an ongoing investment in professional training where service delivery must be accountable to the needs of LGBTIQ+, Indigenous, and LGBTIQ+ Aboriginal and Torres Strait Islander peoples and communities. They also demonstrate the particular skill set and knowledge that only LGBTIQ+ Aboriginal and Torres Strait Islander peoples can provide.

Conclusion

While not in the form of banners, chants, and protests, Black Rainbow's advocacy is demonstrated though its social media presence and outcomes. Much like Indigenous LGBTIQ+ advocacy of the past, Black Rainbow works to achieve change through structural intervention, raising critical dialogue in public domains, and modeling strong and sovereign representations that take aim at settler colonial mechanisms of oppression. It provides a model of care for community that facilitates the celebration and survival of First Nations LGBTIQ+ peoples through small but impactful initiatives. Black Rainbow is an organization that holds ground on social media and beyond as an exercise in agency and cultural autonomy, one of many iterations of social, cultural, and political groups founded by Aboriginal and Torres Strait Islander LGBTIQ+ peoples doing important work in relation to gender and sexual diversity. The historical rise of LGBTIQ+ Aboriginal and Torres Strait

Islander movements provides a valuable insight on LGBTIQ+ Indigenous social and political approaches that have laid the groundwork of a distinct LGBTIQ+ Aboriginal and Torres Strait Islander polity which continues into the future. Contemporary movements depend on work done to achieve reconciliation and equality and have recalibrated to build equity and justice with strong, meaningful, positive, and self-determined outcomes for our community.

Notes

1 "Lesbian" and "gay" are terms found primarily within the historical context discussed. These terms expanded to include transgender, bisexual, intersex, and queer over time.
2 Wendy Dunn/Holland self-describes as Murri rather than a particular First Nation group.

References

ABC. (2019). Canberra's black rainbow. *Afternoons with Paula Kruger.* https://www.abc.net.au/radio/canberra/programs/afternoons/black-rainbow/11300696.

Aboriginal and Torres Strait Islander Suicide Prevention Evaluation Project. (2016). *Solutions that work: What the evidence and our people tell us.* https://www.atsispep.sis.uwa.edu.au/__data/assets/pdf_file/0006/2947299/ATSISPEP-Report-Final-Web.pdf.

Arrow, M. (2018). History-making at the 2018 Sydney gay and lesbian Mardi Gras: Witches, faggots, dykes and poofters, the Museum of Love and Protest, the 2018 Sydney gay and lesbian Mardi Gras parade, and riot. *Australian Historical Studies, 49*(4), 493–500.

Baylis, T. (2014). The Art of Seeing Aboriginal Australia's Queer Potential. *The Conversation.* http://theconversation.com/the-art-of-seeing-aboriginal-australias-queer-potential-25588.

Bonson, D. (2016). Indigenous suicide, sexuality and gender diverse populations. *IndigenousX.* https://indigenousx.com.au/indigenous-suicide-sexuality-and-gender-diverse-populations/.

Bonson, D. (2019). Indigenous suicide, sexuality and gender diverse populations. *IndigenousX.* https://indigenousx.com.au/indigenous-suicide-sexuality-and-gender-diverse-populations/.

Carlson, B. (2013). The "new frontier": Emergent Indigenous identities and social media. In M. Harris, M. Nakata, and B. Carlson (Eds.), *The politics of identity: Emerging Indigeneity* (pp. 147–168). Sydney: University of Technology Sydney E-Press.

Carlson, B., and Frazer, R. (2018). *Social media mob: Being Indigenous online.* Sydney: Macquarie University.

Carlson, B., and Frazer, R. (2020). The politics of (dis)trust in Indigenous help-seeking. In S. Maddison and S. Nakata (Eds.), *Questioning Indigenous-settler relations: Interdisciplinary perspectives* (pp. 87–106). Singapore: Springer.

Clark, M. (2015). Indigenous subjectivity in Australia: Are we queer? *Journal of Global Indigeneity, 1*(1). http://ro.uow.edu.au/jgi/vol1/iss1/7.

Clark, M. (2017). Decolonising the queer movement in Australia: We need solidarity, not pink-washing. *NITV*. https://www.sbs.com.au/nitv/article/2016/03/03 /decolonising-queer-movement-australia-we-need-solidarity-not-pink-washing.

Dodson, M. (1994). The end in the beginning: Re(de)finding Aboriginality. In M. Grossman (Ed.), *Blacklines: Contemporary critical writings by Indigenous Australians* (25–42). Melbourne: Melbourne University Press.

Donelly, B. (2016). Gay minorities speak out against racist slurs on Grindr. *Sydney Morning Herald*. http://www.smh.com.au/national/gay-aboriginal-man-publishes -racist-slurs-on-dating-app-20160418-go8zov.html.

Driskill, Q. L. (2010). Doubleweaving two-spirit critiques: Building alliances between Native and queer studies. *GLQ: A Journal of Lesbian and Gay Studies, 16*(1–2), 69–92.

Driskill, Q. L. (2016). *Asegi stories: Cherokee queer and two-spirit memory*. Tucson: University of Arizona Press.

Duarte, M. E. (2017). Connected activism: Indigenous uses of social media for shaping political change. *Australasian Journal of Information Systems, 21*, 1–12.

Farrell, A. (2017). Archiving the Aboriginal rainbow: Building an Aboriginal LGBTIQ portal. *Australasian Journal of Information Systems, 21*, 1–14. https://doi.org/10 .3127/ajis.v21i0.1589.

Gays and Lesbians Aboriginal Alliance. (1993). Peopling the empty mirror: The prospects for lesbian and gay Aboriginal history. In R. Aldrich (Ed.), *Gay perspectives II: More essays in Australian gay culture* (pp. 1–62). Sydney: University of Sydney, Department of Economic History.

Hanckel, B., Vivienne, S., Byron, P., Robards, B., and Churchill, B. (2019). "That's not necessarily for them": LGBTIQ young people, social media platform affordances and identity curation. *Media, Culture and Society, 41*(8), 1261–1278.

Harris, D., and Prout-Quicke, S. (2019). "It doesn't make me any less Aboriginal": The complex politics of translocal place-making for Indigenous tertiary student migrants. *Population, Space and Place, 25*(3), 1–12.

Hill, L. A. (2017). Black rainbow: Mental health and the Indigenous queer community. *Out in Perth*. https://www.outinperth.com/black-rainbow-mental-health -indigenous-queer-community/.

Hodge, D. (2015). *Colouring the Rainbow: Blak queer and trans perspectives: Life stories and essays by First Nations people of Australia*. South Australia: Wakefield Press.

JD. (2011, April 7). Trans prisoner Veronica Baxter repeatedly called for help. When her jail cell was opened, she was hanging. *Queerty*. http://www.queerty.com/trans -prisoner-veronica-baxter-repeatedly-called-for-help-when-her-jail-was-opened-she -was-hanging-20110407.

Kerry, S. (2014). Sistergirls/brotherboys: The status of Indigenous transgender Australians. *International Journal of Transgenderism, 15*(3–4), 173–186.

Koori Mail. (1995). Anwernekenhe: The Black survivors. http://reconciliation.tripod .com/index.html.

Lucy, L. V. (2017). Native Americans recognise two spirits and five genders. SBS. https://www.sbs.com.au/language/english/native-americans-recognise-two-spirits -and-five-genders.

Morgensen, S. L. (2011). *Spaces between us: Queer settler colonialism and Indigenous decolonization*. Minneapolis: University of Minnesota Press.

OIP. (2019, February 19). Courtney Act picks Black Rainbow as her *Dancing with the Stars* charity. *Out in Perth*. https://www.outinperth.com/courtney-act-picks-black -rainbow-as-her-dancing-with-the-stars-charity/.

O'Sullivan, S. (2015). Queering ideas of Indigeneity: Response in repose: Challenging, engaging and ignoring centralising ontologies, responsibilities, deflections and erasures. *Journal of Global Indigeneity, 1*(1). http://ro.uow.edu.au/jgi/vol1/iss1/5.

Power, S. (2017). Meet the heroes trying to end Indigenous LGBTI suicide. *Gay Star News.* https://www.gaystarnews.com/article/meet-the-people-trying-to-end -indigenous-lgbti-suicide/#gs.9cen4u.

Riggs, D. W. (2006). *Priscilla, (white) queen of the desert: Queer rights/race privilege.* New York: Peter Lang.

Russell, S. (2017). Step by step, the First Nations lead the way at Mardi Gras. SBS. https://www.sbs.com.au/topics/sexuality/mardigras/article/2017/02/17/step-step -first-nations-lead-way-mardi-gras.

SBS. (2017). Comment: Aboriginality is more than skin deep. https://www.sbs.com .au/nitv/nitv-news/article/2017/02/20/comment-aboriginality-more-skin-deep.

Sullivan, C., and Day, M. (2019). Indigenous transmasculine Australians & sex work. *Emotion, Space and Society, 32,* 100591. https://doi.org/10.1016/j.emospa.2019 .100591.

10

Artivism

■■■■■■■■■■■■■■■■■■■■

The Role of Art and Social
Media in the Movement

MIRANDA BELARDE-LEWIS

Protecting Indigenous rights is an ancient Native North American tradition.[1] My Pueblo ancestors were community organizers, strategic planners, and highly skilled at articulating and spreading the word about both high-level goals as well as the mundane acts required to create the revolution now known as the Pueblo Revolt of 1680, a synchronized attack on the colonizing Spanish conquistadores and the violence of their proselytizing Encomienda system on August 13, 1680 (Wilcox, 2009). The coordination between distinct and independent Pueblo communities relied on trade networks, bonds of family and marriage, and the ability to honestly name the brutal regime for what it was—a direct genocidal threat to Pueblo lives, culture, and spirituality. The Pueblo Revolt was successful, and for twelve short years the Spaniards stayed away from their former encampments in present-day New Mexico.

While the nature of Spanish reentry and recolonizing into New Mexico is the source of much debate, the fact remains that the Indigenous peoples of what is now known as North American are no strangers to political activism in staunch protection of our human rights. Now that we are 340 years post–Pueblo Revolt and firmly in a digitally networked society, how do we get our message across and organize disparate Indigenous communities and our allies toward meaningful change and action? In this chapter I contend that art is a primary vehicle for the spread of activism, particularly regarding issues of social justice through an Indigenous lens. *Artivism* (art+activism) shines brightly from our phones, tablets, and laptops, illuminating messages that help other Natives and non-Indigenous allies to understand and ultimately support our ongoing battles to protect Indigenous rights for our children and our women and a safe environment for all. This chapter explores the role of art being transmitted through social media and how ancient networks are shifting and being activated precisely because of social media.

The Power of the Media Spotlight: A Brief History of Turtle Island Activism

The analogy of a spotlight is useful, particularly as Native and Indigenous issues and injustices are routinely left out of major international news cycles, despite the shocking brutality of criminal acts perpetrated against Indigenous peoples and the widespread knowledge of these acts spread through the Koori grapevine and the moccasin telegraph. Activism can be powerfully spread when messages are paired with vivid imagery, and the past five decades of Native activism in North America are no exception. A brief overview of several major activism battles waged between Native protectors and local, state, and federal law enforcement highlights the impact of imagery.

The Fish Wars (1960s–1974)

The 1854 Treaty of Medicine Creek guaranteed the signatory tribes the right to fish the Puyallup and Nisqually Rivers in Washington State. The Puyallup, Nisqually, Muckleshoot, and Squaxin Island tribes had previously fished the waters since time immemorial, and the legal agreement to retain that right in exchange for millions of acres of land, water, and other natural resources was crucial to their signing of the treaty. As commercial fishing boomed in the Puget Sound region in the mid-twentieth century, tribal fishing rights were being blatantly ignored by the commercial and sport fishermen, and soon State Fish and Game wardens were not only refusing to enforce tribal rights to fish their rivers but actively working against the tribal fishermen, aggressively arresting them and taking the side of the commercial and sport fishermen. The term "Fish Wars" is used to describe the era during the 1960s up until the Boldt decision in 1974 (Wilkins, 2011), but the term is not hyperbole; the tribal fisherman were literally in danger as they fished in the Puyallup and Nisqually rivers.

Through the years of the Fish Wars, countless tribal members fished in protection of their treaty-promised rights to fish on their waters and were subsequently beaten and arrested by Fish and Game wardens. One fisherman came to embody the tribal perspective of the Fish Wars: Billy Frank Jr., a Nisqually man who was arrested over fifty times in defense of his and his community's right to fish.

As news of the Fish Wars began to circulate in mainstream news circles, Frank's best friend Hank Adams (Assiniboine-Sioux) developed and mobilized a media campaign that outlined and complemented the political campaign to assert the fishing portion of the treaty rights. Adams was directly influenced from the leveraging of media attention and campaign building by the Civil Rights movement, immediately preceding the Fish Wars. The Adams-led media campaign included coordinated "fish-ins," press releases, and support from celebrity allies like Dick Gregory, Buffy Sainte-Marie, and Marlon Brando. The most successful campaign included Marlon Brando's participation in a fish-in and concluded with him and Frank getting arrested together in March 1964 (Wilkins, 2011). Adams, while not one for the spotlight, even now in his eighties, was absolutely crucial to the media attention and being able to leverage the messaging in support of tribal treaty rights. Ultimately the fight to assert sovereignty over the right to fish was upheld in the seminal case *U.S. v. Washington*, decided by Judge George Boldt in 1974 and affirmed by the Ninth Circuit of Appeals in 1975 (520 F.2d 676). Thanks to the careful planning of Adams and others, they set the precedent for leveraging a media spotlight in support of Indigenous activism through the use of compelling imagery.

The Occupation of Alcatraz (1969–1971)

As tensions built during the Fish Wars in the Pacific Northwest, Native activists were asserting rights in other areas of the country. A legal technicality regarding unused property helped prompt a group of Native activists known as the American Indian Movement (AIM) to occupy the former island prison Alcatraz, in San Francisco Bay (Smith, 1996). The participants of the Fish Wars in Washington were primarily Natives from local communities; the occupation of Alcatraz comprised a generation of recently relocated (and thus recently "urban") Native peoples from a vast range of tribal communities. Similar to the Fish Wars, however, was the rise of several prominent and key spokespeople, most notably Russel Means, John Trudell, and Dennis Banks, with Means and Trudell being the primary "point people" for media interviews. The media attention built off the previous campaign in the northwest Fish Wars and helped to bring awareness to the fight for Native civil rights. The fiftieth anniversary of the occupation of Alcatraz was commemorated in 2019 by a Paddle to Alcatraz (Alcatraz Canoe Journey, 2019; Ghisolfi, 2019) that coincided with the annual sunrise ceremony on Indigenous Peoples' Day coordinated by local Ohlone people (original Natives of the San Francisco region) and the Native community of the area. Canoe families from Washington, Oregon, and California participated in the first Paddle to Alcatraz.

The Fish Wars and the Occupation of Alcatraz both leveraged the power of the media. As images of brutality against Native peoples began to circulate, voices of non-Natives began to echo the concerns expressed by Native people. The images were crucial to building solidarity.

The Social Media Spotlight

Visuals of Indigenous activism captured media attention in the 1960s and 1970s through newspaper and television broadcasts; current visuals take the form of memes, infographics, and photographs that accompany the different movements and issues being spread through social media. The visuals strengthen and complement the messaging. We are squarely within the digital information age, marked by a global digital network that influences nearly all aspects of life. While Indigenous uses of social media incorporate similar aspects of mainstream users, the use of social media to inform a broad and international audience about injustices in specific local contexts has been invaluable for Native water, land, and human rights advocates. The role of social media in the quick mobilization of activists was first seen in Twitter use by the Arab Spring in the Egypt in 2012 (Howard et al., 2011) and quickly was picked up for similar uses in all different parts of the globe. The role of the visual, particularly the arts, cannot be discounted as a compelling factor in the propagation of Indigenous activism in the 2010s.

Idle No More (2012)

As Pascua Yaqui/Chicanx scholar Marisa Duarte noted in her book *Network Sovereignty: Building the Internet across Indian Country* (2017), the Idle No More movement was the first Indigenous movement of the networked age and marked the first widespread use of social media networks to organize in Native North America (see also Wilson and Zheng, this volume). When the Canadian government sought to privatize the water utility across Canada, a group of four women formed Idle No More to spread awareness of the proposed bill (Bill C-45). A core function of the Idle No More movement was the spontaneous mobilization of round dance flash mobs. Round dances are social dances used to build community and solidarity, usually danced at Native events such as powwows and community feasts (Kino-nda-niimi Collective, 2014). The flash mobs began during the holiday season of 2012, with the majority of them taking place in shopping malls across the United States and Canada, culminating with a gathering at the Peace Arch at the westernmost border crossing between the two countries. The flash mobs, the gathering at the Peace Arch, and other direct actions were coordinated through, and posted on, social media networks and later documented by a number of Indigenous media groups (Rock Paper Jet, 2013).

The round dances were peaceful disruptions of the preholiday capitalist enthusiasm and were accompanied by a wave of artwork outlining the issues, calling for action and displaying hashtags to follow—another defining aspect of the social media activism now vividly on display. Guy Fawkes, the molded and stylized, smiling facemask adopted by the online hacktivist group "Anonymous," was re-created but was adorned with Indigenous Coast Salish designs of the West coast, particularly salient after Natives were being racially profiled at the shopping malls that were the sites of the round dances. Perhaps appropriately, an artist affiliation for the Salish style Guy Fawkes masks has not been attributed. A poster campaign of photoshop "mashups"—digitally altered photos featuring historic figures wearing contemporary clothing—with the words "RISE" and "Idle No More" was developed by Kiowa-Choctaw artist Steven Paul Judd. Ligwilda'xw Kwakwaka'wakw artist Sonny Assu adapted the Obama-era "hope" posters to incorporate the words "Idle No More, Round Dance, Never Idle, Teach, Resist," capitalizing on the iconic Barack Obama campaign poster colors created by Shepard Fairey and Indigenized with northern West Coast design elements (figure 10.1).

In many ways the IdleNoMore movement was the galvanizing model for Indigenous communities worldwide; it displayed for us the real-time results of using social media to broadcast time and locations of direct actions as well as helped build solidarity through the shared images of ourselves and our artworks in support of issues that directly threaten our ways of life and our resources.

Water Is Life (2016)

In the summer of 2016, a group of Native youth from the Standing Rock tribal community set up a camp on the banks of the Cannonball River to protest the proposed Dakota Access Pipeline (DAPL). Over the next few months, the camp-in protest garnered the attention first of Native people across North America and the Pacific, then from around the globe. The primary vehicles to disseminate information about Standing Rock were word of mouth and social media (Deschine Parkhurst, this volume). When tribal elder and leader of the Standing Rock encampment LaDonna Allard put out the call via social media that fall, thousands made their way to North Dakota to #StandWithStandingRock, in what became one of the largest environmental protests in U.S. history (Estes, 2019; Estes and Dhillon, 2019).

Immediately, art became a primary vehicle to impart the message of #NoDAPL against the pipeline, and more importantly, as part of the #MniWiconi and #WaterIsLife messaging. There were many different subcamps at the Standing Rock camp, with the Art Action Camp (AAC) being one of them. At the AAC artists, lawyers, media teams, and those training in direct actions worked together to create cohesive messaging, across various audiovisual platforms. The artists in the AAC crowdsourced through fundraisers boosted on social media with T-shirts adorned with the artwork being the primary souvenir of the historic gathering. While discussing the AAC, Sarain Fox from the

FIG. 10.1 There Is Hope, If We Rise #1–12, 2013. Image courtesy of the artist.
(Credit: Sonny Assu, sonnyassu.com.)

show *Viceland* marveled at "the impact that art had on the messaging and the movement at Standing Rock" (Weisenstein, 2017). Fox reflected on the role of the artists in the camp, of the role of art and its efficacy in relaying activist messaging. In direct actions, large signs get damaged, get lost, and the folks holding them get arrested. Small-scale patches of the large banners were printed by the AAC and distributed to all the front-line people (Weisenstein, 2017). The front-line people are the focus in a hyper-documented world; having front-line people wearing the actual signs results in the art being featured in every frame, in every shot, from multiple angles and represents the thoughts and sentiments of the people at the center of that direct action. In an era of fake news and deep fakes, the ability to misrepresent words, to alter images, and to remove statements from context, the messaging through the art remains as a consistent and pervasive visual representing a cohesive message regardless of how the image is staged or revised. The sheer volume of the art being produced and present at every direct action during the more than six-month encampment at Standing Rock echoed the vocal messaging from everyone present and interviewed at Standing Rock.

There were an incredible number of images that followed one of several major themes during what has colloquially become known simply as "Standing Rock." The themes are "Water is Life," "Mni Wiconi" ("water is life" in the Lakota language), "Defend the Sacred," "Kill the Black Snake," and "No DAPL." As was the case with many aspects that set the Standing Rock experience apart from other political and environmental Indigenous movements, the documentation of various aspects of everyday life in the camps was at a level we haven't yet seen. Case in point is the NoDAPL archive (https://www .nodaplarchive.com/), complete with links to artist websites and with more detailed information about many images of art created in support of the Standing Rock tribe, the Water Protectors, as they became known, for the people of Oceti Sakowin specifically, and in support of water and land rights for Indigenous people worldwide in general.

Just as the Idle No More movement had participation from anonymous and well-known artists, so did Standing Rock. Following the initial call to action, the elders advising the leaders of the camps developed community codes of conduct and dress, stating long skirts were required wearing for all women in the camps. Apsalooké fashion designer Bethany Yellowtail donated fabric, ribbon, sewing supplies, and her own time to conduct training in how to make ribbon skirts, a pan-Native symbol for Indigeneity. She also conducted a fundraiser using various merchandise levels as incentives for monetary donations, all of which benefited the Water Protectors at Standing Rock and became social currency, advocacy, and a symbol for ally-ship for those who purchased the clothing items, not just at the time but still today. Blackfeet artist John Isaiah Pepion used the donations of his fundraisers to contribute to the legal funds used to bail out the Water Protectors arrested during direct actions, and in exchange contributors received a T-shirt with a Red Power fist holding a braid of sweet grass breaking a black pipe signifying the DAPL.

One of the most recognizable images is the "Thunderbird Mom/Water is Life" piece created by Isaac Murdoch (Serpent River First Nation) and Michif (Métis) artist Christi Belcourt. "Thunderbird Mom" was adopted and used by many different artists; the images have since been made available in high res form suitable for silk screen patterns, free of charge if used to protest extractive industry, and in direct actions (Murdoch and Belcourt, 2021) (figure 10.2). One of the most iconic uses of Thunderbird Mom was subtitled "water is not a weapon," superimposed on an image of Water Protectors being blasted with

FIG. 10.2 Thunderbird Woman. (Credit: Onaman Collective.)

water cannons, tear gas, and rubber bullets in subzero temperatures on the night of November 20, 2016 (Lafleur-Vetter and Klett, 2016). The live images of Water Protectors being projected over social media via silent drone footage manned by Digital Smokesignals belied the immense fear, frigidness, and disbelief that must have been palpable among the hundreds of Water Protectors huddled together that November night. The fact that footage even exists of that night is a miracle of the technological age we are living in. The use of social media, particularly Facebook Live, provided a large measure of safety for the Water Protectors that night, and a level of accountability for the private security teams that militarized water against the people who were there to protect it; the importance of the live broadcasting from Standing Rock via social media cannot be overstated.

Missing and Murdered Indigenous Women (MMIW) (1492–Present)

For decades, indeed for centuries, Indigenous women and girls in the Americas have borne the brunt of the physical and sexual violence of settler colonialism, racism, and misogyny. The use of social media to increase awareness about the epidemic of missing and murdered Indigenous women (MMIW) in Turtle Island has worked in a variety of ways to increase visibility about this horrible injustice of unspeakable cruelty enacted in disproportionate ways against Native women along racial and gendered lines. The local awareness of women going missing along the "Highway of Tears" in British Columbia has existed for decades, but during the social media age, Indigenous activists and family members have been able to educate the world about just how dangerous life is for First Nations women in Canada. As awareness spread, the epidemic proportions of just how many Indigenous women have gone missing or are the victims of unsolved murders made visible and revealed the many unsolved cases in the United States and Mexico.

#MMIW has been the subject of general and scholarly consciousness (Duarte and Vigil-Hayes, 2017) and has been expanded to include MMIWG—missing and murdered women and girls—as well as MMIP—missing and murdered Indigenous peoples—acknowledging that Indigenous men and boys are also exploited and harmed in disproportionate rates relative to our numbers in the general population (Urban Indian Health Institute, 2018). Duarte and Vigil-Hayes found that the use of #MMIW coupled with #Indigenous across Twitter channels was primarily to alert others about a missing Indigenous person; many times the social media posts were posted prior to police alerts notifying the public about a missing person (see also Moeke-Pickering et al., this volume).

Creating art based on the violent deaths and crushing pain of disappeared Indigenous women and girls is delicate work and has taken a variety of forms, primarily along lines of anger, in memorial, and toward justice and healing. One of the most poignant examples encompassing all of these aspects is the Walking with Our Sisters (WWOS), a commemorative art installation project envisioned by Michif (Métis) artist Christi Belcourt. Belcourt began the project by first creating beaded vamps (the upper portion of moccasins that cover the toe) for each Indigenous woman then known to be murdered or listed as missing in Canada. In 2013 the conservative estimate was more than seven hundred missing or murdered Indigenous women. Belcourt crowd-sourced via Facebook not for funding but for help creating the vamps. News spread through the offline moccasin telegraph as well as through social media, and before long individual bead artists as well as beading circles were creating the vamps. Some of the vamps were created with specific people in mind; others were created to honor the memory and lives of women taken before their time; children's vamps were created to honor the lives of children stolen through the residential and boarding school eras. Bead workers and community members posted their creations to the WWOS Facebook group as they completed them with varying lengths of descriptive text about the design and materials used, what the design represented, and biographical information about the artist of the pair of vamps. Within a short span of five months, Belcourt's initial ask of seven hundred pairs of vamps had swelled to nearly eighteen hundred donated pairs, and what had started as a modest exhibition and memorial idea had turned into a multivenue installation memorial booked in three- to six-month increments from its inaugural year in 2013 through 2017. The popularity of the exhibition was so great that the exhibition run was later expanded through August of 2019—all by the networking power of social media.

Social justice campaigns like MMIW have been able to leverage social media activity for projects such as WWOS. They are rooted in the arts and bringing communities together and provide striking examples of the ways Indigenous peoples are amplifying our activism and our messaging through social media and digital networks in stunning ways.

Considering the Role of Social Media in the Movement

The use of social media to highlight injustices in disparate Indigenous communities to a global audience has the obvious benefit of being able to amplify an underheard message to thousands of "eyes" and potential allies. We only have to look at the direct action standoffs at Standing Rock to see how the use of certain social media functions, particularly Facebook Live, provided a level of safety against further abuses by the private security firms and Morton Country Sheriffs enlisted to protect the capitalist project of drilling and transporting oil. It is my firm belief that the thousands of Facebook users viewing, commenting on, and sharing the video of direct actions prevented further escalation, even in the face of blatant racism, harassment, violence, tear-gassing, intimidation, and arrests. But as we jump in to boost the signal about our struggles to protect land and water, sacred sites, and vulnerable and exploited persons such as the thousands of missing and murdered Indigenous peoples, what privacy rights are we giving up? Information scientists, computer scientists, and data ethics experts have been sounding the alarm about the surveilling power of tracking algorithms coupled with the additional dangers for marginalized communities (Hoffman, 2019) as well as the potential for dystopian social credit tracking systems as has been hyped up about China (Matsakis, 2019). As consumers, we regularly sign over our privacy rights to various "free" social media products, but are these discussions and worries penetrating the Indigenous activist networks, particularly if the "point person" or centralized leadership is nonexistent, as compared to earlier activist movements such as the Fish Wars and the occupation of Alcatraz?

Another tension that requires research through an Indigenous lens by Indigenous information and computer scientists in particular involves how our online profiles contribute to the movements we are seeking to promote *and* that marks us for surveillance (Simpson, 2017). In an increasingly datafied and surveilled society, the use of art can increase the visibility of our struggles and our fight for civil rights, but does it also contribute to the way we are surveilled and targeted for more violence by individuals, hateful online and offline groups, and government agencies? How do we balance the tension between the use of art through social networks and the ability of settlers to exploit/cause further harm, and for our activists to avoid being targeted based on their social media footprint? Aside from reporting harmful, discriminatory, racist, or inappropriate behavior to severely overworked online mediators, or to crowd-source support to get others involved in a "call-out campaign" whereby many followers directly address a problematic post, there is at this point very little to dissuade online violence against anyone, let alone the vitriolic attacks on Native and Indigenous peoples who use social media for activism.

One shining example of solidarity comes from #settlercollector, a Twitter hashtag originating in Canada. Indigenous peoples being attacked by racist trolls can post #settlercollector and any settler-ally can and will jump in to the thread and educate their fellow settlers, relieving the Indigenous person of that burden. This tactic for self-protection, self-care, and mental wellness has been used during the recent era of Reconciliation in Canada, specifically in response to the online and physical threats of violence against the family and filmmakers working to expose the overtly biased investigation and trial surrounding the murder of Colton Boushie, a Cree man whose murderer was subsequently acquitted, exposing long-standing racism in the Canadian criminal justice system (Hubbard, 2019).

Conclusion

The long-standing role of art and visual imagery in the pursuit of reclaiming civil and human rights as Indigenous peoples is manifesting through social media in infinite ways. Earlier activist movements relied on point people, spokespeople, who were usually phenotypically Native—complete with a "Native" look of hairstyles (usually a braid or two, coupled with a folded head-band), dark skin, and features, but who were also men. Indigenous activism in the era of social media no longer requires one person to represent entire move-ments, which in many cases helps prevent one person from being the sole tar-get of online attacks and harassment. There are decentralized but unified messages being echoed across traditional and social media platforms. The active assertion of our treaty, civil, and human rights is being spread across social media from the hearts and minds of Native youth; we are being led by Native women and being guided by Indigenous elders. Our collective action is sur-rounded and supported by the visual imagery that powerfully expresses the activism of our generation.

Acknowledgments

Elahkwah and Gunalchéesh to the people on the front lines, to the elders who have seen this before and who prepare us for what is to come, to the youth push-ing us to fight for a better world, and to the artists who help us to communi-cate that vision.

Note

1   Throughout I use the terms "Native" and "Indigenous" interchangeably unless speaking of a specific Native nation.

References

Alcatraz Canoe Journey. (2019). Canoe journey paddle to Alcatraz. https://www .canoejourney2019.com/.

Duarte, M. E. (2017). *Network sovereignty: Building the Internet across Indian country*. Seattle: University of Washington Press.

Duarte, M. E., and Belarde-Lewis, M. (2015). Imagining: Creating spaces for Indig-enous ontologies. *Cataloging and Classification Quarterly*, *53*(5–6), 677–702. https://doi.org/10.1080/01639374.2015.1018396.

Duarte, M. E., and Vigil-Hayes, M. (2017). #Indigenous: A technical and decolonial analysis of activist uses of hashtags across social movements. *MediaTropes*, *7*(1), 166–184.

Estes, N. (2019). *Our history is the future: Standing Rock versus the Dakota Access Pipeline, and the long tradition of Indigenous resistance*. London: Verso.

Estes, N., and Dhillon, J. (2019). *Standing with Standing Rock: Voices from the #NoDAPL movement.* Minneapolis: University of Minnesota Press. https://muse.jhu.edu/book/70330/.

Ghisolfi, C. (2019, October 14). Native American communities around Alcatraz to honor their history and inspire future leaders. *San Francisco Examiner.* https://www.sfexaminer.com/news/native-american-communities-canoe-around-alcatraz-to-honor-their-history-and-inspire-future-leaders/?fbclid=IwAR0nGF9yYiUxmNJnQ3aSCtPUnCrNqjzdnqfEDajRq16BAA0RGS39dhSOHI4.

Hoffman, A. (2019). Where fairness fails: Data, algorithms, and the limits of antidiscrimination discourse. *Information, Communication and Society, 22,* 900–915. https://doi.org/10.1080/1369118X.2019.1573912.

Howard, P. N., Duffy, A., Freelon, D., Hussain, M. M., Mari, W., and Maziad, M. (2011). Opening closed regimes: What was the role of social media during the Arab Spring? SSRN. http://dx.doi.org/10.2139/ssrn.2595096.

Hubbard, T. (2019). Nipawistamasowin: We will stand up. https://www.nfb.ca/film/nipawistamasowin-we-will-stand-up/.

Kino-nda-niimi Collective. (2014). *The winter we danced: Voices from the past, the future, and the Idle No More movement.* Winnipeg: ARP Books.

Lafleur-Vetter, S., and Klett, J. (2016, November 21). Police blast Standing Rock protestors with water cannon and rubber bullets—video. *Guardian.* https://www.theguardian.com/us-news/video/2016/nov/21/dakota-access-pipeline-standing-rock-water-cannon-video.

Matsakis, L. (2019, July 29). How the west got China's social credit system wrong. *Wired.* https://www.wired.com/story/china-social-credit-score-system.

Murdoch, I., and Belcourt, C. (2021). Isaac Murdoch and Christi Belcourt banners. http://onamancollective.com/murdoch-belcourt-banner-downloads/.

Rock Paper Jet. (2013, January 9). *Idle No More: The next generation.* Video. YouTube. Produced by Brodie Lane Stevens (Tulalip) and Gyasi Ross (Blackfeet). https://youtu.be/m5-n_MDcjJA.

Simpson, L. B. (2017). *As we have always done: Indigenous freedom through radical resistance.* Minneapolis: University of Minnesota Press.

Smith, P. C. (1996). *Like a hurricane: The Indian movement from Alcatraz to Wounded Knee.* New York: New Press.

Urban Indian Health Institute. (2018). Missing and murdered Indigenous women and girls. https://www.uihi.org/resources/missing-and-murdered-indigenous-women-girls/.

Weisenstein, K. (2017). How art immortalized #NoDAPL protests at Standing Rock. https://www.vice.com/en_us/article/d334ba/how-art-immortalized-nodapl-protests-at-standing-rock.

Wemigwans, J. (2018). *A digital bundle: Protecting and promoting Indigenous knowledge online.* Regina: University of Regina Press.

Wilcox, M. V. (2009). *The Pueblo Revolt and the mythology of conquest: An Indigenous archaeology of contact.* Berkeley: University of California Press.

Wilkins, D. E. (2011). *The Hank Adams reader: An exemplary Native activist and the unleashing of Indigenous sovereignty.* Golden, CO: Fulcrum.

11

Interview with Debbie Reese, Creator of the Blog *American Indians in Children's Literature*

JEFF BERGLUND

Debbie Reese (Nambé Owingeh) is a world-renowned blogger and literary social media activist. She founded the influential blog *American Indians in Children's Literature* in 2006 while she was a faculty member at the University of Illinois, where she earned a PhD in curriculum and instruction. Reese grew up at Nambé Owingeh in New Mexico, graduated from the University of New Mexico, and taught elementary school in Albuquerque, Andarko, Oklahoma, and then Santa Fe and Pojoaque, New Mexico, before moving to Champaign-Urbana for graduate school. Reese recalls that as a child there were very few images in picture books of children who resembled her. She reflected on this even more intensely when her daughter was born and she was concerned about how Elizabeth would see herself reflected in books and in lesson plans (figure 11.1).

Reese has been a powerful advocate of accurate representations of Indigenous peoples and has raised vital questions about writerly authority, the need for accurate and nuanced representations, and the impact and violence of stereotypes. Reese has raised the consciousness of authors, editors, publishers, agents, reviewers, and educators. Her work transcends the arena of children's

FIG. 11.1 Debbie Reese reading Simon Ortiz's *The People Shall Continue.*
(Credit: Painting by Julie Flett.)

literature and has influenced the entire field of Indigenous studies. Reese has recently coauthored with Jean Mendoza an edition of Roxanne Dunbar-Ortiz's book for younger audiences: *An Indigenous Peoples' History of the United States for Young People.* It was named an American Indian Youth Literature Honor Book in 2020. In 2019 Reese was honored with the prestigious Arbuthnot Honor Lecture award, which recognized her contributions to children's literature including her monumental work online, on social media, and, very significantly, behind the scenes in relationships fostered through social media; in addition, the award recognized her important advocacy to rename and rededicate in 2018 the American Library Association's children division's prestigious Laura Ingalls Wilder Award to the Children's Literature Legacy Award because Wilder's books perpetuate racist and harmful stereotypes about Native people and African Americans.

The following interview was conducted by Jeff Berglund in September 2019.

JEFF: I saw that to date you've had over 1,656 blog posts in thirteen years and you have nearly 30,000 followers on Twitter and I'm blown away by that. I guess I've forgotten how long I've been reading your work; it is amazing to realize that at least the current version of the blog has been around since

2006. So, I'm wondering when did you first conceive of the idea? Was it in that year and then what was your impetus? Who was your imagined reader?

DEBBIE: Prior to blogger and blogging, everything happened on listservs. When I was in grad school in the nineties, email was a relatively new method for communicating. I was on listservs of people in children's literature. A significant listserv was called child_lit, based out of Rutgers. Editors were there from the major houses, review journal editors were there, reviewers were there, professors and writers from the United States and other countries were there. Philip Pullman was on there. It was the main one, but there were others, too, and I was having the same conversation across five or six different ones. When a new book would come out that was bad [regarding Native content], I would write about it on more than one listserv, trying to get people to think about it. That was really getting old, essentially repeating the same things, but with different audiences. So, I think I was honing my ability to focus on a particular audience given whichever audience the listserv was for. I got tired of having the same conversations across many different listservs. Blogging was becoming a thing, so I studied several blogs and then decided to go for it. This also coincided with the first summer that my daughter was away for the summer. She was at an eight-week Junior Statesman of America program. Her being away that long was so hard on me! I needed something that would grip every cell of my brain, so that's when I made the leap. The personal need to have something that would distract me from missing her and, second, the need to consolidate the time that I was putting into the listserv conversations.

JEFF: Right, and the interest to create something that would be enduring, too. Less ephemeral.

DEBBIE: Right, enduring! The child_lit listserv died (or was killed) two years ago in 2017, It had been started in the 1990s and all of these major figures were writing on there. Too many of us were pushing back there, on the status quo. Michael Joseph, a children's literature professor at Rutgers started that listserv to talk about research in children's literature and it had become something else. It was no longer "scholarship," and was just "complaining." So he shut it down and over twenty years of archives disappeared overnight. Loss of that archive is a tremendous loss to the children's literature community.

JEFF: Do you remember what your very first blog post was?

DEBBIE: The first was a list of recommended books that I used at conference sessions. It's old and outdated now, but that was the first post.

JEFF: One of the things I appreciate about your blog is your willingness to put your ideas out there while you're processing. You'll come across a book, you have a feature now that probably started by accident, the "Debbie, have you seen?" feature where people send you queries—a real testament to the powerful reach of your work. Can you talk a little bit about your evolution with your comfort with what Adrienne Keene (Cherokee) of "Native Appropriations" refers to as learning in public? You put your initial thoughts out there, you come back to them, you encourage people to add on. Is this part and parcel of who you are? It's not typical of academic style. I think a lot of us have learned from it and appreciate and value it.

DEBBIE: I am always willing to help parents, teachers, and librarians by reading a book they have questions about. When they'd write to me, I'd read the book and reply directly to them but realized that others might have questions about that same book. So that's how the "have you seen" feature came about. I make initial comments and do a full review later.

Adrienne's "Learning in Public" is great! First, a few words about it—as applied to changes to books. In the children's lit community, someone would notice that racist or stereotypical content in a book had been changed. Significant revisions were done to *Mary Poppins*. As far as I've been able to determine there was nothing published anywhere that said "we're making these changes, and here's why." I think we learn from our own mistakes but also from studying mistakes others make. The changes made to *Mary Poppins* are significant. Having a public record that acknowledges the mistakes is a public good. So, I created a page at my blog where I keep a record of changes. For old books, we don't know who made the changes but for newer ones, some authors are making public statements about their errors and the edits. I know it is hard but think it has tremendous value for all of us. Second, in 2018, I did a post that acknowledges my own errors. It fits the "learning in public" framework. I had given a positive review to Rebecca Roanhorse's *Trail of Lightning* because I believed she had done right by Diné people and their protocols for writing about their spiritual ways. That turned out not to be the case, and so I did a public apology to Diné people for having promoted her book and I explained why I was withdrawing my initial support.

JEFF: Is there some aspect or teaching from your tribal background that informs your openness and open progression and deepening and deepening of thought and reflection?

DEBBIE: I grew up hearing over and over in the kiva that during prayer, we should not be thinking about ourselves and what we want. We should be thinking about our families, our village, our cities, our state, and the whole world. That way of being selfless is fundamental to who I am and was fundamental to how we got the Native Studies Program at Illinois going. Our model was to emphasize community, to think in terms of "we" rather than the usual research model which is to study someone for one's own career trajectory. It aligned with what leaders in the field, like Vine Deloria Jr.

(Standing Rock Sioux) and Elizabeth Cook Lynn (Crow Creek Sioux) said. They wrote that it is important to get out of the Ivory Tower, that the work we do as scholars is not about us as individuals. I don't want to romanticize this, but what I learned as a kid and what I learned from Deloria and Cook-Lynn dovetail in the emphasis on community rather than individual. I don't know if those teachings—from elders at home and elders in the academy—informs a sense of openness or deepening of thought and reflection in my work, but maybe they do. These teachings emphasis community well-being, and they definitely shaped how I have moved forward from initial praise for Roanhorse's work.

JEFF: This could be fundamentally connected to the blog format, rather than working through the venue of academic publishing that is really slow and doesn't allow this thinking through, this progression. That's also what's expansive about the blog format.

DEBBIE: Yes! Blog posts can address something, immediately. And in subsequent posts, I can refer to older ones, and go back to older ones and insert updates to my thinking or that point to other's writings about the content of the post. There's another aspect of the blog that matters to me, a lot. I was a school teacher and couldn't afford to join the National Council of Teachers of English and get their journal, which is a benefit of being a member of the association. As an academic, I realized that the things I was publishing were going into places like journals and books, where teachers probably wouldn't see them. I was conscious that I was doing work that was published in places that could, in theory, give me tenure, but that were doing nothing for the people that work with kids every day. The blog let me reach them because it doesn't cost anything to read a blog post.

JEFF: Why is representation or the politics of representation "ground zero," or foundational to you?

DEBBIE: I didn't realize how bad misrepresentation was until I went to Illinois to work on my doctorate. When I was an undergrad getting my teaching certification, I learned about multicultural education and bias in what kids are taught. I went on to teach first grade in northern New Mexico and didn't teach that Columbus as a hero. I didn't feel that my physical safety was ever at risk for what I taught. Moving to Illinois, that changed. The university had a stereotypical mascot that was supposed to honor Native people. Before we made that move, the professor who was recruiting us told us about that mascot, and, I remember thinking, "this is not going to be a big deal," but then I got to Illinois and I thought, "*holy crap this is a big deal*." So, moving from a place with a lot of Native people and what I believe was a space of greater knowledge in the public about who we are as a people, to a place where there were very few Native people and a whole lot of ignorant white people who, quite literally, worshipped that mascot . . .

the contrast between those two places made the case about why representation is so important.

JEFF: So, you think it's foundational because you think it's linked to all kinds of other valuations and that it frames all discussions and debates about Native people?

DEBBIE: What people know shapes their valuations and therefore, discussions and debates about anything that impacts the well-being of Native children. I care very much about what Native kids see in books because that content can depress their esteem. Everybody should read Dr. Stephanie Fryberg's (Tulalip) research on the impact of mascots and stereotypical imagery. Her studies prove that stereotypical images harm Native kids. In my effort to understand why people embrace mascots, I started to study images of Native people in children's books. I saw the same thing: stereotypes. I also care about what non-Native kids are getting from these images because those kids will grow up and some will have careers where they can affirm those misrepresentations. I'd rather they interrupt them! I'd like, for example, a non-Native person to be the editor who says yes to a manuscript by a Native writer who is creating story about their life.

JEFF: You have many early posts—something like thirty—that are focused on *Little House on the Prairie*. Sixteen on mascots, twenty-three on Thanksgiving. Those are key moments in the U.S. cultural imaginary. I want to look at the other end of the spectrum. There's a new book coming out in the 2020 publishing season called *We Are Water Protectors* by Carol Lindstrom (Turtle Mountain Ojibwe). Will you talk about that book and how it presents to the two audiences you identify?

DEBBIE: *We Are Water Protectors* is about Native resistance to oil companies whose pipelines put clean water at risk. Native people from around the world went to Standing Rock to support the exercise of their sovereignty, and their efforts to protect the water. They also took part in marches in cities or in their communities. There was one at Pojoaque Pueblo. My sister's grandchildren were in it. For Native kids, *We Are Water Protectors* reflects their participation in resistance. Native people weren't alone in the efforts at Standing Rock or elsewhere. Oil companies are laying pipelines and fracking all over the U.S. and Canada. Everybody's water is at risk. So, non-Native people are also involved in efforts to protect the water. I think they bring an awareness of Native resistance into their homes, and to their children. For non-Native children, *We Are Water Protectors* provides them with information about Native people of today, standing strong. Too much of what I see in children's books are Native peoples of the past, not present. This book pushes on that problem.

JEFF: You briefly transitioned from your blog only to Facebook before transitioning to Twitter as an adjunct to your blog. You use Twitter to amplify your own blogposts, but also to sustain other conversations. What led you to join Twitter and was it a slow process? What do you find most useful about it?

DEBBIE: The immediacy of Twitter appeals to me. It is definitely a place where things happen quickly. You can have a more in-depth conversation on Facebook because it doesn't limit character count. One of its limitations, though, is that a person can delete a post they wrote and everybody's responses to it disappear, too. Sometimes, it is a tremendous loss of substantive content. Here's an example of this: Aaron Carapella, a guy who used to say he's Cherokee, created a set of "Tribal Nations Maps." He posted about them to the Native American Issues Facebook page and got a lot of really good feedback from people who looked carefully at what he said about their own nation. Some told him he needed to do this or that to improve it, and though he said he wanted feedback, he ended up arguing with them. After a while, Aaron got mad and deleted the thread with all of that feedback! That doesn't happen on Twitter.

JEFF: And someone can delete their whole Twitter handle, but they would have to suffer that Twitter death themselves.

DEBBIE: And they can delete individual tweets, but not what others said in reply. There's a hole in the conversation, where their tweet was, but those who saw it can summarize it if people ask what was said.

JEFF: So, you like the immediacy. You have a balance between new posts and reposts. Sometimes you have a thread with posts broken apart because of character count. What leads you to do this rather than a new blog post? Is it a draft of a blog post?

DEBBIE: Tweet threads. I need to be more mindful when I do those. I should number them so people don't see a single tweet and not realize it is part of a longer set of thoughts I was sharing. Sometimes, I do Twitter reviews where I'll tweet as I read a book. I do that because I want people to know I've received a book and am reading it, but am not ready to write a review yet. It is a way to have something like a virtual book club where you read chapter one and share thoughts in the group. When I finish the book, I try to gather the tweets for a blog post. Sometimes I'll do a review and paste the tweets below the review and sometimes I just paste the tweets.

JEFF: Also, it's responding to ongoing conversations on Twitter, whereas if you took it over to the blog, the conversation would be more separate. Has Twitter made some surprising connections with others, organizations, other writers or publishers?

DEBBIE: Yeah! When I first started blogging there were comments to blog posts but that dropped off. People began to respond on social media instead. Surprising connections on Twitter? Yes! The thing that comes to mind is DMs (direct messages) from famous writers asking if I can take a look at the Native content of something they're working on. I'm careful, though, in those conversations. I stipulate that they can't mention my name as having consulted with them because using my name suggests an endorsement of all of the content. Writers decide what feedback to use—or not use—so, I am wary of how my name gets used!

JEFF: An interesting thing about Twitter is that it's seemingly ephemeral because new conversations pop up so rapidly.

DEBBIE: And they go away rapidly, too! For a while, there was a lot of talk on Twitter, about Sherman Alexie, but that ended and pretty much hasn't surfaced again. People who didn't see it the first time don't know there are concerns about him. They praise *The Absolutely True Diary of a Part Time Indian* and talk about using it with kids. That's frustrating. I want to post my links about him again. Same with Rebecca Roanhorse when I see people praising her books. I want to post links about her book again, but I look vindictive, or like a bully. Does our responsibility end when we've said it once, or do we need to keep the conversation going? Lasting change doesn't happen unless we keep talking about problems. I want to figure out how to have sustained conversations in a way that prevents them from being mis-characterized.

JEFF: Could you talk a bit more about how the Diversity Jedis came about?

DEBBIE: There is a group of us—me and Women of Color—who have been talking together about books, for years. We do similar critical analyses, and turn to each other, privately, for perspective and support when things get intense. On October 10, 2015, librarian Edi Campbell talked about *Large Fears*, a new picture book by Myles E. Johnson. It is about a little boy who is queer. Out of the blue comes Meg Rosoff onto Edie's page, just stomping all over her post about the book, literally just stomping all over it. And we're like, "WTF?! Who is this woman?" We learned that Meg Rosoff has written several books. A couple of weeks later, we learned she's friends with Sophie Blackall, the illustrator of *A Fine Dessert*—which has smiling slaves in it. There was a lot of conversation on social media about Blackall's illustrations. Rosoff tweeted that those of us who objected to the smiling slaves are the "Debbie Reese Crimes Against Diversity stormtroopers." Latinx writer Rene Saldana said that I'm not a stormtrooper. He said he thinks of me as a Jedi Knight. A couple of days later, Cynthia Leitich Smith (Mvskoke) tweeted "I might have given up writing #NativeAmerican lit if it weren't for @debreese. She cared when it seemed like so few did. #diversityjedi." Credit for the hashtag, then, belongs to Rene Saldana and Cynthia Leitich Smith. It took off on Twitter on November 2, 2015. On April 4, 2019, Vicky Smith—the children's book editor at *Kirkus*—published a feature article titled "Diversity Jedi" in the print and online edition of *Kirkus*. There, she noted that #DiversityJedi are often accused of being mob-like but rejects that charge. She is grateful, she wrote, for the increase in books by people whose identities have been misrepresented. She thinks that increase is due to the Diversity Jedi. That's a significant observation and affirmation of what we're doing.

JEFF: I'm thinking back to the discussion about *A Fine Dessert*, what others called a controversy. Were you self-conscious working across cultural lines or was there a natural affinity that you've developed through questioning representation and setting straight the historical record?

DEBBIE: I don't think of it as being self-conscious. It is more about being aware that most of us in the U.S. grew up socialized and educated to think about certain peoples in narrow, racist, or derogatory ways. I've learned a lot about that, on Twitter. When I was doing mascot work at Illinois, we were using an illustration that helped people see what is wrong with Native mascots. It had sketches of other ethnic groups portrayed as mascots. I used it on Twitter—I don't remember when, exactly—but a person wrote to me about it. The person said "don't use us to make your point." It was a kick in the gut but I knew instantly that they were right. Using an image of the Cleveland Indians mascot in Blackface to make the point that the Cleveland Indians mascot is wrong subjected African Americans to hurtful imagery. So, I stopped using it. In hindsight, I should have seen the harm of it before it was pointed out to me, but I didn't. That's what I mean about being aware of how we are socialized and educated in the U.S. Now, I monitor myself very carefully for that sort of thing. Being aware and open to criticism helps build the relationships across groups that can drive change in children's books. And being aware of how badly Native people are depicted in the historical record keeps me open to the fact that others are also misrepresented in ways I may not be aware of . . . so I listen and boost their critiques when I can.

JEFF: In the case of *A Fine Dessert*, you're supporting the critical response that's centered from an African American perspective. In that case, you're not making a comparison. You're validating and supporting their evaluation.

DEBBIE: Yes, but probably around the same time it was Thanksgiving and there were smiling Indians. So there's a connection across oppressed groups where mainstream power structures will make us look happy when we're not happy. With smiling Indians or smiling slaves, we can see that we're in this work together, fighting misrepresentations. When I think of us working together, I am reminded of Simon Ortiz's (Acoma) book *The People Shall Continue* when he talks about how everyone comes together, to work against *greed*. His book is so perfect.

JEFF: Yes, that's great. That's what I assumed that your thinking and your work on these other books has shaped your evaluation period, so any book that you come across. And you're also going to support the Twittersphere/

blogger sphere reviewers. And that's the other thing that people have gained from your work is that this is not about *one* reviewer, but this is about valuing each other's work. The best-case scenarios are that you and other reviewers aren't in isolation.

DEBBIE: We definitely learn from each other. For example, we have learned not to share book lists without reading through the list first. One of the things I learned—I don't know where I learned this—but there are lists floating around and people will often retweet these lists without looking at the lists. So, part of what has come from all of that, the emergence of "stay in your lane" conversations—this is not your place to be talking about this—is not good and shuts down a lot of what people should be able to say. It also shuts down the ability to work across and in a collective way.

JEFF: Have you been bullied, have you ever questioned whether this is worth it? Do you grow tired of your platform, of your responsibilities? To your readers?

DEBBIE: One thing for sure is that it is not "tireless" work. I do get tired. There is one recent incident that took me back, that worried me. When the Association for Library Service to Children (ALSC)—it is part of the American Library Association—selected me to give the 2019 Arbuthnot Lecture, I got a couple of emails that said I didn't deserve the award and that I should withdraw. They said I don't deserve the award because I was part of the American Indian Library Association that chose to rescind a book award it gave to Sherman Alexie (Coeur d'Alene/Spokane) and that I am, at heart, a censor, and because of my role in ALSC's decision to remove Laura Ingalls Wilder's name from a book award. So I was getting these emails, and I was copied on others that were sent to people in the American Library Association and in the American Indian Library Association. Similar ones were posted on librarian listservs. I didn't reply to those that came to me, directly. I forwarded them to the president of ALSC who I was also communicating with about planning for the lecture. And then a month before the lecture, somebody wrote to me about a conference in Skokie called "Defeating Bullies and Trolls in the Library: Developing Strategies to Protect our Rights and Personhood." One panel was examining possible responses to harassment. In that session, one of the panelists talked about a person who had threatened to show up at my lecture. As I recall, someone referenced that person's volume of email and called them a "persistent harasser." I decided I ought to find out what was going on.

I learned that the University of Wisconsin–Madison, when they learned about this person, chose to have security at my lecture. They visited her website and knew what she looks like. The event was going to be opened by Wisconsin Dells, a drum group from the Ho-Chunk Nation. It turns out that the guys in the group are in the Bear Clan that does policing and

security for the Ho-Chunk. They were a second source of security. My
family was with me, and Diversity Jedi had flown in for the lecture, from as
far away as San Francisco. I felt okay.

Before the drum did the opening song, I watched from the side aisle as
Elliott, the leader of the drum group, leaned on the podium and said, "We
are on Ho-Chunk land and if you're here to make trouble, we're going to
ask you to leave, and you'll have to leave because you're on our land." He's a
tall guy, and as I listened to him, I thought, *that was interesting.* They did
their opening and I went to the podium and they did *not* leave. I did not
notice, at first that they did not leave. Usually, the drummers leave and
come back to do the closing song. I didn't notice that they hadn't left when
they did that first song. I gave the lecture, they did the final song, and then
there was a reception. That night when hosts walked us to our car, they
said, "That woman was sitting right behind you. The harasser was right
behind you and your husband." The harasser was with her partner and they
had taken the chairs right behind us. I don't know if I shivered when they
told me, but since then, I've thought, *Oh my God* and shivered. Moments
when I think about how close she was to me, with a vindictive spirit,
I think about that, I worry about that. Thinking about the Ho-Chunk's
protection of me makes me feel emotional about that night. Native people
were there that night, to protect me and my family.

JEFF: What insights have you gained from that, or do you have any advice for
people dealing with trolls? Other activists working on social media?

DEBBIE: Yes, speak up when it happens. That's what I see from other people on
Twitter. I see that people don't stay silent about it because other people can
be hurt by silence. A few months later I was invited to give a talk at another
university in the Midwest. I decided I ought to tell them about what
happened in Madison particularly since the harasser was retired from that
midwestern university. I wrote to them and said, "By the way, there's a
retired professor at your institution who went to my Arubuthnot lecture
and whose behaviors resulted in UW providing security at my lecture."
They wrote back immediately, naming a person and asking if it was that
same one. It was, and we got on the phone right away. I learned that the
education professor who had invited me had been targeted by the same
person! They and their students had been pushing against the heroic
reputation of a white woman in that state who had done suffragette work
but who was also very racist. They told me that their campus had a police
file on the harasser because of her behaviors. When I go to that campus in
Spring of 2020, campus security will be on alert for possible disruptions.
I see people on social media who are targeted with harassment encouraging
others to speak up when it happens. It is uncomfortable to do that but it is
important. I felt a bit melodramatic telling the midwestern university

organizers about what happened in Madison but their reaction told me how important it is to speak up.

JEFF: Your work has a life of its own in some ways and you get drawn into discussions and debates. You say you're retired, but you're the hardest working "retired" person that I've ever seen. What kind of parameters do you set for yourself working online?

DEBBIE: I don't have a method. If something moves me then I will say something about it on Twitter, or sometimes, in a blog post. I feel very guilty that I have not done as many blog posts in the last three years (2017–2019) than I had done in the years prior. If you look at the number of posts, it dropped off dramatically. That is because I agreed to adapt Roxanne Dunbar-Ortiz's book into a young adult version titled, *An Indigenous Peoples' History of the United States for Young People.* Doing that adaptation meant working almost every day for several hours with my co-adaptor, Jean Mendoza. I feel bad about the drop in book reviews because there are several books I wanted to say more about, but didn't have time to do more. The primary work that I do is elevating good books and critiquing bad ones. I know that the critiques I do have changed the field, and so that drop off in critiques eats at me.

JEFF: Are there invisible forms of privilege or racism or prejudice that are institutionalized in the book world?

DEBBIE: When I am asked or invited to be on award committees, I say, "No" because the first time I was asked, I was told I would not be able to talk about new books, whether I liked them, or not. There is a moratorium on your free speech while you are on an award committee. You can talk about old books, but not new books. If, for example, Cynthia Leitich Smith had a new book come out, I could not say a single word about it. When I got that first invitation to serve on an award committee, I called Native writers and said, "Here's an opportunity for me to do this...." My words were met with an interesting silence and then a "But, but..." and a *"we need you so badly."* That was said, because part of what I do is point out problematic Native content in books from the major publishers. When I do that, it makes room for people to understand how and why writing by Native writers is so important. Native writers don't create problematic content about their nations. If I said yes to a committee appointment, that would mean a year of silence from me. For some time now we've felt there's a greater interest in books by Native writers. It is important to keep that momentum going. A year of silence would slow things down. So, I turn down those opportunities. For some of us there are other problems. I know a Korean American who had to step off an ALA committee because an author thanked her in the acknowledgments the year she was on the committee. I know a white woman who tweeted that a Latinx kid who came into her library loved

Miles Morales. She tagged the author, Jason Reynolds, in her tweet. She'd done something similar to that before and had been warned that she was stepping into slippery territory. With the Morales tweet, she was booted off the committee. There are interesting threads on social media that are about whether these moratoriums and decisions to kick people off of committees is impacting people who are advocating for people of color. I think they do impact us, the books, and ultimately, kids! What doesn't get talked about is that every single conference you go to, big publishers want reviewers at their table. *Come and sit with the writer!* That socializing is not seen as a violation. I think some people—I'll just say it, *white* people—are getting a pass on what count as a violation and what doesn't count. I think this is an institutional inequity. And, maybe it's because I talk to people of color I'm more aware of them being told, "Be careful!" Maybe white reviewers have been warned but are quite about those warnings.

JEFF: What are you currently intrigued by? You mentioned something to me recently about how librarians and others can manage collections that will have positive impact on readers.

DEBBIE: Several of us who are in the American Indian Library Association get emails from people visiting tribal museums, writing to complain that they see Paul Goble's books being sold in museum stores. They want us to tell museum stores not to sell them. I wish these folks would tell the museum store manager themselves when they're there! They can speak up, too. Anyway, this evolved into a conversation among six or seven of us recently. We wondered if we might be able to make an intervention at ATALM (Association of Tribal Archives, Libraries, and Museums) conferences. It's a relatively new association that is bringing together mostly Native people. It's one of those conferences you really want to go to because it's not populated by a bunch of white people telling us how to do things. It's Native people talking about what they do in their libraries and museums. So, it's a wonderful space. We decided to make a brochure to hand out at ATALM called something like "Do You Sell Books in a Tribal Museum?" We'd describe with some books sold in museums, and we'd ask them not to carry these books. Our list includes books by Paul Goble. Two of the librarians brought up Rebecca Roanhorse. So, she's on that list. And we have a list of recommended books we do think they should be selling and some resources to expand their own knowledge. Two of the resources are Daniel Heath Justice's (Cherokee) *Why Indigenous Literatures Matter* and Greg Younging's (Opsakwayak Cree) *Elements of Indigenous Style*. We are still drafting that brochure and hope to share it soon.

JEFF: What's interesting about people in those positions may not be part of discussions about children's literature, but then they're purchasing children's literature. It's important to connect all of these people.

DEBBIE: Yes, many connections to make! One of the people I've met online is Desmond Wong. He is a librarian in Toronto, and from his tweets, I knew he's got a critical stance and is really smart. When I went up to Toronto in September to give a talk, I thought "Desmond will be there, I hope I do okay." Anyway, he was excited to meet me and before the lecture started, we were talking about David Bouchard and his books for children. Bouchard claims to be Métis. He's done a horribly fantastic job convincing people in Canada he's Métis. They even named a school after him and he was appointed to the "Order of Canada" which is intended to honor Canadians for their work. Bouchard isn't actually Métis. It is a claim he makes but it has no substance. I have an article about him coming out next year. Desmond told me that in his library in Toronto they have a circulating collection and they have a research collection. They put books by people like Bouchard in the research collection. Joseph Boyden's books are there, too. They want teachers to learn about concerns with certain writers and their books. This can help them use the books critically, if they plan to use them. So, these books are in the card catalog, and in the library, but shelved in a special place in the library. I like that idea. My presentation was about Cultural Appropriation. It included a segment about David Bouchard. During the Q&A, someone asked me, "What are we going to do about the Bouchard books?" I asked Desmond to explain how his library handles those books. It was exciting for me that a research library has found a way to deal with this, without censoring the book. So, I want to write about this on Twitter or my blog because it is a strategy that others could use.

JEFF: This year you've received some incredible honors. What are you most proud of?

DEBBIE: Probably, some of the impact that the Diversity Jedi have been able to make. *A Birthday Cake for George Washington* got pulled by Scholastic—its publisher. The ICWA adoption book by Sharlee Glenn, *Beyond the Green*, it got pulled by Charlesbridge—its publisher. Some people try to claim that publishers are being censored by online mobs who "go after" these books, but these are businesses making decisions about their reputation. We are in a new period where there's more attention to misrepresentation.

I guess impact of work comes to mind more than honors for the work. I like knowing that publishers at major houses read my stuff. I hear about this, second-hand. One major writer made significant errors with Native content in a book that had nothing to do with Native people. He wrote to me to say that he wanted to come to my blog right away and say "I screwed up, and on my next printing I'll fix that," but, he went on, saying "my publisher told me I'd be in violation of the clause in my contract that says I won't say or do anything that harms the reputation of the publisher." So, some writers would like to acknowledge the errors in books, but publishers are holding that clause over their heads. Some do reply to critiques, publicly. I have a page on my site that documents these public declarations, because I think others can learn a lot from that.

The tenth anniversary of *Fatty Legs* is coming up! It is by Margaret Pokiak-Fenton, a First Nations woman (Inuvialuk of the Inuvialuit) and her daughter-in-law, Christy Jordan-Fenton. I wrote a foreword for that and was talking with Christy yesterday. She said she had seen my page about "documenting the changes" and said, "we're doing that in the afterword" of *Fatty Legs*. I look forward to changes they made for the tenth anniversary edition, and think that documenting the changes *in* their book will do a lot of good work.

12

United Front

■■■■■■■■■■■■■■■■■■■■

Indigenous Peoples' Resistance in the Online Metal Scene

TRISTAN KENNEDY

Indigenous peoples' resistance to colonization is no new thing. For over 230 years in Australia, Indigenous peoples have protested with their feet, their voices, and the written word. In ever-increasing ways, Indigenous people are embracing new sites on emerging social media platforms to engage in active resistance to ongoing colonization. Social media platforms, facilitated by the rolling development of digital communication technology, have amplified Indigenous peoples' creativity in resistance and political activism online. A key site of resistance is the online metal scene—a site for the production, consumption, and reproduction of not only metal culture, but staunch resistance to colonial ideology. Indigenous and non-Indigenous metalhead allies alike, gather in the online metal scene; what emerges is a negotiated political presence previously unimaginable without the affordances of digital communication technology.

This chapter highlights an emerging trend in the online metal scene. Indigenous metal fans and bands are using social media platforms to disseminate messages of resistance and truth-telling that bypass traditional mainstream record industry channels. Attention garnered by Sydney-based band Homesick, fronted by Indigenous vocalist Peter Jackson, in the online metal scene illustrates the efficacy of social media platforms such as Facebook and You-Tube in solidifying a political presence for Indigenous peoples. It is clear that digital communication technologies afford heightened degrees of permanence and visibility to interactions between metalheads in these disintermediated, digital social spaces.

As highlighted by Carlson et al. (2015), Indigenous peoples have always been early adopters of technology. Indigenous peoples are highly active users of social media. Platforms such as Facebook, Instagram, and Twitter provide opportunities to share stories, build communities, provide support in the face of adversity, and be politically present in a country that continues to actively silence and delegitimize Indigenous voices. The technologies that permit access to these platforms present innovative and sophisticated avenues for communication and mobilization. Social media technology offers sites for social interaction that are disintermediated and deterritorialized. These sites, like the online metal scene, are more accessible avenues for Indigenous peoples' resistance.

The social media sites with which Indigenous peoples actively engage are many and varied. Facebook and Instagram are both used to host pages dedicated to Indigenous resistance, support, and celebration of culture. Twitter sees hundreds, if not thousands, of posts each day by Indigenous and non-Indigenous peoples alike reflecting on current Indigenous affairs. In particular, the online metal scene has emerged as a site for political engagement and debate. Platforms such as Facebook and YouTube, as well as various dedicated metal forums, provide Indigenous and non-Indigenous heavy metal musicians and fans with sites for the production, consumption, and reproduction of metal culture and the subversion of the ongoing project of colonization.

The Online Metal Scene

The online metal scene includes diverse groups of participants, platforms, and digital spaces. The metal community maintains forums dedicated to metal music culture that draw in thousands of metalheads from around the world. Facebook and YouTube are two well-known sites that host audio and video created and uploaded by musicians and fans alike. These spaces are interconnected. Discussion on these platforms often includes links to relevant videos posted on other sites. Videos hosted on web pages include comments sections where fans and musicians can gather and interact. Often these interactions involve links to videos, pages, posts, and other material on other sites. It is a complex web of fans, musicians, non-fans, onlookers, and published material that makes up the disintermediated online metal scene.

Disintermediated social media technology permits new and effective opportunities for self-publication and political activism. According to Brabazon,

"Disintermediation is a characteristic of peer-to-peer networks, where links are removed from the traditional supply and distribution chain" (2014, p. 192). Disintermediation has had considerable impact on the music industry over previous decades. Prior to computer mediated peer-to-peer networks, the offline music industry had a fairly standard process of consumer engagement. "In analogue, pre-Web 2.0 environments, a musician wrote a song. It was recorded in a professional recording studio. The music was stamped onto a vinyl platform. A marketer created an advertising campaign. The product was shipped to a retail store. The CD or vinyl would then be sold to a consumer via a retail assistant" (Brabazon, 2014, p. 192). The process of making, producing, and consuming music was invariably tied to the system of recording, manufacturing, marketing, and distribution. DIY music culture was perhaps an exception to the mainstream rule, however it still relied on a level of mediation through bootleg recording and tape-trading networks. Fast-forward to the early twenty-first century. Through the forums, video posts, comments sections, and various other platforms, metalheads are producing, consuming, and reproducing heavy metal music culture without record industry intermediaries.

The possibility that fans are now intimately tied to the overall production of music culture reflects what Redhead signaled three decades ago when he pointed out the "changing meaning and contours of rock, pop, and youth culture" (1990, p. 47). Heavy metal music culture is no exception here. The online metal scene, replete with the affordances of digital communication technologies, provides a site for fans and bands to coalesce in the dissemination of ideas and opinions that are important to them. These ideas and opinions are not always concerned solely with musicianship—the online metal scene is also a vehicle for political action.

Of course, metal music has always been political. The genesis of heavy metal music can be traced to many different points in time and space; identifying a starting point is indeed the source of much debate. For many, it began in Birmingham in the 1960s, with well-known band Black Sabbath. Many British metal bands followed, and what emerged was a political reaction to deindustrialization and various military movements across the United States and the United Kingdom. Themes of resistance to religion (Kahn-Harris, 2006; Pereira, 2012), war (Moore, 2009), and modernity (Spracklen, 2013) have permeated metal cultures in the decades since. Anticolonialism is also a theme that has emerged in metal music on numerous occasions. Iron Maiden's "Run to the Hills" is a particularly well-known case in point. This song, including the lyrics "White man came across the sea / He brought us pain and misery / He killed our tribes killed our creed / He took our game for his own need," traces the story of the genocide of First Nations peoples in North America. Metal music continues to be an aggressive and explicit outlet for fans to challenge dominant ideological positions.

Homesick, a metal band from Sydney, Australia, uses the disintermediated online metal scene as an outlet for the dissemination of Indigenous resistance. While they are signed to reputable record label Resist Records, they also benefit from opportunities for self-publication of music and associated content on various platforms within the online metal scene such as Facebook and YouTube. Music and lyrics posted on their Facebook page in 2018 include the lines "The decimation of my culture / As you force us to assimilate / Your totality of oppression / Noose around our fate." This content was posted, it appears, straight from the recording studio—no record company, no retailer, no streaming services. The audio and video content was available for anyone with or without a Facebook account to access, and this remains the case today. The content of this video reflects the active resistance to ongoing colonization that is typical of many of Homesick's songs and social media posts. The message, clearly, is that from the beginning of colonization, Indigenous culture has been systematically destroyed. That assimilation policy in Australia was founded on the notion that Indigenous peoples were a "dying breed" (Sheridan, 1988). These policies and actions have contributed to a future that still looks bleak for Indigenous human rights in this country.

Through disintermediated social media and the subsequent opportunities for self-publication by traditionally nonprivileged voices the theme of anticolonialism is one that can now be heard in Indigenous Australian metal too. The online metal scene also provides opportunities for bands such as Homesick to share interviews and other nonlyrical content that further contributes to their active resistance. In an interview with *Rest Assured* posted online in 2018, Homesick's lead singer discussed the politics of their music.

"Nura" and "Never Ceded" are pretty self-explanatory songs. They both go back to pre-colonialism, when our native indigenous people were free to live and roam, as they had done for thousands of years. It also gives a little insight into the cultural song lines and how astrology was used to map out directions, not to mention the co-existence and understanding of humans and mother earth. It then goes on to touch into the immediate halt that came and the dark past that colonialism brought with it. Rape, deceit, lies and massacre. And now society's expectation is that, well now this happened, sooo get over it and assimilate, even though we don't value you anyways. (*Rest Assured*, 2018)

The themes of resistance and political engagement espoused by Homesick in this and similar posts emerge loud and clear on the band's social media accounts. For Indigenous musicians and fans, the online metal scene, and the ability to self-publish via digital communication technology, is a valuable and effective site where voices can be heard.

Not only is social media an advantageous and strategic site for musicians to publish their music, sidestepping mainstream record company executives, it asks fans to participate in the discussion. Digital communication technology also permits connection between musicians, fans, and music. Messages of resistance as well as challenging debate can be entered into across vast distances by anyone with digital connectivity. No longer are messages filtered through mainstream media or the recording industry. No longer are bands and fans separated by record stores, radio, and MTV. Homesick says what they really think; fans hear it and can respond in real time.

Affordances of the Online Metal Scene as Part of the Cultural Interface

New digital communication technologies offer novel possibilities for human interaction. Social media as we know it emerged at the beginning of the current millennium, though of course computer-mediated communication had worked its way into common usage decades earlier with nonsynchronous bulletin board and email communication (Salmons, 2009). The development of these technologies and the associated suite of social media platforms presented several significant affordances for social interaction. Affordances, a term borrowed from Gibson (1979), are the limitations and opportunities presented to human interactions as a result of the presence of technology. Application of the concept of affordances has seen studies into the limitations and opportunities presented by digital communication technology in the fields of education (Churchill, Fox, and King, 2012; Leacock and Nesbit, 2007; Sullivan and Czigler, 2002); e-citizenship, neighborhood, and community (Bennett, Wells, and Freelon, 2011; Wellman et al., 2003); and gender studies (Cirucci, 2017; Shapiro, 2010). There are variations in how the concept is applied. Mostly, these variations are concerned with what counts as an affordance rather than the effect. Cirucci, for instance, refers to the "tools and functionalities" (2017, p. 1) that are offered by specific software and platforms such as the ability to share, post, and the like. Shapiro, on the other hand, looked to the wider possibilities offered by digital communication technology such as the ability to "save, search, and archive" data (2010, p. 122). At their core, affordances are aspects of technology that offer something new to human social interaction.

Affordances of digital communication technology present new possibilities for Indigenous peoples' resistance and activism in a world that is increasingly connected via social media. Of great significance for Indigenous political activism online are the affordances of permanence and visibility. Permanence refers to the potentiality that posts (words uttered or typed, and pictures shared) and other interactions in online spaces remain in these online spaces. Importantly, with the exception of hardware failure or relatively rare cases of deliberate removal, these posts remain long after the individuals who posted them have left. Visibility, in addition, refers to access to these posts by anybody anywhere. Providing one has access to and familiarity with digital communication technology one can view and search for saved or archived data. Together, the affordances of permanence and visibility provide unique opportunities for messages of resistance and political action to emerge loud and clear and to *remain* in the various sites and pages of the online metal scene.

Consider the following scenario: We meet in a crowded bar at the front of a venue at a metal concert on D'harawal Country. We have a conversation about the band and their new album. The only people who are likely to witness this conversation (aurally and visually) will be in close proximity. Once we leave the bar and return to our respective homes, the meeting is no longer audible or visible at the bar. In fact, the only recollection of the event is in the minds of those who were originally present. Now consider a similar interaction in an online space. We log on to a metal forum. We have a lengthy conversation about a band's newly released album. Now once we leave the forum, our interaction remains. Posts that are aligned with our profile pictures and our user names are recorded indefinitely on this forum for any future participant to observe and even interact with. Moreover, it is not just the people who were online and logged in to the forum at the time of our meeting who have knowledge of the content and "vibe" of the conversation. Any person, from almost anywhere in the world, is able to view this interaction (the text and imagery) for as long as it remains on the forum.

A characteristic of the online metal scene is the emergence of a "writing on the wall"—a highly visible and permanent record of online interaction—that espouses the views and opinions of participants in the scene. In the case of metal bands like Homesick, the "writing on the wall" draws metalheads in to engage with staunch political activism and Indigenous resistance to colonization. The importance of the affordances offered for Indigenous participation online lies in the possibilities for a highly visible and permanent record of Indigenous peoples' resistance and political action. Where once our voices would be drowned out, spoken over, and censored we now have a site where our language remains. The messages brought to the fore are saved and retrievable from a digital archive. When we have left the streets and the conversation is over, the message remains highly accessible. The momentum picks up through reposts and retweets and the conversation keeps going.

The "writing on the wall" in the Indigenous online metal scene provides a record of the interactions that take place in what Indigenous scholar Martin Nakata refers to as the "Cultural Interface" (2007). Nakata proposed the Cultural Interface as a theoretical response to the question of "how particular knowledges achieve legitimacy and authority at the expense of other knowledges" (2007, p. 195). Nakata usefully highlights that the Cultural Interface does not involve a static, singular relation of difference; rather it is a "multi-dimensional space of dynamic relations constituted by . . . competing and contesting discourses within and between different knowledge traditions, and different systems of social, economic, and political organisation" (2007, p. 199). Of primary concern here is how Western epistemology and ontology are maintained in positions of dominance over Indigenous epistemologies and ontologies. Nakata's concept is particularly useful to understand the online metal scene as providing new and dynamic opportunities for the continued negotiation between Indigenous and Western knowledges—that is, a site for Indigenous resistance across time and space and in the face of competing and contested discourses and politics.

The "writing on the wall" in our context leaves behind a record of the presentation and representation of "colliding trajectories" (Nakata, 2007, p. 197) of Indigenous and Western knowledges. This representation is, by no means, monolithic. Rather, it characterizes an ongoing *negotiation* of Indigenous metalhead identity at the Cultural Interface. Indigenous peoples' resistance in the online metal scene is sustained by the affordances of permanence and visibility. The "writing on the wall" records and makes visible what Nakata calls the "[active shaping of] new practices and [adaptation of] our own to deal with the encroaching elements . . . [and the] making and remaking in the everyday" (Nakata, 2007, p. 197). A core theme that emerges in this making and remaking in the online metal scene that characterizes the highly visible and permanent "writing on the wall" is the politics of presence and associated alliance building.

An Indigenous Politics of Presence and Alliance Building

The history of Indigenous peoples' relationships with a colonial nation-state that we now refer to as Australia has been and continues to be undeniably difficult. A key mechanism of the colonial project in Australia is the active silencing of Indigenous voices through both passive and openly violent means (Walker, 2003). Through paternalistic policies and action, colonizers systematically outlawed Indigenous language and cultural practices in the interests of "civilising" the Indigenous populations of Australia. This was a policing and silencing of Indigenous voices in order to maintain the myth of Terra Nullius and the ideological dominance of the colonizers.

The struggle to be politically present in the face of such systematic oppression is no new thing for Indigenous peoples. As shown by Heiss and Minter's *Anthology of Australian Aboriginal Literature* (2014), Indigenous peoples have long been active in producing literary works in the form of poetry, novels, music, and letters. The presence of these works in the Australian literary canon is undeniably political. In a country and society that has gone to such great lengths to erase Indigenous sovereignty through the myth of Terra Nullius and through history books, social commentary, and educational policy, the voices of Indigenous Australians continue to survive. Being published, for many notable and highly influential Indigenous storytellers such as Oodgeroo Nunuccal, Anita Heiss, Archie Roach, and many more, once necessarily relied upon Western gatekeepers. Creative works were housed in museums rather than art galleries or were relegated to artifacts of an ancient race, not worthy of inclusion in contemporary art. Indigenous culture was, and still is, seen as old, ancient, primitive, and unsophisticated (Tsosie, 2017). More importantly, when Indigenous voices challenged mainstream ideology they were actively framed as angry, irrational, and selfish (D'Cruz, 2018).

The advent of social media technology is, more recently and in an ever-increasing way, presenting opportunities for a politics of presence for marginalized peoples. It is a site where individuals can "transmit important values by reconstructing them, if necessary, into different forms and practices" (Nakata, 2007, p. 206). Social media renders our voices visible and permanent and provides an opportunity to "untangle ourselves from colonial histories" (Nakata, 2007, p. 207) without the hurdles once raised by mainstream Western media and publishing avenues. Fair and adequate representation in mainstream media is clearly still a long way off as Indigenous peoples "struggle to have a voice in these forums" (Carlson, 2019, p. 225). However, Indigenous peoples' resistance to ongoing colonization, through maintaining a political presence, can increasingly be facilitated through the affordances of the online metal scene. Social media and the opportunities for self-publication allow us to speak back to continued oppression and to actively resist the silencing. Voices can be heard and challenges leveled at those in the mainstream who continue to favor a colonial discourse and discount Indigenous perspectives.

In addition to visibly challenging colonialism through the political presence of Indigenous voices, social media also offers an invaluable platform for alliance building. The support that is offered and the requests for Homesick to travel for shows highlight the broad reception and import of the band's political presence on social media. The online metal scene offers opportunities for allies to listen, to engage, and to affirm their support. As Barker suggests, "To be an ally first requires recognition of the need for action in a real and present struggle: in this case, the struggle of Indigenous survival and resurgence against colonial and neo-colonial power" (2010, p. 316). Through the affordances of visibility and permanence, bands in the online metal scene such as Homesick constantly educate followers about the need for resistance to colonization in Australia. In the online metal scene, there are large numbers of Indigenous and non-Indigenous metalheads whose posts appear to emerge from a perspective of social justice and who clearly recognize and respond to Indigenous peoples' need for active resistance to colonization.

The affordances of social media and the ability to bypass traditional music production processes allow allies to directly voice their support and their continued opposition to a dominant colonial system. Fans are drawn into music from bands such as Homesick and are faced with the highly visible and permanent record of resistance. On Facebook and YouTube, fans can then offer their own messages of support as well as take with them knowledge about the reality of continued oppression. Upon sharing a tour poster for an upcoming Homesick tour one commenter noted, "The importance of this band and their album cannot be overstated. Homesick have a lot to say about important issues including the rights of indigenous Australians, as well as the whitewashing of our nation's deep historical roots . . . if you like to headbang and think at the same time, Homesick are what you need." This message shows a call to potential allies highlighting the wrongs of the past and present that erase Indigenous culture and history. Furthermore, comments such as these demonstrate the efficacy of the online metal scene in making visible messages of Indigenous peoples' resistance. These messages are shared and viewed by metalheads who are active in the online metal scene anywhere in Australia and the world. They are highly visible and permanent reminders that all Australians need to recognize the legacy of colonialism.

Conclusion

The online metal scene is a key site for Indigenous peoples' political presence, resistance to colonization, and forging of alliances. The affordances of digital communication technology, particularly permanence and visibility, facilitate Indigenous peoples' political presence and alliance building activism that continues to challenge dominant mainstream ideologies about Indigenous inferiority and illegitimacy. Resistance to colonization is a clear and constant theme espoused by bands, and fans, in the Indigenous online metal scene. While these sorts of messages of resistance have long echoed through Australian bars and clubs through the likes of Archie Roach, Coloured Stone, No Fixed Address, and many more Indigenous bands and musicians, the advent of social media technology has changed the game. Bands and fans can now bypass commercial channels of music distribution and promotion and enjoy closer, disintermediated interaction. The opportunity for self-publication and the affordances of visibility and permanence provide favorable conditions for the dissemination of messages of resistance and for Indigenous peoples to be politically present in the online metal scene's highly visible and permanent "writing on the wall."

References

Barker, A. (2010). From adversaries to allies: Forging respectful alliances between Indigenous and settler peoples. In L. Davis (Ed.), *Alliances: re/envisioning Indigenous-non-Indigenous relationships* (pp. 316–333). Toronto: University of Toronto Press.

Bennett, W. L., Wells, C., and Freelon, D. (2011). Communicating civic engagement: Contrasting models of citizenship in the youth web sphere. *Journal of Communication, 61*(5), 835–856.

Brabazon, T. (2014). The disintermediated librarian and a reintermediated future. *Australian Library Journal, 63*(3), 191–205.

Carlson, B. (2019). Disrupting the master narrative: Indigenous people and tweeting colonial history. *Griffith Review, 64*, 224–234.

Carlson, B., Farrelly, T., Frazer, R., and Borthwick, F. (2015). Mediating tragedy: Facebook, aboriginal peoples and suicide. *Journal of Information Systems, 19*, 1–15.

Churchill, D., Fox, B., and King, M. (2012). Study of affordances of iPads and teachers' private theories. *International Journal of Information and Education Technology, 2*(3), 251–254.

Cirucci, A. M. (2017). Normative interfaces: Affordances, gender, and race in Facebook. *Social Media + Society, 3*(2), 1–10.

D'Cruz, G. (2018). Breaking bad: The booing of Adam Goodes and the politics of the Black sports celebrity in Australia. *Celebrity Studies, 9*(1), 131–138.

Gibson, J. J. (1979). *The ecological approach to visual perception.* New York: Psychology Press.

Heiss, A., and Minter, P. (Eds.). (2014). *Anthology of Australian Aboriginal literature.* Montreal: McGill-Queen's University Press.

Kahn-Harris, K. (2006). *Extreme metal: Music and culture on the edge.* Oxford: Berg.

Leacock, T., and Nesbit, J. C. (2007). A framework for evaluating the quality of multimedia learning resources. *Journal of Educational Technology and Society, 10*(2), 44–59.

Moore, R. M. (2009). The unmaking of the English working class: Deindustrialization, reification and the origins of heavy metal. In G. Bayer (Ed.), *Heavy metal music in Britain* (pp. 143–160). Surrey: Ashgate.

Nakata, M. (2007). *Disciplining the savages: Savaging the disciplines.* Canberra: Aboriginal Studies Press.

Pereira, S. (2012). Living on the edge: Black metal and the refusal of modernity. *Comunicação & Cultura, 14*, 175–190.

Redhead, S. (1990). *The end-of-the-century party: Youth and pop towards 2000.* Manchester: Manchester University Press.

Rest Assured. (2018, September). HOMESICK interview with singer Peter Jackson. http://restassuredzine.com/interviews/6057-homesick-interview-with-singer-peter -jackson.

Salmons, J. (2009). *Online interviews in real time.* Thousand Oaks, CA: Sage.

Shapiro, E. (2010). *Gender circuits: Bodies and identities in a technological age.* New York: Routledge.

Sheridan, S. (1988). Wives and mothers like ourselves, poor remnants of a dying race: Aborigines in colonial women's writing. *Kunapipi, 10*(1), 9.

Spracklen, K. (2013). Nazi punks folk off: Leisure, nationalism, cultural identity and the consumption of metal and folk music. *Leisure Studies, 32*(4), 415–428.

Sullivan, K., and Czigler, P. (2002). Maximising the educational affordances of a technology supported learning environment for introductory undergraduate phonetics. *British Journal of Educational Technology, 33*(3), 333–343.

Tsosie, R. (2017). Indigenous peoples, anthropology, and the legacy of epistemic injustice. In I. J. Kidd, J. Medina, and G. Pohlhaus (Eds.), *The Routledge handbook of epistemic injustice* (pp. 356–369). London: Routledge.

Walker, P. (2003). Colonising research: Academia's structural violence towards Indigenous peoples. *Social Alternatives, 22*(3), 37–40.

Wellman, B., Quan-Haase, A., Boase, J., Chen, W., Hampton, K., Díaz, I., and Miyata, K. (2003). The social affordances of the internet for networked individualism. *Journal of Computer-Mediated Communication, 8*(3). https://doi.org/10.1111/j.1083-6101.2003.tb00216.x.

13

Interview with Carly
Wallace, Creator of
"CJay's Vines"

■■■■■■■■■■■■■■■■■■■■■

BRONWYN CARLSON

Carly Wallace is a Dulguburra Yidinji Aboriginal woman from the Atherton
Tablelands in Far North Queensland who is now based in Brisbane, Queensland,
Australia. Carly is an AV Myer Award recipient and completed a graduate
diploma in radio broadcasting at the Australian Film Television and Radio
School (AFTRS) in 2010; she was the first Indigenous radio graduate in the
school's history.

Carly has worked in various media outlets across Australia, including Radio
4KiG in Townsville, ABC 702 in Sydney, ABC 612 in Brisbane, ABC Far
North in Cairns, ABC Digital Radio, and, most recently, NITV (National
Indigenous Television) as a television presenter on *Around the Traps, Yabun Festival*, National NAIDOC Awards coverage, and *Our Songs*.

Carly is the creator and writer of the popular Aboriginal comedy Facebook
page "CJay's Vines," which has over forty thousand followers and more than
two million views of videos and widely shared memes and content (figure 13.1).[1]
Her Facebook is accessible at www.facebook.com/cjaysvines/.

Carly was living and working in Sydney in 2010 when her mother passed
away suddenly. Carly took a short hiatus from the media industry and moved
back to the Atherton Tablelands to raise her brother, who was thirteen years
old at the time before the pair both moved to Brisbane in 2013, where they now

FIG. 13.1 CJay's Vines. (Credit: @CJay'sVines Facebook.)

remain. This life-changing experience was both humbling and extremely difficult but built a resilience within Carly that she now uses to inspire and educate others on overcoming life's hardships.

In addition to her media career, Carly has extensive experience working within the social justice and community spaces working alongside Indigenous youth and community members at Atherton State High School, Waterford State School in Brisbane, and the Youth Advocacy Centre in Brisbane as well as with the Australian Indigenous Mentoring Experience (AIME) nationally.

Carly has been a guest speaker and delivered keynote speeches for community events and organizations including the Youth NAIDOC Awards Night for the Gugan Gulwan Youth Aboriginal Corporation in Canberra, the Marni Wingku event at the University of Adelaide, the Australian Indigenous Mentoring Experience on the Gold Coast, Brisbane, Rockhampton, and Gladstone, and the Dreaming at ECU event at Edith Cowen University, Western Australia, in 2017.

Carly is also a proud ambassador for the NSW Health Take Blaktion sexual health campaign and a current serving board member of the National Ad Standards Panel. She has a passion for working with Indigenous people in the media and community sector and hopes to use her stories of success and struggles to inspire more Indigenous and non-Indigenous people to reach their goals and dreams.

The following interview was conducted by Bronwyn Carlson in March 2019.

BRONWYN: Carly, we are great fans of your work and owe many hours of laughter to your videos. We're particularly interested in hearing about your experiences moving into the space of social media with a very public platform. We'd also like to know more about your strategies or processes from concept, to filming, to editing, to upload, to management of user comments. We'd also like reflect on your views on the role of humor in thinking about being Aboriginal or Aboriginal/Australian politics. Finally, we are interested in understanding more about your experiences with cyberbullying and how you stand up to online trolling. Were you always funny? Did anyone encourage you to start filming yourself or was it just for fun?

CARLY: Originally when I first started it was just for a laugh. I think I've always been funny, a lot of people are at me like "you're not funny," but I've always been someone that a little quick witted. I got quick wit from my dad and my mum had a real cheeky mouth so combining the two, I've learnt really quick from a young age to have a comeback so I think it has come from there. I think Blackfellas just have humor anyway.[2] We have a humor about us and we have this one thing that connects all of us and I found that with my videos. Making people laugh is something that I've always liked to do and what I found I can do. Not everyone finds me funny but that's alright. I like to attempt to find humor in something because it's, no matter what race you are, everyone connects to humor and Blackfella humor is just that little bit different and it's a real part of our kinship I think, but I don't think I'm funny. My man though, will encourage me and at first I did it myself and then showed my family and they were like "oh my god what are you doing?" and I'm like "oh shut up, you're just nothing but haters" but my brother said "you're not funny why are you starting a page for?" Then I got twenty thousand followers and he was like "You should probably put me in a videos" and I was like "Nah you was the one running me down."

BRONWYN: You have forty thousand followers now?

CARLY: Almost, I'm at thirty-seven-something-thousand and yeah it's a bit crazy aye.

BRONWYN: Thirty-seven thousand people are watching what you are doing.

CARLY: Isn't that weird? But even more though because people will share it and I'm like that's weird because I just do it from the bedroom. I just do it from my phone. I don't even let my man watch me do it when I do it, just being silly and it's just me. I think I get that from my days in radio when I use to be in radio. It was just me in the studio and I'll be talking to thousands but it doesn't feel like it and it's just me talking to myself really.

BRONWYN: So there were no career aspirations to be a comedian?

CARLY: No, not at all, I've worked in media and I've worked in that communications industry so I love telling stories and I think that's what CJay's Vines is. It's more telling the story in a funny way. It's funny because the whole comedian title kind of weirds me out. I'm not like a stand-up comedian. I'm not like Eddie Murphy or any of them, even our Aboriginal comedians like Sean Choolburra and others. I don't do what they do. I can't stand on a stage and do jokes because that's not my style of comedy but I guess what I still do is comedy just in a different way. This whole social media has really amplified comedies to different genres and in different ways.

BRONWYN: So social media now creates space for naturally funny people?

CARLY: Yeah as well as personality-based comedy I think is what it is more than anything.

BRONWYN: Who do you find funny? Which comics, or comedians? Any on social media?

CARLY: On social media I love "Bush Tucker Bunjie."[3] I love "Ted's Vines," I love Stephen Oliver, I love "Take Blaktion" which is a sexual health page.[4] I love just watching anyone and everyone. I've got a cousin who's a stand up, Steph Tisdale; she's doing her thing.[5] I appreciate anyone who's giving it a go because it's not easy. I know for a fact. Half the time I'm just trying to make our own family laugh, let alone if I can make a total stranger laugh that's a bonus. Some of the things are a bit of a gamble but you know what, I'll just chuck it out there. I love Sean Choolburra and Kevin Kropinyeri, everyone that our mob loves, but I also love just my own cousins or like aunties and uncles, just real funny ones that can crack ya up.

BRONWYN: Were you using Vine at the beginning? Is this how you came up with your online name CJay's Vines?

CARLY: I watched a lot of vines so I loved that whole like world star vine type compilation stuff. I really loved all that when I first started and vine was around at the time so I wasn't using vine but the concept of vine was that short, sharp, little videos put together or silliness put together in one big compilation. So, I just came up with this idea of what am I going to name the page because it literally made it overnight. I thought I had to come up with a name and my man's like just use vine or something, there was no thought into it because I didn't know what to call it. The only other thing out there to compare it to was "Bush Tucker Bunjie" or "Ted's Vines" just because there's only a couple of us that do this stuff. Then vine disappeared like two months later or something but the name I kept because it's still the same concept even though vines not around or as popular anymore. That's how I came up with the name.

BRONWYN: Have you always used the filters?

CARLY: Yes, I started with the filter because I was on my Snapchat and just started doing that and went oh well I'll keep it because people seem to like the animation of it. It speaks to young people but also just the voice, it was part of the filter, so I just used the filter and thought it was funny. The voice made it a bit more of a comical fantasy type thing that's more of a character so it's not entirely me but it elevates the comedy a little bit more as if an accent would. So, I become something different to just me. Honestly I just did it on Snapchat with the filter and people were like "which filter are you going to use again?" I originally used like a reindeer one and that was around for ages and filters had only just come out. Then people began expecting the filter so I was like alright I'll stick to the filter. And I tried to do one without the filter because some people don't like the filter but it wasn't as popular. So, I was like obviously the filters got to stay. I think people maybe have already associated themselves with the character.

BRONWYN: So then what led you to switch to different platforms? or are you still using Snapchat a lot?

CARLY: I used to have a Twitter profile, not as CJay's Vines but as me, Carly Wallace. Snoop Dogg retweeted me once and what happened next led me to shutting down my account. I made a post using the hashtag #When-inAustralia. People were posting using the hashtag with things like— #WheninAustralia you go and pat a wallaby or whatever. I just chucked one in, went on my Twitter and I'm like #WheninAustralia respect and acknowledge the traditional owners of the country the Aboriginal people.

He obviously liked it, retweets it and instantly I'm open to three million people. I'm like holy hell and that led to my first dose of real trolling, because people started posting things like, "nothing but drinkers" and other negative and derogatory comments. It just started blowing up my phone. I was getting instant messages for over an hour. I couldn't even answer my phone, it was crazy. So I end up having to get a friend to jump online because I couldn't even get on my phone to do it. I asked if they could jump on the computer and shut it down because I can't have this blowing up my phone. I also had another person create a fake profile aimed at me. My experience with trolling and especially on Twitter was enough to really go ughhh look this space, it is like really negative. I'm a story teller so that's not the platform for me like to be able to tell stories how I want to tell them.

So Facebook or Snapchat or Instagram where I like photos as well is more what I like and if I want to engage in something in a social sense or like ya know whatever's happening or trending I can always look on Twitter. I know how to use Twitter, I know the community that's on Twitter but I just choose not to get into it but I use Snapchat first where I do my videos. That enables me to put all my videos in one place and so then I just download that as a video and put it on to Facebook. It saves me needing any type of editing equipment, plus the filters on there are good.

BRONWYN: Which of all those platforms do you think is really the most productive for you in terms of engagement?

CARLY: Facebook definitely because our mob is on it like the biggest users of it so anything I put on Facebook gets way more shares and likes on it than I do on even YouTube so I don't really even use my YouTube.[6]

BRONWYN: I use your YouTube videos in my classes.

CARLY: Yeah and exactly if I knew I'm doing something like that, teaching, where I need to show the videos and I don't want to go on Facebook and I use it as a backup as well for my content so in case it gets taken off Facebook, I've still got it. But I don't usually use YouTube too much I don't find the pick-ups enough.

BRONWYN: Do you have many followers on Snapchat?

CARLY: I think I've got over a thousand or something it doesn't really tell you on Snapchat. I've got a lot because I know when I go to post a story on Snapchat it will show me how many viewers and it's like over a thousand but it's just for CJay's Vines so anyone that adds it I'll accept it so it's kind of an open thing, I don't know how many is on there though.

BRONWYN: Do you have different accounts on Facebook—your personal page and one for CJay's Vines where anyone can follow as well?

CARLY: Yeah and that's where it kind of started because I did it on my personal page to begin with then I got all these friggin people trying to add me. It was open to everyone and everyone kind of knew me and I was like aww nah I don't really like this. If I'm gonna do something like this I'm gonna make a page for that. I like my privacy so I ended up just creating a page so I can put all the content there and kind of keep it separate.

BRONWYN: That's probably a good idea. Give us a description of each of your personas; so including Felicia and Precious.

CARLY: Oh my god. You know it's funny, when I first came up with Precious the flight attendant, the Murri flight attendant, I got this idea because I was flying a lot so I can legitimately recite everything they say, and I love flight attendants (figure 13.2).[7] I actually got through to the second round to become a flight attendant and then another job came up so I took that one instead. I could have been a flight attendant for real, but with that Precious flight attendant I was like "Okay, I really want to do this properly and I want to feel like it" so I dressed up, you know like I did my hair, I got a scarf, and I got the black jacket, and put the lipstick on, and I came out of the room and I was like to my man: "Hello I'm Precious the Murri flight attendant." My man was like oh my god like who's gonna pop out, you know?

And then it was Felicia the Murri reporter; same thing. I got a gammon earpiece, it was just headphones. I got all these real gammon props.

And then I've got Aunty Bron, not you, not based on you; Aunty Bron the Aboriginal Prime Minister of Australia. She had something Aboriginal

FIG. 13.2 CJay's Vines in action filming a skit. (Credit: @CJay'sVines Facebook.)

and she had her glasses on and looked like an academic but they're busted up sunglasses with no lenses, you know? I'm a poor comedian. I don't have money for props I just grab something. I think I had a deodorant bottle once with a microphone thing on top of it and used it as a mic. I think my followers find that even funnier.

They have all kind of got their own personalities. Honestly, it's so strange sometimes I'll do two characters in the one sketch. I did one about how everyone was talking about the Kardashians and it was two Blak girls talking to each other: "Heard Kourtney Kardashian had a baby?" because everyone was talking about it like they knew that woman. So I did this complete conversation of these two characters talking to themselves on the phone while I'm getting dressed in my room, then getting undressed, then putting a jacket on and then I'm taking it off, then I've got a different filters. I'm having this three way conversation with myself. I walk out of it totally confused like: "Who's who? I don't even know who it is."

A lot of them are based on friends of mine or Aunties or people I know. I think everyone imagines what if there was a Blackfella flight attendant, how would she be? Everyone knows that one Precious, or knows that Ebony, or knows that Felicia, you know?

BRONWYN: Is there any particular choices behind which filter you use?

CARLY: I go with the cutest one. No actually, I loved a few different ones: I love a little rabbit because they move when you talk and it gives you a bit more animation. But I first started just using which ever one was there. The reindeer one was quite popular and then the rabbit was up for ages but I use the ones now that have a little bit of a tweak in the voice but not too much so people can understand what I'm saying without being super annoying. I realize that the filter can get annoying, it gets annoying to me sometimes.

BRONWYN: The high-pitch chipmunk voice?

CARLY: Yeah that chipmunk kind of animated voice. But when I don't use it, people don't like it so you can't win! I try to go with the filter that's the clearest and that you can hear but it's also nothing over the mouth, nothing that restricts the face so it's a full character there all the time, so it doesn't distract the viewer too much.

BRONWYN: This is the question we did speak about briefly this morning. The animal component of the filter of your persona could be interpreted in some interesting ways, in terms of Aboriginal culture and identity so as relations with nonhumans, ancestors, etc. Or it could be a big middle finger back to racists who have categorized us as flora and fauna? What have you thought about that?

CARLY: Yeah, I know and I didn't even think about that actually until now, until you asked that. But I don't think we've ever had a little bear with sunglasses as flora and fauna, that's not a native animal so I can't claim that.

BRONWYN: No deeper thinking into it?

CARLY: No, no deeper thinking in it when I'm looking like a reindeer, ya know? We don't have that as native flora and fauna but it's interesting, yeah, when you look at it at that lens.

BRONWYN: It's more about popular culture?

CARLY: Yeah, it's really about what's available. I'm all about doing things on my own. I don't have a graphic designer, I don't have like a full on website, everything you see on CJay's Vines down to my logos, down to my pictures, profiles, everything is done on filters or an app because I like to be able to do it there and then.

BRONWYN: You do have some merchandise available that you spoke about today which most of it has sold out so obviously its popular. Is that something you're going to continue to do?

CARLY: Yeah I've still got shirts up. So, a few of my sayings from my videos, people really liked it. https://cjaysvines.bigcartel.com/.

BRONWYN: "In Ya Hole Troll" I love that one.

CARLY: Yeah, I have another one: "Aboriginality is not a mathematical equation."

BRONWYN: Yes, I saw that, it's quite good too and especially the endless debates about blood quantum and the politics of identity.

CARLY: A lot of people have liked that and got shirts for their kids and stuff so I've still got them available. Yeah but I don't really make any money off it. I use whatever money is made to make more. I just put it up there because people ask for it, that's basically it.

BRONWYN: And I think that your logo is obviously a kind of cartoon version of you?

CARLY: Yeah, of me. It's so weird, this is how it came about. I took a photo with the filter on Snapchat, saved the photo then I used another app which added like another filter on top of it to make it look more cartoony. And then, I added another app which was the Thug Life app and then it's got all different thug life things like bandanas, sunglasses, chains, whatever and I added the sunglasses so it's taken three apps to do that one thing. And then it was on a shirt and I'm like bloody hell.

BRONWYN: Awesome editing.

CARLY: Right? All from my phone.

BRONWYN: That's fantastic.

BRONWYN: What are your two most successful or your two most favorite videos that you've produced?

CARLY: I think the flight attendant one, that one really took off, that's what made CJay's Vines I think.

BRONWYN: Why do you think that one is popular?

CARLY: I dunno, I think a lot of people obviously fly and they know the wording and then to see it in a Blak version is just funny. People just go "Oh that's funny like imagine." And the things that we think when we are passengers like extra leg room, you can't lift that door. I had someone look at me real dirty the other day because I accidentally stood in the emergency section. Even in America when I was in Hawaii I got on a flight and they're all looking at me, I said "Aye don't look at me like that, I can lift this door, you're all safe with me you know? We all know it." Yeah so if there was a Blackfella doing it and she was real Blak that's how she'd probably be.

So, I think the flight attendant one and anything to do with Blak mums. The videos I do like "Blak mums say this" or "act like this" because it gives me good memories of my mum growing up in my childhood and they're the ones our mob really share in. They seem to really resonate with a lot of our mob.

BRONWYN: What of the non-Indigenous audience?

CARLY: Yeah, I have a lot of non-Indigenous followers and I think it's because it's something that they can laugh with and share in, they kind of feel a little bit guilt free. I've had a lot of people say "oh I've learnt so much just watching your stuff" and I've even had university lecturers tell me they use my videos like you do. I've got teachers that use my stuff to engage with their kids or with Indigenous issues so it's become a safe space I guess.

BRONWYN: How does that make you feel to know that people are using your stuff for education?

CARLY: It's cool, it's really cool because if I can make one person laugh or if I can change a stereotype and make people think about it. But I love to play up the stereotypes don't get me wrong and I've had people say "oh that's nothing but a stereotype why do you show us like that and all in that light" and it's like well is it wrong? Is it false? Or is it true? Because everything I do is a reflection of my life, and my childhood, and our mob that I know, that's in my life personally. It's observational so it may not sit right but it's what happens.

BRONWYN: That's so true.

CARLY: But yeah people learn from it, that's cool. That's the inspiration I guess, just real life! From real life, from watching our mob hanging out with mob. I think I got it from my radio days of making something out of nothing you know? And looking at something and going how can I make that a topic or how can I make that funny. And mine with CJay's Vines is how can I make this relatable to appeal to mob because I know that's what our mob really love, they really love to see themselves in the skit because we're not portrayed good in the media. So when they find the platform, or when they see some of my Bush Tucker Bunjie or Stephen Oliver you know they go "yeah that's a little bit of me" or "they're talking about my culture" or "that's in my family."

BRONWYN: So you mentioned before at the Indigenous youth and cyberbullying symposium that you are sometimes a little reluctant or you filter or censor some of the videos several times before you put them up. Some particular topics, so what are some of the topics?

CARLY: If it's risky, I don't like to put anything out there that's gonna damage our mob or looks like I'm running our mob down or anything like that. Like I said, I like to be as truthful as I can but in a comedy aspect. I know that identity is sensitive but I also know it's a real issue. We'll think it or we will know someone that's gone "well where they from . . . I dunno" but no we'll speak to each other and everyone will run something down but no one will ever actually say it. I've always been someone that's, growing up with my Blak mother her mouth was on point, and she would be the person that would say what everyone was thinking and I've just modeled that behavior. I think it's just part of my personality. I like to be able to talk to things but do it in a respectful manner. Comedy is my way of dealing with that trauma sometimes. I've been through a lot of traumatic stuff in my life, as have a lot of our mob and like I said in the symposium "If you don't laugh you cry and if you don't cry you laugh." As positive as I can be and as respectful as I can be with pushing that line, I'm kind of making people uncomfortable but doing it in a truthful way.

The things I do get reluctant about are anything to do with identity (even though it's something we talk about), white people or Blackfellas—how we go about the white people, even some of the language that I use. I really do try to think about how I'm gonna do the skit with also remaining true to myself because that's the hardest bit. I don't wanna filter myself too much where I'm just playing it safe because that's not what comedy is about really.

BRONWYN: Do you have a script?

CARLY: I come up with an idea, so it could be "Blackfullas on public transport" right? It could be nothing. Or I might just look at something and go like "Blak people catering" or something I've seen or heard or whatever. Johnathan Thurston (an Indigenous former professional rugby league player), perfect example on the weekend, everybody on my Facebook: "Oh Johnathan you're the man," "oh he's retiring," and everyone was going on, EVERYBODY. I was like "oh my god." Anyone would think this fella was dying the way our mob go. I took that idea and then I just emulated what I'd seen online, what everyone was saying and doing. And so I'll write a bit of a script in my notes on my phone and sometimes I'll find like top headlines or topics or ideas and I'm like "what the hell is that?" but I've done it and gone "ooh it's not today but I know I'll come back to that." It's just easy for me to then when I record it, I'll just copy and paste. So you know like "How Blak Mums Go . . ." or something and then put the caption, so I'll write it first. And then I don't stick to the script, I'll kind of write little bits and then I'll just kind of add a little at the same time. It's good to have a structure so I know where I'm going.

BRONWYN: I guess you get a lot of positive comments about your work as well. What have been some of the more positive comments that people have responded with?

CARLY: My partner asked me this the other week, he's like "who's been some of your stand out followers or comments?" Because I was dealing with some trolling and he's like "Think about the good ones" you know? There's a little boy I met last year at NAIDOC.[8] His mum came up to me, his name is Mason, he's got a little Instagram page called @facebymase and he wants to be a beauty blogger. Mason's only young, oh god I can't even remember how old he is, I'm gonna say between eight and ten. Beautiful, little Aboriginal boy and his mum came up and his other little brother and she's like "oh CJay we came here just to see you today . . . this is Mason, he really wanted to meet you" and he's just looking at me with like admiration in his eyes. I took some photos with them and you know yarned and stuff and then I got home and I had a tag on Instagram. He'd posted and said you know "I wanted to wear makeup at NAIDOC today but I was too shamed but now that I've met CJay I'll wear it again next year." That just melts my heart. He bought my shirt and like he wears it proudly. It's just so nice to have people that I've made a difference to by being me, you know? That's cool, that's who I do it for.

But there's been a lot of people. I get a lot of people, even down to mental health, people who have felt suicidal message me saying "I have depression and your videos really lifted me up" or "I've got cancer, I'm in hospital and I watch your videos to lighten up my day." The impact that I have just blows my mind. I never set out to do that, that was never part of the plan but it's kind of like an extra bonus that I get. That's why I do it now.

BRONWYN: That's pretty big.

CARLY: It's big, yeah. I feel a responsibility to them. I feel like as much as trolls or cyberbullying can get you down or mob running you down or whatever, it's like you don't get the messages that I get, you don't see the texting that goes back and forth, or people that come up to me randomly at shops wanting to hug me. That stuff spins me out. That's why I keep doing it.

BRONWYN: Have you ever been asked for your autograph?

CARLY: I think that's kind of old school now? I think, yeah, it's a bit old school, it's selfie now. I get asked can I get a photo. I had a woman chase me down. I was at late night shopping and we were buying a washing machine. I was in my work clothes. She was going up the escalator, I was coming down with my man, I was zoned out because I'd had the longest day ever and looking like a rat. She saw me and she reached over and looked like she was touching my man. I was thinking "aye who's this touching my man?" Then she goes "oh CJay!" and I'm looking at her thinking do I know her? I've got the worst memory so I'll meet people and completely forget where I meet them. She says "Oh CJay! Oh my god! Can I get a photo?" She was going frantic, holy hell. So, I was like yeah, and she ran up the escalator, ran down, pushed all these poor, Asian mob out the way, they're all looking like who's this? She's there trying to get a photo with me on the escalator so I'm like let's go down here and we'll get a photo. And then you know I'm yarning with her. Yeah so there's random little moments like that. But it's more if I go to a community event or if I'm at somewhere with schoolkids. Stuff like that. It just depends aye.

BRONWYN: So even without the filter they recognize you?

CARLY: Yeah, I used to be able to hide behind the filter a lot but I think I also do live updates every now and then on my feed, you know, if I'm feeling slack. I do little shout outs and mob like to engage in that. So, I think because of that people have started to be able to recognize me. But I'm not at the point of being any type of celebrity status where I can't go shopping. You never know. I can't buy a washing machine I know that, nah [laughs].

BRONWYN: So, you talked today about, of course, the cyberbullying and trolling. So, it would be really good to include that in the interview if you wanted to speak to us a bit about the page getting taken down, the trolling, and some of those comments you experience.

CARLY: Yeah, I've gotten a lot of racist type comments from predominantly white men. No real white women, you know? It's white men that seem to target anything to do with my race, or anything I put out there that's something to do with my skin color, or the way I speak. They will find it, and if it's getting a lot of views, a lot more people see it and then they wanna engage with it. I've had things from people calling me anything from a "coon" to "you're white as snow, you're not a real Black." You know, all that type of stuff, which is just like crazy.

BRONWYN: What about threats of physical violence?

CARLY: Yeah, threats of physical violence, I've had that before. I posted a meme one time and there were about two-thousand-something comments, it was about identity and our mob really liked it and made comments like, "True, this is true," "Oh my god." They were sharing and sharing it saying things like, "Man, this is something we all wanted to say, but she just said it. Holy hell." Then there were a handful of people that were like "you can't say this, this is lateral violence" or "you can't talk about this or that." They can't read between the lines of comedy and they're just seeing it for what it is and making their own interpretation of what it means, not what it actually means. So, I wrote a comment and I said: "If you're upset about this meme, it's probably because you are who I am targeting, you're probably the one that I'm talking about." That wasn't towards anyone, it was just a general comment. Then, I had this girl, who I obviously blocked, I couldn't remember what she even wrote, to be honest. She wrote something and I thought "oh she obviously don't like it. I don't have to have you on my page, it's not a democracy, I can get rid of whoever." So, I deleted her and a few others, and she found my personal Facebook page because we had mutual friends. She inboxed me. Someone had screenshotted my comment of: "If you're upset about this, it's probably aimed at you." She thought I was talking about her, personally; someone had seen it, sent it to her, and she's in-boxed me: "Oh how dare you! You think you're so deadly . . . you're not even funny . . . wait till I see you in person . . . how dare you write this about me." I was like "I've got like 30,000 people, why would I be talking about you? I don't even know you." That was the first time I replied to somebody, I said: "Sis, calm down, for one, I wasn't talking about you, personally, I actually don't even remember what you wrote. I just know it was negative and I got rid of you. Like chill." And she was going off. Writing me paragraphs and I was like: "listen, the convo is not going anywhere I'm just gonna leave you now. Be good."

Wow, that really spun me out. It was like okay, alrighty this is next level. And it's like probably not unusual that I come across this girl sometimes. We're both in the community.

BRONWYN: And she'll wanna fight with you?

CARLY: That's it! We'll be one of those fight videos on YouTube. But for me I thought she really took it out of context and really took it to the next level. It's actually nothing to do with her personally, it's the people who really take what they see and they interpret it however they want to. Even though, I had no intention of it looking like how she received it, she took it there. But you know, it comes with it hey? The good and the bad, but it doesn't make it right. Trolling has definitely been a part of the CJay's Vines journey that's for sure.

BRONWYN: You mentioned before, there was a meme made about you. Tell us about that meme and how it made you feel.

CARLY: That was only like the other week. I was like: "What the hell!" I hadn't had trolling for a while or any hate, I was kinda like "oh this is good, no crap to deal with." But someone tagged me in it, tagged my actual name in it and I hadn't seen it because it was on somebody else's timeline. So, it was already a meme, he had taken my image, which is copyright by the way if you're listening, don't worry I've already checked with my lawyer. He had taken my image from CJay's Vines and put it on another thing and was like: "Oh I stepped in shit" and it was a character lifting their foot up and it was my image on the bottom of the shoe.

BRONWYN: How did it make you feel seeing that?

CARLY: Oh it's a meme, I was like congratulations, you went to a bit of effort there, so good on ya.

BRONWYN: That could still be considered cyber bullying.

CARLY: Still cyberbullying, yeah. But it was like "okay who's gonna see this? Only mob." I actually looked at his page and he was probably eighteen to twenty-one. I could get upset and go oh you're an idiot or whatever, but I'm like he's an eighteen- to twenty-one-year-old, his brain's not even fully developed, I can't be mad at the dude. He just doesn't like me, that's alright. But I would never go and make a meme with his face and put it on my shoe.

I think people detach themselves and think that I'm not real life. They see me as some type of character. I think he also was trying to dabble in the online comedy space. Maybe he was a little bit threatened or it was jealousy or whatever.

I had a thought to actually reach out to him and go "bruh do you actually wanna have a yarn about it?" Let's have a yarn about this because I could go "oh you're an absolute idiot" and share and get him reported or I could maybe go let's have a chat about why you did it. I'm interested, ya know? It could be "oh I hate you," okay cool like "how do you think that made me feel?" or "how do you think it portrays you as a person sharing that?" I thought about doing that but like oh I don't have time or the energy. I think that people live and learn. He might get popular on social media and he might start receiving some hate, to be on the other end of it. You know, see how he feels.

BRONWYN: Have you ever had to take a break from social media, from the fatigue of it all?

CARLY: Yeah, like the last three months.

BRONWYN: So, you've taken three months off?

CARLY: Yeah, I've taken a couple months off, every now and then. I never know when I'm gonna post something. I used to want to do one a week. But it's actually harder than it looks to come up with content and to constantly be entertaining people, or to come up with something funny, original and new that's not copying someone else. In our space, in Aboriginal comedy and Indigenous comedy, its small, we all kind of have mirrored thinking with the sketches that we do. So, like Bush Tucker Bunjie did something similar to me on Saturday with Johnathan Thurston. Not the same skit, but we both had the same idea without even thinking about it because it's such a small space and we both have the same type of followers and family, that we've seen the same thing. So, of course it's gonna be mirrored stuff, you know?

BRONWYN: Do you reckon there is a big difference between trolling from Indigenous mob and non-Indigenous mob?

CARLY: Yeah, you know it hurts more when it's from mob. It hurts more because I started CJay's Vines as a joke with my family. I actually started too by taking off Kooris, because I'm Murri, and there's a little rivalry between Murris and Kooris.[9]

BRONWYN: Yeah, of course.

CARLY: We all have that little, it's like state of origin with the culture really.

BRONWYN: Plus, the Blues won didn't we?

CARLY: Well my man's a Koori and I'm Murri so we constantly have this little rivalry in our household where I'm like "Murris are funnier . . . nah not even" you know? And so I started CJay's Vines to chuck off at his stuff you know? To chuck off at Kooris and I would talk like them and act like them.

I get people thinking that I'm Koori because I can do their voice down to a Tee. It started kind of from that. But yeah, because I started with that intention of just a bit of fun and mucking around, just imitating stuff and being observational, and now it's grown and more people are following and I get all these nice people telling me the difference that I'm making, and then I get someone from mob running me down or whatever, like that hurts more. When people interpret what I'm doing as creating stereotypes, that's not what I'm aiming to do but I can't help the way you interpret things, I'm not gonna be able to control that. I can only be me, and I can only do what I know to do. Comedy is different levels, different tastes, and it's important to respect everyone's different tastes. I know that I'm not for everyone, but I've always said I made CJay's Vines for our mob, and if you're a non-Indigenous person that gets it and understands it, you're welcome to it. But it's not really for you, no offence, none of that, it's just I do it because I like to make our mob laugh and be happy. But when I get trolled by non-Indigenous people, it's not really surprising because that's the people I'm taking off. Of course, you'd be angry because I'm taking the piss out of you. That's fair.

BRONWYN: You could do a skit on all the trolling comments that you get. You did talk today about when your site was taken down, do you wanna tell us a bit more about that?

CARLY: Yeah, well it got to the level where I was starting to get a lot of views and a lot of followers. I think the more popular I got, obviously, more people were like oh what's this about, you know? And they would see me on their timeline heaps and, again, the different tastes in comedy or whatever, and I had started to do things more controversial. So, at first it was kind of taking imitation-type stuff about Blak mums or Koori pickup lines and just funny little things like that.[10] But then I started to move more into things that get said when we're light skinned.

BRONWYN: A bit more political?

CARLY: Yeah, and not that I was trying to be political but it was just like this is how it is. I'm just being observational and how we would like to talk back to you is like this. And how we do talk back to you is like this. When I started to get into that political lens, people started to really come out of the woodworks. The more views there were, the more hate, you know? It got to the point where enough people hated me and reported my page for whatever reason.

BRONWYN: What did they report? You don't know?

CARLY: I don't know. I have no idea.

BRONWYN: Was it community standards?

CARLY: They were just reporting my page because I think if it was a video they were reporting, the video would just be taken down or the post would have been taken down, but the page got taken down. The whole page. They were reporting the page. It would have had to be enough, from my guess, like more than one person doing it because at this point I had about sixteen thousand followers. I can't imagine one person reporting the page would have been enough to get it down. I think there would have had to be more than one.

BRONWYN: Yeah, I'd imagine.

CARLY: Yeah, I think it was the shift from when I started doing that more political, kind of flipping the script on racism and all that stuff that got to the point of getting taken down. It got banned for like three weeks. I was devastated. I had no answer besides: "You've breached community standards." What community standards? What can I fix? What can I do? I actually genuinely wanted to know; I still want to know so I don't do that thing again. But I think the answer was: "Too many people hated you and you've been taken down."

BRONWYN: How long did it take to get your page back up?

CARLY: It was gone for about two, three weeks. This one day, I kind of got to the point of accepting it was gone. At this point I hadn't backed any of my stuff up. All of my videos were gone and my views and all the likes and I was like "oh, man." I put a lot of time and effort into that.

BRONWYN: Did you get it all back?

CARLY: Oh, yeah. When the page got reinstated it was all still there. I was just like peaking. I was thinking "oh my god, I wonder if it's still all gonna be there, if it even comes back."

BRONWYN: So, given that you weren't told anything do you think it's some cultural bias going on there? Racism? Sexism?

CARLY: I don't know. I think, we all know as mob, anything with the word "Aboriginal" it's gonna get negative traction. No matter what. I'm talking about racism, and I'm actually finding ways to combat it and people don't like that. They like to have control. We've been oppressed people for a long time, and we're not oppressed anymore. We're not gonna do it, we got fire in our guts now. We've always had fire but we've got this power of social media to take control, and when we take that power away from people, they don't like it.

BRONWYN: So, how did the fight go to get it back?

CARLY: So, I had a meltdown, wrote a status: "Someone, anyone, can anyone help?" I tagged a whole bunch of people who were savvy in online space. Leesa Watego, gotta give her a shout out to her because I wrote something blabbering to her like help! Like does anyone actually know how to do this? Because this was something I had never done before. How do I navigate this? And a few people contacted me from National Indigenous TV (NITV) and other media (https://www.sbs.com.au/nitv/article/2017/06/12/internet-star-cjays-vines-removed-facebook).

I had a follower start a petition to get me back: "Bring CJay's Vines Back." Like two thousand and something people signed it within a week, and left all these lovely comments. I was just like "wow, people actually care about this page. It's their page, it's not my page." That's kind of when I started to realize it was bigger than just me, it's the community's page now, it needs to come back. I had a lawyer friend working on it and I also had someone I had contacted on Facebook who was working behind the scenes in America, so there was that time difference I was like "Anything? Anything? Anything?" Then I had one of my good mates, Martin, he did a lot of ground work. He was on the phone to them, Facebook, at like three in the morning going, "I'm not getting off the phone until you reinstate the page, until it comes back."

BRONWYN: That's a lot of effort!

CARLY: Yeah I had so many people fighting for it.

BRONWYN: Did that make you feel better about your worth after they deleted your page?

CARLY: Yeah, I guess so. Then it just came back. It was like "We've reviewed it and its all good, here it is again." You idiots. No actual reasoning, just "You've breached community standards." I don't know what that standard is I breached. So, I don't even know how to avoid it again and I always think its gonna happen again. But yeah I had a lot of people fighting for it so it was nice.

BRONWYN: What advice would you have for people to combat bullying, trolling, cyberbullying, and how to keep safe?

CARLY: I think the one thing with people online, whether it's somebody you even know who's trolling you down to a complete stranger or complete troll made up just to write negative things. That person is wanting your reaction. They're wanting you to engage with something. They're not gonna stop, they're just gonna keep going because they're actually just sitting there living for this. You gotta realize, you're a normal person going about your day and they want to hurt you. There is a level of sadism in it. There's narcissism in it. There's a whole bunch of personality disorders behind these trolls that you're not gonna be able to fix by responding to them. They're not going to listen to you. They're not going to go, "oh I'm really sorry." They're just gonna keep going. For your own mental health, my tip would be screenshot something. Its lucky I've screenshotted because now I am able to use that in symposiums, like the one today, where I can share that for other people to learn from.

BRONWYN: How do you feel when you reread them?

CARLY: Yeah, I found one the other day and I was like "oh that's yuck." Especially when you read them one after the other. I like to compare it to an assault to the mind, it's like a physical punch to the mind every time you read it. It can really drag you down and drain you. So, I screenshot it, I keep it somewhere, not always if it's just something really simple I'll just block and delete. But when it's something racist or something that's vile I'll screenshot because I think you need to talk about it. But I ban people and I block them, and I won't sleep until they're gone off my page. A lot of the time if I know it's someone in community that's gone too far, I'll find that person's page and I'll ban them from my own personals so they can't contact me on my personals now. So, that's important: banning them, not replying to them. Just don't reply because that's what they want. A lot of the time they want to feed off your profile, they want to feed off your name to get themselves' attention. It's like "nah, you can't use me to get attention, not happening."

BRONWYN: How did you come up with your #InYaHoleTroll? What was that over? That's a cool hashtag. I love it.

CARLY: I just came up with it. I was sitting on the couch and I had a lot of trolling going on. I love Arthur, the cartoon. Growing up, it was on ABC channel and it's just the cutest little cartoon and there's a little girl called DW (Dora Winifred), that's Arthur's little sister. She's so funny. So, there's all these memes with her and Arthur now. It's actually like a trending thing and it's the best thing ever. I saw a little photo of her and she was up against a fence with glasses on looking real cool. I put that up and said "Blocking my trolls like this" and it was just like #InYaHoleTroll. I don't even know how I came up with it but then I got people since then using it. I just see random people using this hashtag and I'm like "Hey, that's from my page."

BRONWYN: So, have you been able to monetize or earn any profit from all this positive interest in your work and all the platforms you're working on?

CARLY: Not online I haven't. YouTube takes a lot now to actually earn money, Facebook as well. But I've earnt money by doing talks, you know, going to schools or going to NAIDOC or an MC. So, I've actually had to go and get an ABN (Australian Business number) because people are like "do you have a business card?," no, but I'll make one. I've made one, I've had to do an email address too. I've had to set this up as a little kind of business because you never know who you're gonna meet or who wants you to come somewhere. I've done the sexual health campaign Take Blaktion to appeal to young, Indigenous people in communities about being safe around their sexual health. So, we've used skits and I've been able to promote that on CJay's Vines. I endorse things. There's not been a lot of money, it's not a steady income. I can't make a full-time career just yet.

BRONWYN: But with thirty-seven-thousand-plus viewers on all the platforms etc., would you consider yourself a social media influencer?

CARLY: I think that's what people call me. It's weird saying that, "an influencer" aye?

BRONWYN: I've seen it on some shows on TV when that's the title of their job.

CARLY: That's the title! I know! I don't want that title! I've still gotta work. "I'm a social media influencer"—it's weird!

BRONWYN: It is a weird title. What does it mean?

CARLY: What does it mean? Who do I influence? Influence is a big word.

BRONWYN: Clearly with thirty-seven thousand people following you that's like insanity. What the hell? That is huge!

CARLY: I know! Yet I have no friends. I'm the most antisocial person you'll ever meet. Imagine if those thirty-seven thousand people gave me a dollar each, that'd be awesome.

BRONWYN: You should put a call out for that, do a skit.

CARLY: Yeah, yeah.

BRONWYN: Have you been approached by producers or networks to write or perform like Black Comedy (A TV show featuring Aboriginal and Torres Strait Islander comedians)?

CARLY: Yeah, I did the Black Comedy workshop last year. They put a call out, like they do every year, for a new set of writers. I had so many followers tagging me in it. I was like "oh my god stop tagging me!" So, I was like "alright, I'll apply, please stop tagging me." I don't really want to be on television, I don't want to be an actor. I would love to be like the Australian Oprah, that would be deadly, like have my own talk show. That would be mad, aye? NITV if you're listening.

BRONWYN: I think that would be popular, actually.

CARLY: Right? It would be fun as. But I don't want to be a stand-up comedian, I don't wanna do those types of things. That's not what I'm in it for. What I do is very different to acting but I do have presenting skills. I've done a lot of public speaking and I love sharing stories. That stuff there I have had a lot of people contact me like "can you do skits for this? Can you do skits for that?" I'm a little bit picky with it because I am also aware that people would like to use your followers. Not that that's always their intention but they'd be silly not to. But I'm picky because I like to keep CJay's Vines as that. I know that every time I step out of that realm, my followers don't always necessarily like it. They like me to do the same thing. I've tried different things; I've tried maybe without the filter but my followers are so used to what I do. This is why we follow her so don't change. They back me when I speak up about issues. I try to use the platform for that as well. I know I've got an influence and I know I've got a responsibility as well. I've always been a political person. I've grown up with a very strong, Blak mother and family so I can't sit quiet when I've got thirty-seven thousand people following me, you know? I'm gonna have my say if there's a death in custody or a young Aboriginal boy has been run over like I can't not. It is hard.

BRONWYN: After being at this academic environment here, talking about cyberbullying, Aboriginal youth, and sitting with us for this interview, how would Felicia, the Murri news reporter, report out on what she's experienced today?

CARLY: It's hard to do CJay's Vines characters in front of other people, I get real shame. No filters and I can't do it when people are watching me because I get too shame. But I think if there was some type of commentary it would be like: "What these migaloo ones talking bout? They don't know our mob!" or like: "Cyberbullying . . . I never heard my aunty say lateral violence before? What the?"[11] I love to be silly, I'm not a serious person. I just can't be. One of these things I'm sure if I could sit and think about today, I could probably write something about it. And I'd like to actually write some sketches on responses to trolling or to reading things online and do my own type of thing around it because I think I am someone who can influence and who has had that experience, who can live it and speak on it.

BRONWYN: I think that #InYaHoleTroll is empowering too because it's like "get stuffed."

CARLY: Yeah, get stuffed and in ya hole, this is how we deal with that. I've actually replied to trolls with a picture of my face with the Thug Life and went "In Ya Hole Troll." Then they will go, "oh this is so stupid" and I'll just keep posting it and it drives them mad. It's so funny. Its only very rare that I reply to trolls because they're just so stupid and half of them can't spell, but I'll do it just because I'm in a stirring mood, you know? And I'll just reply with my own meme so it is empowering.

BRONWYN: So maybe CJay's Vines will do some cyberbullying stuff?

CARLY: Hopefully. Watch this space.

Notes

1. The video-sharing app Vine limited videos to six seconds in length. While the app was very popular at one time, the introduction of the ability to upload videos to other social media platforms such as Instagram and Snapchat instigated a decline in the use of Vine. Twitter purchased Vine in 2016, and it has ceased to be used for video sharing.

2. "Blackfella" is a term used by Aboriginal and Torres Strait Islander people to describe themselves and other Aboriginal and Torres Strait Islander peoples. See Carlson et al. (2014).

3. See Bush Tucker Bunjie at https://www.youtube.com/channel/UCvvtAeolyx21 LufKsnEMr_A.

4. See Take Blak Action at https://takeblaktion.playsafe.health.nsw.gov.au/.

5. See Steph Tindale at the 2019 Melbourne International Comedy Festival Gala, https://www.youtube.com/watch?time_continue=3&v=GKzHvHaKGVc&feature =emb_logo.

6 "Mob" is a colloquial term used by Aboriginal people to describe Aboriginal people as a collective.
7 "Murri" is a term generally used to describe Aboriginal people from the state of Queensland.
8 NAIDOC is a weeklong celebration of Aboriginal and Torres Strait Islander peoples and cultures. See https://www.naidoc.org.au/.
9 "Koori" is a term generally used to describe Aboriginal people from the state of New South Wales.
10 Indigenous people in Australia often refer to themselves as "Blak" as opposed to "Black." It is an expression of taking back power and control within a society that doesn't offer Aboriginal and Torres Strait Islander peoples the opportunity for self-determination as individuals and communities. For more information, see https://sites.google.com/site/australianblakhistorymonth/extra-credit.
11 "Migaloo" refers to non-Indigenous people or white people specifically.

14

"We're Alive and Thriving . . . We're Modern, We're Human, We're Here!"

••••••••••••••••••••

The 1491s' Social Media
Activism

JEFF BERGLUND

The gravity and magnitude of colonization make it all too simple for non-Indigenous peoples sympathetic to Indigenous causes to focus on dire inequities and the lack of economic, political, social, and educational access to the rights and privileges of the nation-states who colonized their sovereign nations. Indigenous artists, authors, and filmmakers have similarly been pulled to the "gritty realism" end of the representational spectrum and have fallen prey to similar limitations. Some critics have called the works of academics—the works of documentarians, filmmakers, and writers alike—who focus only on dysfunction and deprivation, "poverty porn" (Ross, 2013). By contrast, the 1491s, an Indigenous comedy troupe that broadcasts through YouTube, Twitter, and Facebook, vigorously work against this reductive take on Indigenous realities, not by ignoring truths but by highlighting the everyday incarnations of beauty, intelligence, survival and wit manifest in the humorous scenarios they construct. Bobby Wilson (Sisseton Dakota), one of the founding members of the 1491s, summed this up succinctly during a 2013 TEDx Talk in Manitoba: "The big thing we're trying to fight, man, is go cry over somebody else's tragedy, 'cause we're alive and thriving, we have absolutely. . . . The thing that gets forgotten in the middle of all the other things is that we're modern, we're human, we're here!" (TEDx Talks, 2013).

This chapter examines the activist role played by the 1491s in social media spaces, particularly on YouTube but also on supportive platforms such as Facebook and Twitter. While their work is humorous and deeply ironizing and quite simply brings happiness to people, their work connects fans together and uses the positive energy of comedy to galvanize others, with a particular emphasis on shaping the ways Indigenous peoples are seen, how Indigenous peoples see themselves, and how changes might be implemented that lead Indigenous people to think critically about the conditions that they may resist and change (see also the interview with Carly Wallace in this volume). Certainly, individual members of the 1491s have their own activist engagements in social media spaces, ones that are more overly and recognizably politically activist in orientation. Most notably, Dallas Goldtooth (Santee Dakota and Diné) has been extremely active on Facebook, Facebook Live, and Twitter as he broadcast from the Standing Rock, North Dakota, resistance to the Dakota Access Pipeline from August 2016 through January 2017. While Goldtooth's recent efforts deserve particular consideration in a separate analysis, I contend that his and his colleagues' work as the 1491s is equally profound and impactful and deserves to be understood as activist in orientation and intent. The magnitude of their reach and their subversive power rests in their ability to lift up others through razor-sharp critiques and energizing, often humorous and positive messages, directed inside as well as outside of Indigenous communities.

In addition to Goldtooth, the 1491s are composed of Bobby Wilson (Sisseton Dakota), Ryan Red Corn (Osage), and Migizi Pensoneau (Ponca and Ojibwe). Occasionally, two other regular contributors make appearances: Sterlin Harjo (Mvskoke) and Tito Ybarra (Red Lake Band of Ojibwe). Core members have been producing their work and uploading videos to YouTube since 2009. Their name posits a point of origin prior to western colonization, as 1492 marks in the western hemisphere the onslaught of the Columbiad and European empire building and genocide throughout the Americas. Early on someone suggested the name "1492" to mark the starting point of Western imperialist expansion in the Americas, but they quickly realized that it would be more poignant and humorous to subtract a year, to imagine a world free of the devastating impacts of colonization. After all, their work, by and large, is to decolonize, to push back against ongoing neo- and para-colonialism. As of January 2020, their YouTube Channel has had 9,781,861 views with 54,800 subscribers. They have 60,668 followers on Facebook and 21,046 on Twitter.

My aim in this chapter is to contribute to a growing body of scholarship on Indigenous social media use and to a deeper understanding about the role played by YouTube in connecting Indigenous and non-Indigenous viewers through work by Indigenous performers such at the 1491s. In part 1 I situate this analysis within scholarship on YouTube and Indigenous social media use. In part 2, of the dozens and dozens of choices to draw from, I turn my attention to their most popular humorous video, one that keys in on debilitating cycles of behavior (including internalized colonialist logic) within communities, particularly centering on men. The logo for the 1491s is an arrow turned in on itself, a symbol of the group's willingness to turn the critique on themselves and the communities of which they are a part. I situate this analysis in the tradition of humor within Native culture. In part 3, I look at their more typical activist-based work such as public service announcements (PSAs) and celebrations of cultural strength and resilience. Undoubtedly, the audience base for these more serious works in which they are the producers and not the stars in front of the camera has been built and sustained by the comedic performances I focus on in part 2 of the chapter. Together, the great variety of their work strategically disseminated to a global audience through the platform of YouTube positions the 1491s as a major force in social change, inspiring Indigenous and non-Indigenous audiences alike (figure 14.1).

Part 1: YouTube as a Performative Social Media Platform for Indigenous Activism

Before 2009, Sterlin Harjo explains, "No one had really picked up a video camera and made YouTube videos for Native people. There was a space for us to do it, because no one else had done it" (Bullock, 2015). With the advent of technology that can be held in the palm of one's hand, and which is more affordable than ever before, expressive artists like the 1491s who plug into social media now possess the potential to reach broad audiences quickly and efficiently. Social media has transformed the typical power relationships between media technologies and media makers. Mobile technologies mean that like no other time in the history of the world, technologies can be used to connect us, to help us understand one another.

While the role of YouTube is currently understudied in the U.S. context of Native American social media use, social media, generally, has undeniably reshaped the nature of community and provided ways to bridge the time-space divide, bringing people together around common causes and vision. This was well documented with the ascendancy of Idle No More in 2012 and 2013 from one province in Canada to a national and then global phenomenon. Diné/Navajo writer Natanya Ann Pulley reflects on the powerful connections that continue to be made among Native people in online spaces that plug into

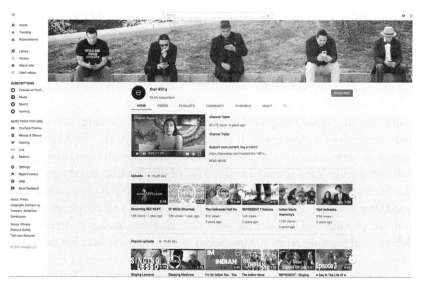

FIG. 14.1 The 1491s' YouTube channel. (Credit: Screenshot by author of the 1491s YouTube channel.)

Indigenous peoples' cosmologies of time and space in her essay "Indigitechs": "I exist outside the Western grid of time-space, in a space where my encounters with my Native brothers and sisters strengthens our connection to the cosmos. It is the air-spirit of the first world alive and kicking" (2014, p. 99). "Of course," she continues, "I can, at any time, socialize with my Native relatives and future-friends on Facebook. I can also keep in touch with Native artists, writers, and poets. But more than this, Native people acquire a political pulse online that in the past was sequestered on the reservation—and beaten down there, as was the American Indian Movement at Pine Ridge" (pp. 99–100). Though surveillance of politically engaged Native gatherings continues even online, status updates, the circulation of petitions, announcements of events, and shared memes and jokes join people together in ways that mainstream media and in-person events cannot. "The 'Natives be like' joke memes are just as important as shared links to pages about the latest rally against the Keystone XL pipeline" (p. 100). Pulley emphasizes here that the "micro utterance," perhaps something like a meme, has macro consequences as it "reverberates across hyperspace" (p. 100).

New scholarship is emerging on the expansive role played by social media in Indigenous communities with clear reminders that Indigenous peoples are early and frequent adapters of new technologies. Research by Bronwyn Carlson (Aboriginal Australian), Acushla Dee O'Carroll Sciascia (Māori), and Alex Wilson (Neyonawak Inniniwak from the Opaskwayak Cree Nation) has examined the role played by social media in Aboriginal, Māori, and First Nations and international Indigenous contexts (see Carlson and Frazer and Wilson and Zheng in this volume). Previously, in an article in *AlterNative*, I wrote about what Indigenous theorists would describe as the "visual sovereignty" of the 1491s comedic stylings on YouTube, particularly in light of misrepresentation and narrow visions of Native American peoples. In addition to looking at the role played by social media in revitalizing communities and connections across great distances, this research also highlights the impact on activism and social justice initiatives. As Carlson (2013) notes, "We still have a lot to learn about Aboriginal use of social media and the potential that social media may offer in terms of social and cultural interaction. But one thing is quite clear—social media is here, Aboriginal people are online and are posting and interacting with one another, having conversations, debates and forming relationships. Social media is a social site but as I have demonstrated, it is also a political site where Aboriginal struggles and identities are being out in the 'new frontier'" (p. 164). In terms of scholarship on YouTube, very little has yet been focused on Indigenous content and subscriber and viewer comments. That said, one of the first full-length scholarly books on YouTube, *YouTube: Online Video and Participatory Culture* (Burgess and Green, 2009), did focus a few pages on the rapid proliferation on YouTube of Australian prime minister Kevin Rudd's 2008 apology to the Stolen Generations and video reactions and edited responses and reinterpretations of this political landmark event. The reaction to this event marked one of the first sustained and rapidly unfolding dialogues on YouTube surrounding Indigenous causes. The reaction of Indigenous peoples circulated because on YouTube voices that mainstream media outlets would have ignored or marginalized and perspectives that might have been rendered in Indigenous newspapers and even in limited newscasts at later dates because of production delays can be disseminated immediately.

In addition to scant attention paid to Indigenous content on YouTube, little attention has been paid to the variable ways that YouTube functions as a social media format. While it does offer the space for interaction and some limited collaboration—as detailed below—its primary function for many users is sometimes outside of social media spaces as yet another disseminating conduit for entertainment, tutorials, news, and self-expression, all of which are commercialized or monetized to varying degrees. The website YouTube went live in 2005 and was purchased a year later by Google for $1.56 billion, leading quickly to its commercialization and monetization. The 1491s uploaded their first video in 2009, well after YouTube had gone commercial, providing a platform for professional and amateur videos alike. Fan bases elevate the status of all works, irrespective of origin, and dictate the terms of further monetization and thus commercial viability of particular sites. Some independent producers of videos have engineered their careers to earn up to $12 million a year (Berg, 2015).

Building an audience base that increases revenue streams depends on industries' perception of the profit potential of the audience. A play-through gaming site or a children's toy site is directly linked to consumer purchasing—both of these types of YouTube channels and stars routinely make the *Forbes* top-ten list of richest YouTubers (Berg, 2015). What's the profit potential in Indigenous sovereignty? While this might be taken as a sarcastic, rhetorical question, there's actually an answer: educational and business-oriented services. Colleges, Grammerly—directed at college students in need of help with their writing—and GoToMeeting, an online service to facilitate long-distance business partnerships, are all currently advertisers on the 1491s' YouTube site (although, admittedly, one wonders, if this ad placement is dictated by analytics about my own online identity). By the time readers of this published chapter turn to the site, there may be different advertisers. Even with regular sponsorship, YouTubers such as the 1491s make income only if audiences click on the ads or watch the initiating ads (ones that roll before the video content will display) in their entirety, both of which are unlikely if consumers are concerned about conserving data streaming charges (an even more likely the case if there's a mismatch between the advertisement and the consumer interests). On top of this, for their use of the platform, YouTube commands a 45 percent cut of profits. According to comments made by Bobby Wilson at Mesa Community College in 2014, the 1491s earn a modest $150 to $200 per month and depend on sales of T-shirts and performance fees to supplement income earned in their other "day jobs" (Haskie-Gonzalez, 2014). "It costs money doesn't it? When we get together we do videos. We're Indian guys so we do other things. . . . Then we're getting live shows and make money. Our YouTube channel pays us $150–200 a month. We sell shirts, and once a year we get together and make videos, plan. We budget, we plans things, we figure out how we'll pay for things, etc." When someone asks, "What do you do in real life?" Bobby explains that he manages the group and its schedules. He's also a graffiti artist and does murals. "Dallas Goldtooth works with the Indigenous Environmental Network and does a shitload of planning for this. Ryan Red Corn owns two businesses, a Fry Bread Mix company, he inherited from his grandfather, and a marketing firm. Migizi is a student working on his masters in creative writing. Sterlin Harjo makes real movies, not this bullshit like we do" (Haskie-Gonzalez, 2014).

Currently there is no analytic to track ethnic or gender identities of viewers. YouTube tracks numbers: the number of viewers (from unique IP addresses; return viewers from the same computer are not tabulated); the number of likes (thumbs up) and dislikes (thumbs down), allowed only by registered users; and the number of subscribers to the 1491s' channel. Registered users are allowed to leave comments on the 1491s' videos. Registered users can reply to others' comments. Each video has many more viewers than commenters, as might be expected. It's hard to know how many viewers read comments left by other viewers; this information isn't tracked. Viewers may sort by two categories, "Top Comments" and "Most Recent Comments." If a viewer is interested in reading more than twenty or so comments, they may click "Show More" to go further back in the comment archive (comments are preserved unless the 1491s delete comments).

In her in-depth study of YouTube and its unique facets that alter the reception of digital film, Carol Vernallis (2013) explains, "[YouTube's] online distribution also encourages participation. In miniature, the video's performers may carry more weight than they would on television—the technological magic that brings them to us feels palpable. We may also experience greater agency with viral media, because a click allows us to seek out the video's performers, who address us directly—one more click or turn away from the monitor would break a fragile bond. As we forward the link to those in our affinity groups, our sense of connection branches outward" (p. 171). To enjoy the 1491s' work, all one needs to do is Google their name or enter their name in the YouTube search bar. But if that's not enough, you may follow them on Twitter, you may subscribe to their YouTube channel, and you may like them on Facebook. These various multimedia platforms serve to notify viewers of new postings, keep them updated about other news, and, importantly, maintain a relationship across space and time. Depending on one's smartphone settings, announcements about new postings can immediately reach followers. While there are differences of opinions about the possibilities of YouTube to build a community that receives and creates progressive and innovative media of value, there are some scholars who contend that the circulation and sharing of videos fosters "kinship networking." Vernallis notes, "YouTube provides intense media experiences . . . sometimes a clip sent by a friend or colleague produces a moment of intimacy, as if we were in a conversation and one of us had suddenly turned the witty phrase that concretized gathering experience. The three-minute clip swells in the light of our shared feeling. The clip's cleverness helps it merge into our paths of dialogue and mutuality" (p. 149). The ongoing responses and comments by viewers is a surprising feature of YouTube and grounds the experiences in the real lives of people. In previous generations, fans could have written a letter, formed a fan club, and bought a ticket to an event, but YouTube enables direct engagement.

Part 2: Humorous/Satirical Engagements

In *Engaged Resistance* (2011), Dean Rader coins a term to articulate the activist contributions made by artists—"aesthetic activism," which is "a manner of political and social activism that finds representation in the artistic realm."

I find it useful to think about the 1491s work as "aesthetic activism" because while they're not writing policy statements, and they're not leading marches, they *are* forcefully shaping the discourse about the value and rights of Indigenous peoples, and their work definitely issues responses to relevant and timely incidences and everyday occurrences in "Indian Country." This is an especially useful interpretive tactic when analyzing works that seem humorous, silly, and sometimes downright "lite." An understanding of the function of humor within Indigenous cultures, though, recognizes that humor is a tactic used to move people, to change attitudes, to critique behaviors, and to lead to change. Laguna Pueblo writer and theorist Paula Gunn Allen considers humor "the best and sharpest weapon we've always had against the ravages of conquest and assimilation" (as cited in Lincoln, 1993, p. 7). Perhaps it is the transformative possibility of humor that led playwright Hanay Geiogamah (Kiowa and Delaware) to say, "I see the Indi'n capacity for humor as a blessing. . . . It's a miraculous thing that's pulled us through so much. It's a force that's part of religion" (as cited in Lincoln, 1993, p. 336).

One of the most popular of the 1491s' humorous videos is "Slapping Medicine Man" (2011), with a simple format and direct purpose: to dismantle a culture of rationalization that displaces blame for one's conditions to others (figure 14.2). While the video risks oversimplification of the complexities of obesity, depression, gossip, unemployment, broken relationships, and so forth, the healer in the series asks a series of questions of three young men who visit him and gives them a hard dose of reality: a real question that cuts to the heart of the men's own complicity in their hardship followed by a physical rebuke—a slap in the face. A fixed over-the-shoulder shot puts viewers in the position of the medicine man who is consulting with three young men played by Tito Ybarra, Dallas Goldtooth, and Ryan Red Corn. When Tito's character talks about being overweight and sick, he's asked if he drinks or parties; when he replies in the affirmative, he's met with a "Well, knock it off!" and a slap. When Ryan's character says, "I'm a student, and I don't think I'm eligible but I'd like one of those free Indian scholarships," he's met with a slap. And, when Dallas's character worries, "I don't know what to do to get 'em [my family] back," the medicine man asks, "Well, are you still drinking?" to which Dallas replies, "Well, yeah, from time to time!" Then, without missing a beat, the medicine man delivers a sharp slap. The unexpected hard truth and the physical surprise of the slap combine to elicit laughter from viewers. The scenarios with the different characters cycle through and the medicine man continues to dispense with truths about hard work, employment and education.

With 1,179,552 views—one of their most popular videos—since it was uploaded in May 2011, "Slapping Medicine Man" has elicited a staggering 815 comments. The extreme ridiculousness of the scenario combined with physical humor and predictable, repeated patterns, has all the ingredients of classic

Slapping Medicine Man

1,195,739 views • May 26, 2011

10K 172 SHARE SAVE ...

the1491s
55.6K subscribers

SUBSCRIBE

A super traditional Indigenous Medicine Man (Noah Ellis) slaps around
comedian Tito Ybarra. Dallas Goldtooth and Ryan Red Corn
SHOW MORE

FIG. 14.2 The 1491s' "Slapping Medicine Man." (Credit: Screenshot by author from the 1491s YouTube channel.)

comedy. Michael RedCrow's response highlights typical audience reactions: "BWAHAHAHA poor Ryan, i felt so bad for him (ok, i was laughing so hard i almost fainted but i promise, i was feelin bad, too), and the SLAP (aho!) i literally fell out of my chair onto the floor, my wife thought i was havin some kind of attack! i loves me some 1491's, and this one was almost the best ever!" Other typical responses focus on the medicine man's logic. For example, Wa-Ya Hilderbrand wonders, "Is it kind of sad that my school beyond needs this medicine man?" Another, Gobbles Wells (KetchupPopsicles), also wishes this hard medicine were in readier supply: "If only today's medicine man was this serious about slapping some sense into the younger generations. Nowadays you find that most are in it just for the financial opportunities to be had, much like the white man that many of them complain about." Shiidenzhoneshash comments on the way the 1491s are able to deliver these insights through their humorous scenario: "You know watching this video from time to time is good for a laugh BUT what a message it sends us through humor. The slap of reality, wake up and smell the coffee, so to speak snap outta it, . . . if you want change then change. What a jello community we have become. So because I can't go around slapping my Natives this video is some way good therapy for me . . . hahahahahhah."

The satirical humor of "Slapping Medicine Man" targets self-pity and self-abuse by issuing a call for a commitment to action and control over one's own life, a sovereignty of self that will build the possibility of transformation and resilience for others. "Slapping Medicine Man" shows the need for self-accountability and the sobering prescription of discipline, dedication, and hard work. That is why the 1491s' logo consists of an arrow turned back on the shooter (Bobby Wilson describes it as "an arrow shooting ourselves in the ass" (Haskie-Gonzalez, 2014); their target is not just beyond themselves, outside of their communities, but includes themselves and their family and neighbors, their fellow tribal members.

Part 3: Resistance, Resilience Building, and Celebrations of Indigenous Brilliance

The 1491s use the YouTube platform to establish and maintain a community that can bear witness to and honor the many ways to be Indigenous which empowers others to tell their stories and join the conversation. Their work creates models of engagement and resistance, models of problem solving, models of resilience building and Indigenous resurgence, testimonials of Indigenous brilliance, beauty, and talent.

A specific genre of serious and noncomedic activism by the 1491s is the PSAs they routinely distribute through their YouTube channel. Disseminating PSAs online is not unusual, but their placement alongside the 1491s' comedic playlists *is* unique and models an interdependent relationship, in terms of both production and praxis, or theory in action, reminding viewers of their serious commitment to Indigenous peoples and communities even in their comedic engagements. Their production infrastructure and celebrity affords the group a reach that extends far beyond local activist engagements; moreover, the 1491s openly share their equipment, filmmaking knowledge, YouTube platform, and existing fanbase, all to support work outside of typical commercial media infrastructures.

One provocative 2011 PSA joined a public dialogue about the epidemic of violence against Indigenous women, both at the hands of Indigenous and non-Indigenous men alike during a period when the U.S. Congress was considering the renewal of the Violence Against Women Act, originally passed in 1994. Based on a poem written by Randy Red Corn, "To the Indigenous Woman" was uploaded in October 2011. While Red Corn reads the poem in voiceover, viewers see images of Indigenous women, loving and caring for their families and being loved by them in return—the reality that *should* exist but that does not match the stark reality facing the majority of Indigenous women. Details supplied with the video remind us of shocking, disturbing statistics: "Native women are murdered at 10 times the national rate; 1 out 3 Native women will be raped in her lifetime, and 3 out of 5 physically assaulted. Even worse, 88% of the perpetrators are non-Indian and cannot be prosecuted by tribal governments. Stand and take action now to restore safety and justice for Native women. Do Something! Visit www.indianlaw.org." Red Corn's words give voice to feelings of regret and complicity and the need for everyone, all people, men and women, adults and children, Native and non-Native, to stand up and take action. To ignore this stark reality is to be complicit.

> To the Indigenous woman
> I'm sorry we have not fought harder for you
> I am the dysfunctional man
> I will borrow your forgiveness like I always have,
> and you will be there for me like you always are
> Ask her, and she will tell you I stole her tongue
> Replaced it with guilt
> Saddled it with blame and rode off on it like a horse
> . . .
> To doctors without clues
> for say nothing neighbors
> do nothing attorneys
> and quiet parents with no memories
> Thank you.
> You make all of this possible.
> We couldn't fail these women without your help.
> For the woman and her baby left for dead by the police in her home,
>   while they gave a ride to her attacker back to his house
> To the girlfriend punched in her pregnant stomach
> To the wife who took the beatings so her kids wouldn't have to
> To the daughter who found a man as abusive as her dad
> To the coed who will never ever go to the nine again
> To the restraining order as strong as the paper its made from
> To the shelter with not enough beds
> I give 1000 sweats for rape victims
> 1000 doctorings for husbands
> 1000 prayer ties for courage
> 1000 meetings for silence
> 1000 songs for patience
> 1000 fires . . . for enough light . . . to fill a room . . .

to reflect off a mirror the size of the moon
just so we can see ourselves for what we are.
Complicit.

And if this recognition of complicity—the word "Complicit" flashes on the screen as Red Corn pauses—in inaction is not enough to move viewers of the video poem, Red Corn reminds those watching that these victims are all of our relatives. As he continues to speak, close-up shots of women follow. The women stare directly into the camera, making eye contact with viewers, imploring us not to ignore their plight. Red Corn shifts to first-person in the closing lines, giving voice to the women themselves:

I am your wife
I am your sister
I am your mother
I am your daughter
You are supposed to protect me
You are supposed to be a warrior
Protect me from you,
from him,
from all of them.
Tell me you have daughters
Tell me you don't want this for them
Tell me you won't joke about this with your friends
Tell me you won't forget we talked
Tell me you will do something
Do something.

This last line, like "Complicit," flashes on the screen. The logic is clear. If you don't "do something," you'll be complicit and things won't improve.

Viewer response to this video was intense and positive. One viewer, "star kiona," writes, "When I feel like crap because of statistics and due to being a Native women, also feeling like I am going nowhere because of my history, and where I am from. I watch this. Makes me feel like I am cared for, it inspires me to try my hardest to make it different and easier for us Native people. I can almost see my future occupation when I watch this video. Many thanks, 1491s. <3." Lucretia Lovato, another viewer, comments, "So moving and raw. . . . Thank you for calling out to the Native men to help keep the women safe. . . . You're opening their eyes to what they are doing to their own women. Thank you for being the voice of all those that are too scared, too beaten, or can no longer ask for justice. . . . Many thanks and bless you all for being brave." One male fan, Rocky Rockholt, stands by Red Corn's call for all men, as well as Native men, to recognize their responsibility toward Indigenous women: "Thank you, thank you, thank you, for calling out the 'warriors' in our Native American culture who will look away from a 'family matter.' My mom in an NDN Woman Super Hero!! She raised three of us unruly kids to be solid citizens. Along the way, she was raped, beaten, and treated as if she was disposable. She is not disposable!! She is the mother of a man who is hard wired to keep trying for his kids. She is a businesswoman. She doesn't even recognize her past. Nor do I!!!" Rockholt speaks to the endurance of his mother and the way she transformed her past, but he also speaks to the intergenerational responsibility to be watchful and protective of women and children and to recognize this drive as a fulfillment of being "a warrior."

The 1491s refined this message about putting an end to violence against women in later videos as well, including a brief, thirty-second one that has garnered 14,925 views since March 2012. Titled "Ten Little Indians," and underscored by the sing-song of the outdated and racist nursery rhyme of the same name, the simply formatted black-and-white video features extreme close-ups of Indigenous women looking into the camera. After viewers are shown a succession of ten women and are reminded that six out of ten Native women will be physically assaulted, they are implored to "Do Something." The dissonance between the all-too-familiar song, not to mention its inappropriateness in today's world, estranges the familiar and works to draw attention to an important cause. In 2013 Congress did reauthorize the Violence Against Women Act and then two years later, under President Barack Obama's leadership, for the first time in U.S. history, the most significant update for Native women was finally implemented: a provision allowing tribal courts to investigate and prosecute non-Native men accused of abuse of Indigenous women on federally recognized tribal reservations. Unfortunately, in 2019, under President Donald Trump and a conservative majority in the U.S. Senate, the act expired.

In addition to these PSAs, the 1491s have produced a number of videos that beautifully and forcefully represent the diversity of Indigenous lives. Several focus on language: one issued on Valentine's Day with dozens of speakers sharing a litany of words for love in different tribal languages; another NSFW video hilariously features phrases and strategies for indicating one's attraction and romantic or sexual interest in others. In this category are also spoken word performance poems such as "Bad Indians," which feature multiple contributors, all Native, collectively performing lines of the poem also written by Ryan Red Corn and built around a simple yet profound argument. Each speaker looks and sounds different; most speak English; some use their tribal language. Collectively, their voices assert a contemporary Indigenous presence, one that claims sovereignty and control over their own destiny and a renewed and collective sense of empowerment. Speakers look confidently and proudly into the camera showing respect and honor for their subject, models of strength and endurance. They show how to turn on its head General Philip Sheridan's equation, "The only good Indian is a dead Indian." Alive and thriving, the speakers in the video are very "bad Indians," indeed, but bad in all the very best ways possible: they are here.

The 1491s' work revitalizes Native communities through a modeling of resistance to pernicious, damaging stereotypes, but they also do so, specifically, through their "REPRESENT" series (which more than just nominally) embodies Linda Tuhiwai Smith's (Māori) "Representing" project she lists among other indigenizing research projects (see also Carlson and Frazer and the interview with Debbie Reese in this volume). And, furthermore, the REPRESENT series fulfills Tuhiwai Smith's goals of "Creating," "Networking," and "Sharing" as this series is the outcome of collaborations (referred to as "collabs") with people whom the 1491s meet on university campuses or within communities they visit. The 1491s offer the opportunity for others to tell their own stories by using their equipment, their editing software, and the social media platform the group has built. Migizi Pensoneau explains the group's motives: "We've put cameras in people's hands and have asked what would you like to see. It goes in direct contrast to that sort of Aaron Huey National Geographic thing where it's like you know we're just gonna showcase all the sad. Look at this poor destitute Indian and we're like, you know what do you want to see when you culture is vital and thriving? . . . We've created these outlets for people to tell their own stories because it's not something that it's our place to, it's someone else's" (TEDx Talk, 2013). The multiple, varied stories are all connected by the series title that is superimposed at the beginning and close of every video; a fixed camera is used in all videos; cuts are minimal to nonexistent. These minimalist choices focus attention on the subjects' talent.

The REPRESENT films create the opportunity for other Indigenous peoples to showcase their talents, to demonstrate their presence, intelligence, and what Gerald Vizenor (Ojibwe) would call "survivance," "an active sense of presence, the continuance of native stories, not a mere reaction, or a survivable name. Native survivance stories are renunciations of dominance, tragedy, and victimry. Survivance means the right of succession or reversion of an estate, and in that sense, the estate of native survivancy" (1999, preface). REPRESENT becomes a means of resisting stereotypes through the process of honoring and valuing the full humanity of Native peoples. For Native viewers, the REPRESENT series recognizes and honors Indigenous viewers' own knowledge and experiences, provides aspirational models, and shows that transformations of age-old traditions are not merely a rejection of tribal identity or Indigeneity, but a new strategy of empowerment, a means of indigenizing other spaces. A young man moonwalks like Michael Jackson in front of a natural history museum display; a teacher speaks Ojibewemowin to teach math in an Ojibwe school; a jingle dancer (without regalia) in jeans, with earbuds in, dances on the quad at

Dartmouth College; several young hip-hop artists rap about Indigenous resurgence and Idle No More, surrounded by friends and family at a community center in Detroit; a young mother places her child in a cradleboard; an award-winning recording artist sings of the riches of family while Bobby Wilson beatboxes at her kitchen table; Berkeley students who are Native go about the mundane business of being college students; a Nambé Pueblo woman, then a student at Yale University, throws candy in a "Pueblo Throw" at young men passing by; three young women, students at Fort Lewis College in Colorado, sing a '49 about love and desire.

Uploaded in October 2012, the REPRESENT video featuring Fort Lewis College students Sherri Willeto (Diné, a sociology major/minor in Native American studies), Teahonna James (Tlingit/Athabaskan, a humanities major), and Mariana Harvey (Yakama, an Indigenous studies major) has received 344,598 views, the most of all of the REPRESENT series. The video, as with all others in the series, is filmed with a fixed position camera, framing the women in a medium shot that fosters a sense of intimate familiarity; the camera filter casts the three women in golden light. The video opens with the three waiting to begin, smiling, and laughing. They sing a '49, a secular popular musical form, typically sung in English with vocable elements about everyday subjects; '49s are sung at pow-wows, at parties, and when friends get together and are extemporaneous fusions of pop and traditional elements. The lyrics the three women sing are simple and repeated with each one taking turns singing the lead in a round: "I got this loving feeling / Ya-he-he-yah / I got this loving feeling / Come a little closer / I'll hold onto you all night long / Hey-a-hi-hey-a-hi-yo." Their harmonious voices are striking and moving to listeners. They sing of love and desire, components of personhood, and a full humanity, for too long absent from any representation of Native peoples on film (albeit something that has been changing over the course of the last two decades). Viewer ChehalaRose comments, "Beautiful to see my Indigenous sisters out there representing our strong and resilient culture! Makes me proud to be nehiyaw. And for anyone who has left negative comments, I feel sad for you because our roles as human beings, as women is not to tear each other down but rather it should be about empowering each other, supporting each other on our journeys. Anyway hiy hiy for sharing 1491's!" Another reviewer critically questions the combination of vocable stylings in a love song about desire—"so i guess if u add a few way yah has in a country ass song its all of a sudden cultural . . . damn how our ways have changed smh:/[shaking my head]." While Derick Gill, the previous commenter, may be SMH (shaking my head), another viewer takes him to task and questions his expectations for Native singers. Bulldoggrrr writes, "lmao, what? . . . you expect them to play the flute on horseback. True, 'our' ways have changed, but you are projecting about what you think a reflection of our culture is. Have you ever been to a 49? I would guess not."

Videos that are part of the REPRESENT series combat stereotypes and change common narratives about Native peoples. Often they celebrate the efforts to maintain and revitalize important tribal traditions; in other cases, they offer clear juxtapositions of unquestionable Indigenous pride in the midst of supposedly non-Native contexts. In this way, the videos push back against expectations—that Native culture has been lost or died out, that Native people are part of history, not the present, and that Indigenous people lead separate existences outside the purview of mainstream culture. The videos remind non-Native viewers that Indigenous people are everywhere and that their presence is vital and enriching.

And this is the real activist effort of the 1491s, a project supported by their expansive national and international reach on YouTube and the fanbase that responds and communicates with the performers and with one another about important political matters affecting the lives of Indigenous people everywhere. As Natanya Ann Pulley puts it so succinctly, "A Native American presence online is always a political act. It is a testament to our staying power and to the people's ability to surge onward . . . I no longer need to open a book or work through my mother's memory of Navajoland to reach my people (though I deeply miss its sand and growing winds). I simply have to open an app. And I am not faced with static images, but with emergent and pulsing paths of inclusion and action" (2014, p. 100). There's no room for fixating on tragedy in this space. There's too much to be done, and a little bit of laughter and appreciation of beauty courtesy of the 1491s will make the work easier to undertake and sustain.

References

The 1491s. (2011a, March 17). Bad Indians. https://www.youtube.com/watch?v=3FUgDutdauQ.

The 1491s. (2011b, May 26). Slapping medicine man. https://www.youtube.com/watch?v=MVWLHMZ-ceE.

The 1491s. (2011c, October 18). To the Indigenous woman—a poem by the 1491s. https://www.youtube.com/watch?v=6fxP95eu8Xs.

The 1491s. (2012a, March 12). Ten little Indians—violence against Native women. https://www.youtube.com/watch?v=TJHQutcSFQU.

The 1491s. (2012b, October 26). Represent-singing on campus—Ft. Lewis College. https://www.youtube.com/watch?v=OblFCoxsMfw.

The 1491s. (2013, February 15). Indigenous love words project. https://www.youtube.com/watch?v=Zvt4Eba_EJM.

Berg, M. (2015, November 2). The world's top-earning YouTube stars 2015. *Forbes.* http://www.forbes.com/sites/maddieberg/2015/10/14/the-worlds-highest-paid-youtube-stars-2015/#3e560a26542c.

Berglund, J. (2016). "I'M Just as Indian Standing before you with no Feathers Popping Out of my Head": Critiquing Indigenous performativity in the YouTube performances of the 1491s. *AlterNative: An International Journal of Indigenous Peoples,* 12(5), 541–557. https://doi.org/10.20507/AlterNative.2016.12.5.8.

Bullock, M. (2015, June 8). The making of the 1491s: Native humor goes viral. *Tulsa Voice*. http://www.thetulsavoice.com/June-8-2015/The-making-of-the-1491s/.

Burgess, J., and Green, J. (2009). *YouTube: Online video and participatory culture*. Cambridge: Polity.

Carlson, B. (2013). The new frontier: Emergent Indigenous identity and social media. In M. Harris, M. Nakata, and B. Carlson (Eds.), *The politics of identity: Emerging Indigeneity* (pp. 147–168). Sydney: University of Technology Sydney ePress.

Haskie-Gonzalez, J. (2014, October 13). The 1491s Bobby Wilson's visit to MCC September 24, 2014. https://www.youtube.com/watch?v=4GvAOogxFFg.

Lincoln, K. (1993). *Ind'n humor: Bicultural plans in Native America*. New York: Oxford University Press.

O'Carroll, A. D. (2013). Kanohi kit e kanohi—a thing of the past? An examination of Māori use of social networking sites and the implication for Māori culture and society (Doctoral dissertation, Massey University). http://www.whariki.ac.nz /massey/fms/Colleges/College%20of%20Humanities%20and%20Social%20 Sciences/Shore/reports/OCARROLL%20A%20D%20-%20PhD%20Thesis.pdf?o 7BE5C6EBFE9AAFF2ACA54DD8AD295D4.

Pulley, N. A. (2014). Indigetechs: The original time-space traveling Native Americans and our modern world hyper-pow-wow. *Western Humanities Review, 68*(2), 95–101.

Rader, D. (2011). *Engaged resistance: American Indian art, literature, and film from Alcatraz to the NMAI*. Austin: University of Texas Press.

Ross, G. (2013, December 12). Don't believe the hype: Beyond poverty porn, pain and drunk Indians. *Indian Country Today*. http://indiancountrytodaymedianetwork .com/2013/12/12/dont-believe-hype-beyond-poverty-porn-pain-and-drunk-indians -152673.

Smith, L. T. (1999). *Decolonizing methodologies: Research and Indigenous peoples*. London: Zed Books.

TEDx Talks. (2013, August 7). 1491s play with themselves, imagery, and reclamation: 1491s at TEDxManitoba 2013. https://www.youtube.com/watch?v=MqKvwRrgW_Q.

Vernallis, Carol (2013) *Unruly media: YouTube, music videos, and the new digital cinema*. New York: Oxford University Press.

Vizenor, G. (1999). *Manifest manners: Narratives on postindian survivance*. Lincoln: Bison Books.

Wilson, A. (2015). Idle no more round dance: Revolution at the Hemispheric Institute of Performance and Politics Montreal Encuentro: A discussion with Roewan Crowe and Alex Wilson. *Caribbean Rasanblaj, 12*(1). http://hemisphericinstitute .org/hemi/en/emisferica-121-caribbean-rasanblaj/crowe.

Acknowledgments

We must first acknowledge the powerful and brave Indigenous activists whose commitment to justice, equity, self-determination, sovereignty, and decolonization is inspiring. The world would not be the same without your efforts. We hope this book honors your work.

An edited volume is a joint effort between a community of scholars, and we thank each and every author who contributed a chapter to this book. Thank you for entrusting your work with us and thank you for the productive conversations in which we were able to engage through the process of creating this book. We very much thank Charlotte Allingham for providing such a strong image for the cover—the Blak warrior will always be a force to be reckoned with. We would also like to acknowledge the Forum for Indigenous Research Excellence (FIRE) of which we are both long term members. FIRE has brought together many of the contributors of this volume and as an Indigenous research network has provided a space where collaboration is encouraged and facilitated. In 2021 FIRE has reestablished itself as the Centre for Global Indigenous Futures as it moves toward a more globally connected network.

We're grateful that Frederick Aldama, series editor, saw promise in our book proposal. We thank Nicole Solano and her editorial team at Rutgers University Press for their support and guidance seeing into print *Indigenous Peoples Rise Up*.

I would like to acknowledge my coeditor Jeff Berglund for all the support you have shown me over the years. From our first meeting when I was given the title of "Honours Bronwyn" being the only person in the room still working on my doctorate back in 2010, to now having worked collaboratively with you on numerous projects. I am ever grateful to the "Working group on emergent Indigenous identities" led by our colleague Michelle Harris and supported by

Harvey Charles, which enabled me to travel to Northern Arizona University (NAU) for the first time. It seems a long time ago and we have achieved so many things including the edited volume *The Politics of Identity: Emerging Indigeneity* (2013) and the establishment of the *Journal of Global Indigeneity*. Some of my favorite times have been road trips and there have been many in the United States, Aotearoa, and Australia visiting Indigenous people and communities and spending time with students. Our students here in Australia often speak about Jeff's fabulous "shut up and write" workshops. I have always felt like family coming to Flagstaff and working with colleagues at NAU. I was always included in fabulous social events, and I extend my thanks to Monica Brown for her generosity and making time for me and to Ricardo and Shawn for also providing wonderful hospitality. A special thanks to the Native American Cultural Center, which provided a welcoming space for us and where I have had the pleasure of presenting more than once on my research.

I would like to acknowledge the productive environment created by colleagues in the Department of Indigenous Studies at Macquarie University where the new Centre for Global Indigenous Futures is situated. Macquarie University is built on the lands of the Wallumattagal people of the Dharug nation, and we are fortunate to work with Dharug scholar Jo Rey who teaches us a lot about Dharug Ngurra (Dharug Country/homelands) and whose scholarship has led to the development of our unit of study focused specifically on Dharug peoples and knowledges. Three of my colleagues are authors in this book. My coauthor Ryan Frazer, whom I have had the pleasure of working with now for a number of years exploring Indigenous engagements on social media—thank you for your brilliant and ever thoughtful contributions. Both Ryan and I are grateful to the Aboriginal and Torres Strait Islander people who have shared their stories with us over the years, which has allowed us to try and make sense of the challenges people face when engaged on social media platforms and also the opportunities they afford us. Tristan Kennedy, fellow sociologist who is always a fabulous collaborator and colleague—I very much enjoy plotting and planning with you and look forward to all the projects we are yet to imagine. Andrew Farrell who inspired the creation of our Indigenous Queer Studies program—you continue to amaze and amuse me; a sense of humor cannot be understated and Andrew can always be relied upon to find the funny in any situation. Sandy O'Sullivan has recently joined our team and like the others has been a long-term member of FIRE; Sandy is ever generous in their feedback on ideas and writing and knows just about everything! We are really glad they have joined us. Madi Day, there are simply no words that adequately thank you for your incredible generosity and brilliance; I do not know what I would do without your humor and ability to make sense of everything and the way you always manage to find solutions. I am sure the journey to complete this book would have been made far more difficult if I couldn't text you day and night sharing ridiculous memes and endless commentary on settler reality shows. I am also ever grateful to all the administrative support Tetei Bakic provides—having you in our department is delightful. I am privileged to work with such brilliant scholars who are all doing amazing work. It is not every day that one gets to work with a team of people who are intellectually amazing but are also part of a strong scholarly network who share a vision where Indigenous Studies is at the forefront of imagining a future centered in Indigenous ways of knowing, being and doing.

To my family, my partner Mike and my four children, Anastasia, Jason, Rebecca, and Connor and my seven grannies, Scarlet, Jack, Aurora, Evie, Phoenix, Isaac and Grace—it is because of you that I persevered and it is my pride in you that gives me hope that you too realise you can do anything you set your minds to do. The future is Indigenous.

—Bronwyn Carlson

I would like to thank the brilliant and creative Indigenous activists who continue to find new ways to mobilize and bring about change. I have learned so much from you, about human nature, Indigenous values, about strategies for representing social justice causes. As someone trained in literary, film, and textual studies, I'm fascinated by the mix of tools, modes/genres, rhetorical appeals and the complex of symbolic networks that are deployed in different contexts and that emerge and evolve over time. I'm grateful for the comedic productions of The 1491s that led me to work in the arena of social media. And for the work of Indigenous comics on social media like Carly Wallace (a.k.a., CJay Vines) and Tonia Jo Hall (a.k.a., Auntie Beachress). Students in my classes at Northern Arizona University (NAU) have enjoyed their productions on social media and helped me think about the role that YouTube and social media play in their everyday lives. Debbie Reese's work on her blog, *American Indians in Children's Literature,* and now on Twitter, has always been a go-to resource and inspiration to me. I'm pleased this book afforded us the opportunity to have a substantial conversation about the serious work she engages in as a public-facing intellectual who challenges publishers, editors, reviewers, librarians, and readers to think differently about the powerful foundations laid by good books about Indigenous peoples. I'm grateful for what she teaches me and am grateful for her friendship and support of my work.

I'm grateful for my friend and colleague Bronwyn Carlson. I knew you "back then" when you were still working on your PhD and we were gathered together with a group of other Indigenous Studies scholars discussing the subject of Indigenous identities. Your work on Facebook opened my eyes to what was a new field of study. Your support opened a whole world to me. Some of the best moments of my professional life are linked to your initiatives, particularly the study with graduate students in Aotearoa/New Zealand, University of

Wollongong, Bateman's Bay, and, especially, my "Bulli Beach residency" in Wollongong, and then our epic road trip with Ryan Frazer up the center of Australia. We sure had a lot of good laughs as we wound our way from Alice Springs through Tennant Creek, Katherine, and then Darwin—and met a pig and a kangaroo who were very good friends and who made us famous for a minute in the tabloids! I also want to acknowledge Michelle Harris and Harvey Charles, who inspired us to start a working group in the first place—at NAU and beyond. Thank you for being visionaries. Your support led to a vital new chapter in my professional life. Some of my work on The 1491s first appeared in a special issue of *AlterNative* that Bronwyn and Michelle edited. I'm grateful for the friendships with Mike Carlson, Dave and Marena Kampers, Evan Poata-Smith, Sandy O'Sullivan, Jodi Edwards, Andrew Farrell, Ryan Frazer, Tris Kennedy, Madi Day, and so many other great colleagues at Macquarie.

At NAU, I thank my colleagues in Indigenous Studies, particularly Chad Hamill, Ora Marek-Martinez, Darold Joseph, and Kathleen Frank for supporting the 2019 Indigenous Peoples Rise Up Symposium where many of the contributors in this volume shared their work. Thank you to the many NAU students and faculty—including my friends Shepherd Tsosie, Ricardo Guthrie, Shawn Thomas, Benning Tieke, KT Thompson, and, especially, Mounia Mnouer, a contributor to this collection—who joined us in the crowded Native American Cultural Center on a beautiful October day in Flagstaff, at the base of the sacred mountain, known in English as the San Francisco Peaks. I acknowledge, honor, and respect the many diverse Indigenous peoples connected to the land on which NAU is situated, within the homelands of the Diné, Hopi, Zuni, Paiute, and Havasupai.

Finally, I want to express gratitude for my family who continue to inspire and embolden me. In particular, Juliana, Isabella, and Monica, you have all taught me so much about social justice and creating an equitable world—building a better world to meet everyone's needs, providing for everyone's health and well-being, and ensuring that everyone's voice is honored and represented. Your work gives me hope about a better world.

—Jeff Berglund

Notes on Contributors

CUTCHA RISLING BALDY (Hupa, Yurok, Karuk) is associate professor and chair of the Department of Native American Studies at Humboldt State University. Her research is focused on Indigenous feminisms, California Indians, and decolonization. Her book *We Are Dancing for You: Native Feminisms and the Revitalization of Women's Coming-of-Age Ceremonies* (2018) received the Best First Book in Native American and Indigenous Studies award at the 2019 Native American Indigenous Studies Association Conference. She is also the author of a popular blog that explores issues of social justice, history, and California Indian politics and culture: www.cutcharislingbaldy.com/blog. She received her PhD in Native American studies with a designated emphasis in feminist theory and research from the University of California, Davis and her MFA in creative writing and literary research from San Diego State University. She also received her BA in psychology from Stanford University. In 2007, she cofounded the Native Women's Collective, a nonprofit organization that supports the continued revitalization of Native American arts and culture.

MIRANDA BELARDE-LEWIS (Zuni/Tlingit) is assistant professor of Native North American Indigenous knowledge in the Information School at the University of Washington, Seattle. She researches how Native arts are used to protect, document, and reclaim Indigenous ways of knowing, in physical and online spaces, and how Native communities are leveraging social networking sites for activism and the assertion of cultural protocols during ceremonial events. She is a practicing curator and scholar of contemporary Native arts, having curated exhibitions for the Frye Art Museum in Seattle and the Museum of Glass in Tacoma. She has worked with tribal, city, state, and federal museums to create exhibits, public programming, educational content, and symposia that challenge and educate both Indigenous and non-Indigenous audiences.

JEFF BERGLUND is director of liberal studies and professor of English at Northern Arizona University (NAU) in Flagstaff. His research and teaching focus on Native American literature, comparative Indigenous film, and U.S. multiethnic literature. His books include *Cannibal Fictions: American Explorations of Colonialism, Race, Gender, and Sexuality* (2006), *Sherman Alexie: A Collection of Critical Essays* (coeditor, 2010), *Indigenous Pop: Native American Music from Jazz to Hip Hop* (coeditor, 2016), as well as *The Diné Reader: An Anthology of Navajo Literature* (coeditor, 2021). He is the author of articles on Native film, poetry, global Indigenous terminologies, and the pedagogy of American Indian literature. His other publications focus on Esther Belin, the Diné band Blackfire, Diné filmmakers, Simon Ortiz, and the 1491s. In addition to serving as the treasurer of the Association of Studies in American Indian Literature, he is a member of the Australian-based Forum for Indigenous Research Excellence (FIRE), the Working Group on Emergent Indigenous Identities, and DINÉ (Diné Institute for Navajo Nation Educators), NAU's partnership with the Yale National Initiative.

BRONWYN CARLSON is professor and head of the Department of Indigenous Studies at Macquarie University, Australia. She was awarded an Australian Research Council (ARC) Discovery Indigenous grant in 2013 for research on Aboriginal identity and community online (IN1301000360) and a second ARC in 2016 for research on Indigenous help-seeking on social media (IN160100049). In 2019 she was awarded a third consecutive ARC grant (IN200100010), specifically focusing on Indigenous experiences of online violence. She is the author of *The Politics of Identity: Who Counts as Aboriginal Today?* (2016), which includes a chapter on identity and community on social media. She is widely published on the topic of Indigenous cultural, social, and political engagements on social media, including coediting and contributing to two special issues; the *Australasian Journal of Information Systems* (2017) on "Indigenous Activism on Social Media" and *Media International Australia* (2018) on "Indigenous Innovation on Social Media." She established the Forum for Indigenous Research Excellence (FIRE), an international research network, and is the founding and managing editor of the *Journal of Global Indigeneity*.

SHEILA COTE-MEEK is Anishnaabe-Kwe from the Teme-Augama Anishnabai. She serves as the inaugural vice president, equity, people, and culture at York University, Toronto, Ontario, Canada. She is an active social media user who is committed to facilitating change for those who are marginalized in society, including Indigenous women and girls. She has extensive research experience with Indigenous peoples in Canada and has expertise in leading large national community partnership research grants, is renowned for her work on the impact of racism on Indigenous peoples in the education system, and has extensive connections with Indigenous communities in both academic and community settings. Along with Taima Moeke-Pickering and Ann Pegoraro, she is the codeveloper of the hashtag #girlpowereffect @girlpwreffect, dedicated to making a better place for women and girls.

MARISA ELENA DUARTE (Pascua Yaqui/Chicana) is assistant professor of justice and social inquiry in the School of Social Transformation at Arizona State University, Tempe. Her research focuses on Native American and Indigenous peoples' approaches to information and communication technologies, specifically for the purpose of advancing sovereignty and resisting colonialism. Her book *Network Sovereignty: Building the Internet across Indian Country* (2017) reveals the relationship between U.S. colonialism and the capacity for Native American peoples to build their own internet infrastructure. Her most recent work includes social network and decolonial analyses of Native American peoples' uses of social media toward political engagement. She teaches courses in justice theory, Indigenous methodologies, learning technology for Indigenous education, and surveillance in society.

MOHAN DUTTA is the dean's chair of communication and director of the Centre for Culture-Centred Approach to Research and Evaluation at Massey University in Palmerston North, New Zealand. His research interests include antiracism and activist interventions, Indigenous health, social media, and critical communication studies.

PHOEBE ELERS is a postdoctoral research fellow in the Centre for Culture-Centred Approach to Research and Evaluation at Massey University in Palmerston North, New Zealand. Her primary research interests include health communication, digital inequalities, critical and cultural studies, and Māori health.

STEVE ELERS is senior lecturer of communication at Massey University in Palmerston North, New Zealand, and is a researcher in the Centre for Culture-Centred Approach to Research and Evaluation. His research interests include the critical analysis of representations of Māori and Indigenous peoples and culture in news and social media, public relations, and advertising. He is a member of several Māori iwi/tribes: Ngāti Kauwhata, Ngāti Hauā, Ngāti Maniapoto, Ngāti Raukawa, Ngāti Kahungunu, Rangitāne, Ngāi Tahu, and Ngāti Hikairo.

ANDREW FARRELL is an Indigenous early career academic fellow and PhD candidate at Macquarie University in Sydney, Australia. His work is multidisciplinary across Indigenous and gender and sexuality studies, with a focus on Aboriginal and Torres Strait Islander gender and sexual diversities situated across the LGBTIQ+ community. His thesis is on Aboriginal and Torres Strait

Islanders' experiences of identity and community online. He is a queer-identified Aboriginal person of Wodi Wodi descent.

RYAN FRAZER is a postdoctoral researcher at Macquarie University in Sydney, Australia, and is currently working on a project that explores Indigenous peoples' experiences of online violence. In 2019, he completed his PhD at the University of Wollongong, which drew on the work of Deleuze and Guattari to understand the role of volunteer refugee resettlement organizations in producing territories of care, home, and belonging. Since 2014, he has worked as an associate research fellow in Indigenous studies and has published extensively on Indigenous peoples' use of social media for activism, identity, and community.

TRISTAN KENNEDY is an Aboriginal Australian with an academic background in Indigenous studies and cultural studies. He is a lecturer in the Department of Indigenous Studies at Macquarie University in Sydney, Australia. His current research interests include masculinity in digital spaces, metal music culture, and Indigenous peoples social media. He is currently leading an investigation into Indigenous peoples' navigation of harmful and hate speech on social media platforms. He is a managing editor of the *Journal of Global Indigeneity* and member of the Forum for Indigenous Research Excellence (FIRE).

MOUNIA MNOUER is an independent scholar. She is originally from Morocco. Both her parents and their families are Indigenous people of Morocco, Imazighen. She grew up in Meknes, Morocco, and identifies as Indigenous North African. She graduated with an English degree from Moulay Ismail University in Meknes, Morocco. She was active in human rights matters, as she worked with the Moroccan Organization of Human Rights during her college time in Morocco. After obtaining her bachelor's, she went to the United States to pursue her master's degree in TESL. She finished her PhD in education at Northern Arizona University in 2018. Her research projects focus on the embodied narratives of study abroad and intercultural understanding. She works on autoethnographies that pertain to Amazigh identities in the diaspora and issues of decolonizing the Arabic classroom and engaging in social justice education.

TAIMA MOEKE-PICKERING is a Māori of the Ngati Pukeko/Tuhoe tribes. She is a full professor in the School of Indigenous Relations at Laurentian University, Sudbury, Ontario, Canada, and is an active social media user committed to making a better change for Indigenous women and girls. She is an advocate of Indigenous pedagogies and has methodological expertise in Indigenous research. Along with Sheila Cote-Meek and Ann Pegoraro, she is the developer of the hashtag #girlpowereffect @girlpwreffect, dedicated to making a better place for women and girls. They are also the coeditors of the book *Critical Reflections and Politics of Advancing Women in the Academy* (2020).

NICHOLET A. DESCHINE PARKHURST (Standing Rock Sioux/Diné), MSW, MPP, is a justice studies PhD student at Arizona State University, Tempe. Her research focuses on the representation of Native Americans at the intersection of activism, social media use, and American Indian federal policy. Her article "Protecting Oak Flat: Narratives of Survivance as Observed through Digital Activism" demonstrates aspects shaping contemporary American Indian social media activism through a case study of the activist group Apache Stronghold. Her current research project examines ways that American Indian child welfare advocates use social media to correct misinformation about American Indian tribal sovereignty. She is a policy analyst and program evaluator. Her background is in American Indian health disparities research, specifically in the role of culture in American Indian youth substance abuse prevention. She managed an NIH-funded community-based participatory research study that developed and implemented a randomized controlled trial of a culturally grounded prevention curriculum in three urban American Indian communities.

ANN PEGORARO is the Lang Chair in Sport Management and full professor in the Lang School of Business and Economics at the University of Guelph in Ontario and is an active social media user who is committed to making a better change for Indigenous women and girls. She has expertise in communication, specifically in the realm of social media. She has methodological expertise in meta-synthesis and content analysis of text, specifically the use of qualitative software to enable analysis of big data research. Along with Taima Moeke-Pickering and Sheila Cote-Meek, she is the developer of the hashtag #girlpowereffect @girlpwreffect, dedicated to making a better place for women and girls.

JULIA ROWAT is a master of Indigenous relations student at Laurentian University, Sudbury, Ontario, Canada, and is an active social media user who is committed to making a better change for Indigenous women and girls. She completed her thesis on MMIWG and Walking with Our Sisters. She is a research assistant on an MMIWG grant for Moeke-Pickering, Cote-Meek, and Pegoraro.

MORGAN VIGIL-HAYES is assistant professor of computer science in the School of Informatics, Computing, and Cyber Systems at Northern Arizona University, Flagstaff, where she teaches courses on computer networking and network science. Her research leverages methodologies from network and data science to characterize how internet infrastructure is used by Native American communities and uses these characterizations to drive new innovations in wireless infrastructure. She envisions a future where Native American communities are empowered to design, build, and use information systems that support self-determination.

ALEX WILSON (Opaskwayak Cree Nation) is a professor in the College of Education at the University of Saskatchewan, Canada. Her research and teaching focus on land-based education, queering education, and the protection of land and water through sustainable housing. Her scholarship and community work focus on Indigenous rights, education, and environmental protection. Over the past several years, she has volunteered with and been a central member of the communications team of the social movement Idle No More. Most recently, her activism has focused on the One House Many Nations campaign, an initiative centered on working with First Nations community members and leadership to develop solutions to the housing and water crisis in First Nations communities. In 2017, she, along with B. Carlson and A. Sciascia, coedited "Reterritorialising Social Media: Indigenous People Rise Up," a feature issue of the *Australasian Journal of Information Systems*.

CORALS ZHENG is a master of environmental studies in planning student at York University, Canada. Her research focuses on land-use planning, sustainable urban development, urban systems, and waste management in Toronto.

Index

Printed and bound by CPI Group (UK) Ltd, Croydon, CR0 4YY

09/06/2025

14685724-0001